# the devil in tim

## travels in Tasmania

# the devil in tim
## travels in Tasmania

# TIM BOWDEN

ALLEN&UNWIN

This edition published 2008
First published in 2005

Allen & Unwin
83 Alexander Street,
Crows Nest NSW 2065
Australia
Phone: (61 2) 8425 0100
Fax: (61 2) 9906 2218
Email: info@allenandunwin.com
Web: www.allenandunwin.com

National Library of Australia
Cataloguing-in-Publication entry:

Bowden, Tim, 1937– .
The devil in Tim : travels in Tasmania.

ISBN 978 1 74175 237 3

1. Bowden, Tim, 1937– . 2. Tasmania – Description and travel.
I. Title.

919.4604

Set in 12/15pt Caslon 540 by Midland Typesetters
Printed by McPherson's Printing Group, Maryborough
10 9 8 7 6 5 4 3 2 1

# contents

For Ros

# foreword

Why is it that mainland Australians have rounded shoulders and sloped foreheads? Because when you ask a mainlander, 'where is the best place in Australia?' they hunch and scrunch their shoulders and reply, 'geez mate, I dunno'. And when they hear the answer 'Tasmania', they slap their foreheads with gusto and say '. . . knew it all the time'.

Maeve Binchy wrote in the foreword to Tim's irreverent memoir *Spooling Through*: 'Not only would I like to have been raised in Tasmania, I would love to have known Tim Bowden's selection of relatives and friends . . .' I share her envy about growing up in Tassie and after reading *The Devil in Tim* feel like I know some of the friends and rellies, plus an island load of other characters.

If you are lucky enough to know Tim and Ros personally, you will understand the childlike delight Tim has in all manner of things and the gift he has for seeing the humanity and beauty in the simplest of situations. He has this knack of making history as exciting as the present moment with words that are as crisp and clean as a Tassie spring morning. Like his description in this book of the

Strahan waterfront which makes it hard to separate the 100-year-old ship-building noises from the present day clatter of caffé latte cups.

What a delightful transition it is to see Dr Bowden go from transported mainlander, convict of the north, to once again being a patriotic Tasmanian freely roaming the highways and byways of his native land, seeking out sacred sites and page by page becoming a true Tasmanian again.

Above all else you know that a man who is prepared to take the piss out of himself in his writing is honest in thought and word. The effect of this is that you sit up and take notice when you read the horror of Truganini's story and descriptions of the scars left by clear-felling in the Styx Valley where the world's largest flowering trees are disappearing fast. It packs quite a punch, like a Southern Ocean gale. And behind the storm front there is fresh, clean air, albeit a bit chilling. In other words, a candid and rib-tickling appraisal by a keen observer whose sharp mind and well-considered opinion take the sting out of a complex debate.

From the opening words onwards, this will grab you where it counts.

Bless Tim Bowden. Shame there is only one of him.

GREG MORTIMER
Mountaineer, mate and travelling companion

# acknowledgements

Everyone who received honourable mention in this book was helpful—you expect that in Tasmania. In particular, though, I would like to thank Snow and Shirley Thomas not only for their hospitality but, as local historians, for their forensic (and helpful) dissection of my forays into north-west coast history. Brian Mansell shared his personal story about growing up as an Aboriginal Tasmanian and made a special trip from Hobart to the west coast to show us Aboriginal sites we could never have found by ourselves.

Graham Cook of Federal Hotels in Strahan arranged for Ros and me to voyage up the lower Gordon River on *Lady Jane Franklin* and experience the recently reconstructed West Coast Wilderness Railway—including a ride in the cabin of steam locomotive Abt No 3.

Tony Coleman and Richard Davis took us into the Styx Valley to show us the 'Valley of the Giants' and spoke courageously and passionately against the logging of old growth forests.

Tourism Tasmania provided quick and informative information over the year-long gestation of the manuscript whenever I asked—which was often.

My wife Ros shared the journey, took most of the photographs (they are the classy ones) and contributed to the narrative which was edited by Nina Riemer, a thoughtful and excellent editor, who also diplomatically reins in my tendencies for adjectival over-exuberance and, it must be said, occasional lapses of good taste.

Thanks also to Rebecca Kaiser and the 'Dream Team' of publishing at Allen & Unwin.

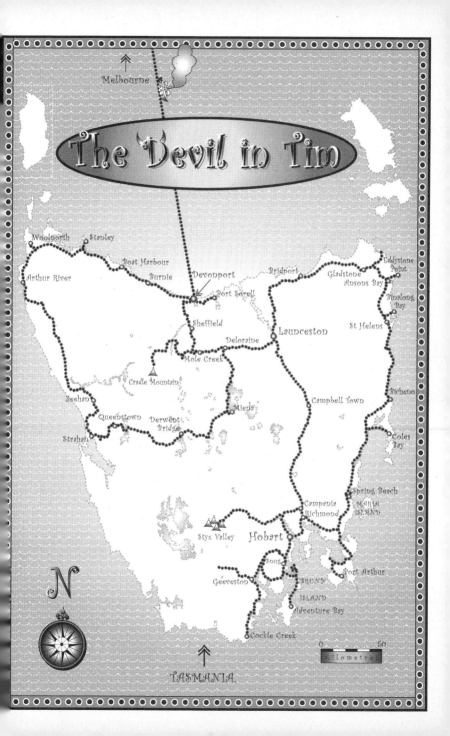

This road sign says it all.

# one

## Crossing the Rubicon

*'Tasmania is the testicle of Australia—suffusing The Mainland with strength and vigour. What a pity there is only one of them.'*

I can't recall exactly when I came up with that little number—perhaps I was still an adolescent in Hobart. It is an inevitably sexist metaphor, although the actual shape of Tasmania has other connotations which I will come to in a moment. The saying does, however, reflect the fierce pride that the island people have in themselves and their perceived values. Doubtless, as Australians, the denizens of the big island to the north have that same sense of 'special-ness', but Tasmanians, who inhabit the only state to be detached from the mainland, are passionate islanders. If asked where they are from, the response is certain to be 'Tasmania' before mentioning the name of the continent across Bass Strait. They may not get around to that.

Like the Western Australians, Tasmanians are particu-larly impatient with the notion that Captain James Cook 'discovered' Australia in 1770. The Dutch explorer, Abel Tasman, visited Tasmania in 1642, mapped the coastline's bottom half, and even 'discovered' the great mineral deposits of the west coast more than two hundred years before they were located by prospectors in the late nineteenth century. It was the west coast's large magnetite iron ore deposits that caused the compass needles of his two ships *Heemskerck* and *Zeehaen* to swing wildly as the gales of the Roaring Forties blew the Dutch mariner towards the island that was named after him. Two days before sighting land, Tasman noted in his log that, 'There might be mines of loadstone about here'. Tasmanians don't get too excited about Captain Cook.

Some graphic designers have considered the island state an inconvenience, and had the temerity to lop Tasmania off their depictions of Australia—to the fury of the locals. Others have taken considerable delight in the distinctive triangular shape of Tasmania, and I was asked by the State Library of Tasmania early in 2004 to open an exhibition featuring the various ways the state has been depicted on everything from ash-trays, badges, fruit bowls, tea-towels and even a gigantic chocolate freckle. And to redress my sexist saying above, the curator of the exhibition, Tony Marshall, even found 'an impressionistic image of a woman's body with the map of Tasmania where you'd expect it'!

Tasmania is still sometimes referred to as the 'Apple Isle'. That is a throwback to the middle of the last century when Tasmania exported apples to the United Kingdom and Europe, cargo ships lining up in the River Derwent to be loaded in the port of Hobart. England's entry to the Common Market shrivelled that industry, and Tasmania's right-wing Labor governments turned to mining on the west coast (including the rich deposits of iron ore that had swayed Tasman's compass needles) and hydro-electric power to attract heavy industry to Tasmania. But 'the tyranny of distance' worked against the island state, and Tasmania was traditionally considered an economic basket case, propped up by the Commonwealth government's grants scheme.

The growing conservation movements of the late twentieth century saw Tasmania's last major wild river, the Franklin, saved to run free—but most other significant rivers had been dammed by then. Seeking alternatives to industrialisation, Tasmanians became clever at devising niche business schemes, ranging from growing opium poppies (for the legal pharmaceutical trade), using their cool temperate climate to establish vineyards and a world-renowned wine industry, farming trout and Atlantic salmon as well as scallops, oysters and mussels, growing apples (of course), raspberries, strawberries and other more exotic berries for the national and international market. Some of the industries weren't so niche—such as the success story of Incat that manufactures huge high speed catamarans for the world market at its Hobart shipyard.

Even so the 'economic basket-case' label stuck to Tasmania until fairly recently. The population was dropping as young people left the state to seek opportunities they could not find at home and real estate values were laughably low, compared with the mainland states. But the commissioning of the two large vehicular ferries, *Spirit of Tasmania I* and *II*, in early 2003 seemed to fuel an astonishing economic revival. With the ferries shifting up to 1000 people twice every 24 hours (including day and night sailings during the summer season) tourists poured in to visit the island. Always important to Tasmania, tourism is now its biggest industry. (In January 2004 a third ferry, *Spirit of Tasmania III*, began direct Sydney to Devonport sailings.)

I was astonished to find out that from January to December 2003 visitors spent 1.17 *billion* dollars in Tasmania. Tourism was responsible directly for 22 600 jobs, and indirectly a further 15 350 (an example of an indirectly created job would be a taxi driver only employed in the peak summer season). But I thought the most staggering statistic was the number of visitors. In round figures, the island's population is 400 000. Some 800 000 tourists now come every year. As one tourism spokesman told me: 'Not so long ago our corporate plan centred around how to attract more people. Our next plan will be how to manage them without altering the character of Tasmania!'

Growing up in Hobart, and starting in journalism in the mid 1950s, I had travelled widely within Tasmania as a young man, covering stories for newspapers, radio and television. But that was all half a century ago—and since that time I had neither lived nor travelled there as a tourist. I thought it was time to re-explore my state of origin.

At our home on the mid north coast of New South Wales, where a freshly serviced Penelope (Toyota Series 80 Landcruiser) and The Manor (our off-road Jayco camper) were being stocked and prepared for six weeks of Tasmanian exploration, Ros and I pored over maps and camping lists. On an expedition to the Kimberley we'd had to carry extra jerry cans of diesel fuel and water. Neither would be needed in Tasmania, however, where water is not scarce and where we knew we could cross the island from north to south—and probably back again—on Penelope's main and reserve tanks. We did keep the roof rack on for old time's sake, although we really didn't need it. We carried a gas barbecue on it (not used once!) and occasionally firewood if we were taking some into a national park or camping reserve.

As usual for major excursions, I took the back seat out of Penelope and brought the cargo barrier forward to make room for such essentials as the wine cellar, storage of non-perishable food and folding tables and chairs for lunchtime stops. Even in February and March Tasmania can turn on brief bursts of cold and wet weather, so we included our parka rain jackets and woollen pullovers as well as our walking boots. At the other end of the scale we would need swimwear and thongs. Tasmanian weather can surge in summer into the high thirties which generally abruptly ends in a crashing, cold, south-westerly change. Those who take a gloomy view of Tasmania's cool temperate climate allege that summer does not reliably arrive until the end of January so we thought mid February to the end of March was probably a safe bet for our journey.

I had The Manor's wheel bearings lubricated and repacked and the electric brakes checked, which was just as well as there were no linings at all left on her brake shoes. We carried two gas cylinders on the front of the camper, one empty because of restrictions on how much portable gas could be taken onto the new *Spirit of Tasmania* ferries. We had been told we would have to vent the extra cylinder into thin air if we exceeded the quota. (As it happened, this was total nonsense as the rules had changed.) I also had a three metre electrical cable made up to connect Penelope's auxiliary battery to The Manor in camping mode away from 240v power so we could have an interior 12v light, and a very handy transformer to convert 12v power to 240v for my computer. Provided we travelled enough to keep the auxiliary battery topped up, we could stay away from powered sites indefinitely if necessary. We were soon to discover how useful this independence was, given the pressure on Tasmania's camping grounds and caravan parks caused by the influx of tourists from the big new ferries. Our small fridge in The Manor could operate on 12v power while we were travelling, gas or 240v mains power at other times.

In the rear section of Penelope we also carried an even smaller three-way fridge which we used as a kind of permanent esky for lunch stops and day excursions away from camp. This was a bit of an indulgence, but Ros and I like to think indulgence is what camping should be about. It was run from the auxiliary battery, and on occasions was given a boost with a 240v lead if we camped in a powered site.

### Travel Diary Thursday 13 February

It's simply fantastic to be on the road again, heading off to fresh adventures. We got away at 6.35 am, a good early start. It's a fine morning with scattered cloud, great travelling weather. It's always a good omen to start with fine weather.

Made good time to Sydney and were quickly under the harbour and into the new southern outlet tunnel which fed us straight on to the Hume Highway by 11 am. Penelope seems sluggish on the hills, and it is a struggle to stay above 100 kph, probably because of the slow climb up into the Southern Highlands and a slight head wind. The roof rack creates extra drag as well. Ros reminded me that we hadn't really needed to bring it.

The countryside is heartbreaking, just baking with drought: skinny sheep nibbling at stones and stubble on bare fields; cattle lying in the shade and seemingly too exhausted to try to glean sweet bugger all from the brown fields. The only green is a narrow ribbon on each side of the highway because of run-off from the bitumen when there has been a little rain.

We had planned to stop at Holbrook before getting to Melbourne the following day but we were doing so well we decided to go on to the Lake Hume Tourist Park near Albury. We were glad we did. The advertised tourist park in our out-of-date literature was no more, but there was a caravan park by the shores of Lake Hume where we scored a fabulous site overlooking the water, facing east, surrounded by gorgeous eucalypts with smooth pink trunks under a late afternoon sky streaked with high cirrus cloud. We sat at our folding table with glasses of red wine in hand as the sun set behind us and three cormorants skimmed low over the water sustained by an occasional lazy flap of their wings. It seemed time to break out our portable CD player and speakers to add the soothing obbligato of pianist Glenn Gould playing some of Bach's preludes and fugues from *The Well-Tempered Clavier*. We didn't expect to have such an idyllic camp on what was to be a 'service' stop on the Hume Highway.

As twilight overtook us, an old bloke (well, he was older than me I think) walked past from a fairly battered caravan even closer to the water than we were. As tends to happen in camping grounds we exchanged pleasantries. Ros asked John where he lived normally. 'Australia,' he replied. He has family in Albury so travels east for Christmas to see his grandchildren. Then back to the Kimberley to a piece of coastal paradise called Port Smith about a hundred kilometres south from Broome, where for the past eight years he has been crabbing and fishing to his heart's content. Just listening to him made us nostalgic for the Kimberley. He said there was only one hill between Albury and Broome and that was at Port Augusta!

As we were just a few hours from Melbourne we didn't have to rush away in the morning from our waterfront idyll. We had booked into the Ashley Gardens Caravan Park in Braybrook on Melbourne's western fringe and recommended by the TT Line as being a good jumping off point for the ferry. The two *Spirit of Tasmania* ferries run overnight and throw in day sailings for good measure in high season and at weekends during the 'shoulder' season from February to the end of April. We had chosen a day voyage, but booked a cabin so we could have an afternoon nap. We turned off the Hume Highway at the ring road, and hurtled around Melbourne's admirable but sometimes intimidating freeway system. Certainly the heavy trucks are daunting. Their drivers know exactly where they want to go and while I don't think they really want to kill nervous tourists trying to change lanes, they don't give much quarter either.

Most of the other denizens at Ashley Gardens were preparing to board either *Spirit I* or *Spirit II* and the caravan park, in a light industrial area, seemed fairly new and well organised. (But I can't *stand* loud musak in the toilet blocks. Why do they do it?) Campers always eye off each other's rigs at such times and you never know when you might pick up a good idea about something as mundane as a folding table, or a clever way to store gear on a roof rack. Most of the time, though, you reassure yourself that your way of doing things is superior to the camper or caravan in the next bay.

It had been a few years since we took Penelope and The Manor on a major excursion to the Kimberley and we now noticed there seemed to be far more mobile homes on the road. Not that you would expect to find many way out on the Gibb River Road, come to think of it, but scads of them were heading to Tasmania. Some were enormous, rivalling in bulk some of the articulated trucks that had terrorised me on the way in. One pantechnicon, just across from where I had erected our modest camper, was called 'The Aussie Dream'. I think it was also called a Swagman, although no swaggie could ever have imagined such luxury. The problem of having only the width allowed for the road was solved in the caravan park by somehow winding a great section of it out sideways, creating a wider living space, with an expandable awning as a roof. It had to be three-quarters of a million bucks worth of on-the-road accommodation. It towed a 4WD festooned with bicycles and on the roof was a big satellite dish.

I sticky-beaked as I walked past and saw a huge plasma-screened telly, broadcasting World Cup cricket on Foxtel, straight from South Africa. We give television a miss when we are on the road, and just carry a small radio for news and weather and some good books. But the owners of The Aussie Dream probably had no other home, unlike us who were on holiday for only a couple of months, so I reminded myself it was entirely reasonable that they had their creature comforts. We camped near a similar rig in Strahan on the west coast of Tasmania a week or so later, and Ros talked to the owners who cheerfully told her they had sold their house and bought a Swagman instead. They now lived on the road.

It may seem churlish to say again that I am not an admirer of motor home camping, and the more we travel, the more I am confirmed in that opinion. By and large you can't take them off the bitumen, certainly not the hired ones which have such restrictions built into their contracts. They lumber along majestically, burning up vast quantities of fuel and often hold up traffic. When motor home campers do get to a camping ground and find they need to drive to a shop for a litre of milk, some grog or groceries, they have to pack up and take their whole camp with them.

At Ashley Gardens, the office thoughtfully provided a mud map for navigation to the ferry. We set off in plenty of time the next morning, which was just as well as the map did demand local interpretation. Joining Melbourne's early morning commuter and truck stampede and with Ros navigating, we successfully made it from Albion, on the western fringes of Melbourne, from the M80 Ring Road onto the M1 heading for the West Gate Bridge, pursued and surrounded by the entire commuter pack from Geelong. The trick was to get off the elevated highway before we found ourselves heading over the West Gate Bridge towards an uncertain navigational fate. We managed this with some relief, but instantly ran out of ferry signs in the maze of roundabouts and underpasses under the M1. We dithered about until I saw a 4WD and caravan I assumed were heading to Tasmania and followed them. They behaved uncertainly for a time, and I managed to draw level at some traffic lights to check they were heading for the ferry. 'Sure,' said the driver, 'if we could find the bloody thing. We were thinking of following you!'

By keeping Port Phillip Bay on the right we both found the Station Pier at Port Melbourne and joined the queue beside the imposing bulk of *Spirit II* in time for our security check, ticket inspection and boarding. No one seemed the slightest bit interested in our two exterior gas cylinders on the front of The Manor, or whether they were full or empty. It was early days for the *Spirit*s, and the rules kept changing. We had to pay more for Penelope and The Manor because of the extra length. Had we just had a car, that would have travelled free except in high season. Cars go free for forty-five weeks of the year though, so it's not a bad deal.

The *Spirit*s are large, well appointed vessels with restaurants ranging from the canteen self-serve style, through to table service and white damask tablecloths and napkins. After we boarded we noticed that some passengers had staked out seats in the lounges with hats and small backpacks. These were the smarties who knew that the day sailings were more populated than the night, where everyone has to have either a cabin berth or a reserved sit-up seat. Night sailings carried up to 750 people, but by day there were more than 900. There were plenty of plastic chairs and tables in the screened outside areas, but using them depended on good weather, not always available in Bass Strait. We were glad of the sanctuary of our twin cabin, which we felt was worth the slight extravagance of $184 extra (seniors discount) as we read our books and dozed off for a post-lunch nap. We had an interior cabin without a porthole, which some might find claustrophobic, but didn't worry us. Even the two berth cabins have four bunks, but only two are used. (I discovered later that the TT Line had increased the capacity of the interior lounges for day sailings.)

Bass Strait was in an overcast but benign mood as we headed out the heads from Port Phillip Bay through the famous Rip, and the rest of our ten-hour sea road with *Spirit II* was almost as steady as the proverbial oil platform. Early in the afternoon we crowded to the port side to wave at *Spirit I* heading north on its daylight crossing from Devonport to Melbourne.

The Mersey River at Devonport looks hardly big enough to handle these new ferries, but the skipper had obviously done it before, and we berthed spot on time at 7 pm. Because trucks, semi trailers and vehicles with caravans and campers are carried on the main vehicle deck, we were off within ten minutes of the big bow door opening. Our fridge in The Manor was not yet stocked or operating so we had booked ahead to spend our first night in a Devonport motel, only a few cables' length from the ferry terminal. It was just as well we had. I happened to go into the office of the Argosy Motel at 7 pm to find a desperate fellow *Spirit II* traveller and his family asking for accommodation. Not only was the Argosy booked solid, but the proprietor told him, 'You won't find a motel room or a B & B bed between Devonport and Launceston'. He suggested the traveller head west towards Burnie (which was not where he wanted to go) on the slim chance of finding something up that way. That was only one of the effects of the day and night sailings of the new ferries. We were about to experience other impacts on Tasmania caused by the flood of eager mainlanders onto the island.

The next day, Sunday, promised to be intriguing, because of an odd mix of coincidence, history and Tasmanian connections. Some months before I had been flying from Melbourne to Sydney and had found myself in need of one of those minuscule bottles of red that airlines provide—at a price. I pulled a coin purse out of my pocket to pay for it, and the person sitting in the window seat next to me (we had not spoken up to that point) said, 'I see you have one of "Snow" Thomas's coin purses'. The purse was

an ingenious circular leather purse with no zip or clasp.
The folded and creased sides compressed to a series of star-
like points and opened when you squeezed the sides, then
folded back to contain the coins. Snow had given it to me
at a university alumni dinner in Burnie many years before.
There are coin purses, I have to report, that are made out of
the scrotums of kangaroos, but Snow said his were better,
and indeed they are as the whole purse opens out ingen-
iously to form a flat rosette of leather. Snow saw and bought
a similar purse in Hobart's Salamanca Place (he thinks it
was Polish in origin) and worked out how to make it. Snow's
version, as he said when he gave his creation to me, 'Looks
more like a horse's arse'. Apparently Australian bushmen
first gave that appellation to a similar style of tobacco
pouch. Mates, wanting the makings, would say, 'Lend us
yer 'orse's arse'. Despite its sphincter-like appearance it is
a very useful, compact coin purse and was well worn when
my fellow traveller noticed it.

My airborne companion and I exchanged pleasantries,
and it turned out that Andrew Andersons, a Sydney architect,
had recently visited the Thomas property, North Down, in
Tasmania on the coast between Devonport and Port Sorell.
He had designed a house for Daniel Thomas, Snow's twin
brother, who had a long career in arts museums. Daniel
worked as a curator at the Art Gallery of New South Wales
and the National Gallery of Australia. I remembered meeting
him as the director of the Art Gallery of South Australia—
which he headed from 1984 to 1990, when he retired. His
brother, Snow, is a farmer, living on the same property the
Thomas ancestors first occupied in 1828. Andersons was
naturally proud of the house he had designed for Daniel, on
land bought near the family property, commanding views of

both the mountainous hinterland and the waters of Bass Strait. I forget how our conversation turned to music, but I happened to mention to Andrew that, to my chagrin, I had not yet been to a concert in Sydney's relatively new City Recital Hall in Angel Place, but that I had heard it was not only an exciting space but had superb acoustics.

'I'm pleased to hear that,' he said, 'because I designed it!'

I could not think of an immediate response, but the idea took root at that moment to ask Snow if Ros and I could come to North Down when we were in Tasmania, and now that day was about to dawn. Besides, I needed a new coin purse and I knew that Snow was manufacturing them as a cottage industry so as to keep out of the way of his son, now farming the property.

Although not reaching back to the 1820s, I had my own nostalgic connections with the Port Sorell district. As a small boy I used to go there for Christmas holidays, even during World War II when my father was in the Middle East, and in the post war. My aunt and uncle, Mary and Stuart Maslin (Mary was my mother's eldest sister), had a wooden, corrugated iron-roofed shack there called Sorlrite and I had cousins, Janne and Toni, to share the holidays. The sound of wattle birds calling and that distinctive smell of bracken and hot sand always take me back to those idyllic summer days in an instant. Sometimes Uncle Stuart used to take us out in the evenings, if the tide was right, to spear flounder. We would walk along waist deep in water, towing a small dinghy behind us with a car battery for the flounder lights. It was hard to detect a flounder, lying camouflaged on the sand, and spear it. Usually you could only spot its eyes. You had to allow for the angle of refraction in the water or it was off in a flurry of sand and fins.

I wanted to see if the cottage was still there because like many sleepy coastal towns, Port Sorell is now succumbing to development. The origins of the cottage's name Sorlrite were arguable. It was thought it was owned, perhaps originally, by some people named Saul. But it was more likely a play on the words 'it's all right', which was endemic in Port Sorell shacks. Not far from Sorlrite was Weona ('We Own Her'), with Soda Wee next door and Same Here bringing up the banal trilogy.

Port Sorell is only a twenty-minute drive to the east of Devonport, and we booked The Manor into a caravan park and left her there before retracing our steps to North Down where we found Snow in his workshop stamping out his latest batch of coin purses. He has had a special press made which cuts out the flower-shaped circles of kangaroo leather (in all colours of the rainbow these days as well as the dark brown of my original) and then folds and compresses the distinctive 'horse's arse' finished purses with their ingenious claspless tops. Snow makes and distributes his coin purses himself—all over Australia. He and his wife, Shirley, recently spent eleven months on the road finding new outlets.[1]

Over a cup of coffee in the homestead Shirley and Snow (no one calls him by his given name, Bertram) revealed the plans for the day: a tour of the property, a beach picnic, and a visit to Daniel's new house by mid afternoon. It turned out Shirley and I had been to the University of Tasmania at the same time in the late 1950s. I was a part-time student, which meant I didn't participate in student social life so we had no clear memories of seeing each other on campus. We were both born before World War II but she was far

---

1 He has a website: www.clever-kangaroo.com

more intimately involved than I with that conflict. I spent it snugly and safely in Tasmania, not needing to use the air raid shelters (other than play games in them) that were dug in the playground of my pre-school. Shirley, on the other hand, was dodging real bombs and artillery shells. Her father, Henry Hirst, was appointed colonial adviser in stock management to the Maltese government in 1938, so the Hirsts were caught by the war and while Malta was never captured by the Germans, it was very heavily bombed, and Shirley has written a memoir about her experiences.[2]

North Down is superbly situated high above a plain with sand hills separating its pasture from the wild waters of Bass Strait. Thomases (and their extended families) have occupied North Down in various houses all of which, alas, except the present homestead, have been destroyed by fires or the ravages of time since Jocelyn HC Thomas and his brother Bartholomew B Thomas were associated with the property in 1828.

The history of North Down is built into Snow and it was a delight to have a personally conducted tour of the property, taking in the site of the original homestead which is closer to the sea than the present house, and to see evidence of how his pioneer ancestors cleverly drained the brackish lagoons behind the coastal dunes and turned them into productive grazing land. The land was seasonally occupied by Aboriginal people when the first Thomases arrived and Snow said he still comes across stone tools, grinding stones, stone 'knives' and other implements which he used to pass on to the Queen Victoria Museum in Launceston until the Aboriginal Relics

---

2 Shirley Thomas, 1996, *Greetings from Malta: World War II*, Regal Press, Launceston

Act required they be left *in situ*. He is proud of the way the original Thomases were determined to have peaceful relations with the Tasmanian Aborigines living there—a contrast to the behaviour of many other trigger-happy pastoralists. Unfortunately this was to cost Bartholomew B Thomas his life, as well as the life of his overseer, James Parker. Snow's father, Harold Thomas, researched and wrote a family history that outlines what happened.[3]

Harold Thomas quotes an early settler, James Fenton, who wrote of Bartholomew Thomas:

> Captain Thomas was a gentleman of the most kindly and generous disposition. He indulged a philanthropic desire to befriend the poor savages who at that time inhabited the wilds of Devon. The Port Sorell tribe became docile and semi-civilised under his mild treatment.

But Harold Thomas added that Bartholomew's good work among the blacks came to a bad end because the Big River Tribe, driven out of their own domain, the Derwent Valley in the south of the island, were wandering at large homeless and hostile. They had reached Port Sorell and were camped by 'the big water' on the stream later known as Poyston Creek. Fenton thought:

> The gallant Captain should have known the danger and futility of attempting to parley with the wandering blacks, but his enthusiasm for a good cause led him to this foolish action in spite of remonstrance from Parker . . .

---

3  Harold Thomas, 1975, *Sam Thomas and His Neighbours*, North Down, Latrobe, Tasmania

Harold Thomas concluded:

> The story of the killing, as gathered from the blacks and reported after the inquest, is that as the two white men were led by a local black into the bush to visit the Big River Tribe, Parker was first speared and clubbed and B. B. speared as he fled . . .

BB Thomas and Parker were killed in 1831, almost a year after Governor Arthur's failed attempt to round up the island's Aboriginal population by what was called the Black Line, a cordon of soldiers and civilians advancing down the island and beating them like game towards the Forestier Peninsula in the south—ignominiously capturing only an old man and a boy. Although the Black Line was a farce, it did signal the end of Aboriginal resistance, because by the end of 1831 the demoralised and dispossessed native Tasmanians were convinced by George Augustus Robinson to accept his promise of their own homeland on Flinders Island. Instead they got a kind of concentration camp and their numbers declined rapidly through disease and demoralisation. So now the pastoralists could develop Tasmania's arable land unhindered by the presence of, or attacks by, hostile blacks. By 1876, in the space of one lifetime, the last full-blooded Tasmanian Aborigine, Truganini, had died. Perhaps Thomas and Parker were among the last European casualties of that unequal contest.

Such dark history seemed far away as we sat enjoying Shirley's excellent picnic lunch, sitting on the rocky foreshore beside a small peninsula on the north-east corner of

North Down. By some geological chance the multi-coloured sea-rounded pebbles heaped around us looked like a lapidarist's fantasy, and the lichen on the rocks where we sat was bright orange. Later as we walked barefoot along the beach in the warm early afternoon sunshine we found more pebbles clustered in the base of sandy pools, like exotic bird's eggs in a watery nest. I tried to photograph them with our new digital camera, but failed to capture their beauty. Perhaps some natural things should only be seen to full advantage in the wild by the naked eye and remembered in the mind's eye.

Daniel Thomas's house came next on the North Down tour and he had said we could drop by after 3 pm. Snow unlocked some farm gates and we were able to drive up a track not normally used from our shoreside picnic spot. The brothers are twins, but not identical—Snow the bulky farmer has his trademark thatch of white hair, and Daniel, slightly smaller in stature, has a neatly trimmed white beard. I photographed them among Daniel's big abstract paintings, so well featured in his remarkable Andersons-designed home of unassuming farmhouse weatherboards outside but with surprising minimalist modernity inside. (Daniel Thomas and Andrew Andersons were associated with state gallery extensions in both New South Wales and South Australia.) Daniel likens his present location to living on the 'Tasmanian Riviera'.

The house nestles into a hillside, with generous views not only of the sea but also of the surrounding landscape—no other building can be seen. There are dry gravel gardens around the house with salt tolerant plants which morph into casuarina groves to the west—themselves like an extension of the gardens. While Snow and I walked up to the top of the hill to a lookout point, Ros and Daniel roamed the casuarina groves, which Ros said had been 'tidied' by their aesthete owner so that a fallen branch seemed to have its ideal place among rock outcrops in Japanese-style harmony of the space. The dry garden is grey, silver and white, but boxes of vivid red geraniums overlook it from inside the long sunroom and from a bedroom bay window. The unfenced 'garden' has to be distasteful to rabbits and to native marsupials like wallabies, pademelons, potaroos, possums and wombats—although snakes are frequent visitors to the gravel 'lawns'.

Over fine tea of our choice from a Wagenfeld pot on an Alvar Aalto trolley, Daniel discussed some of the difficulties of having such a sophisticated house in the bush. Finest tea required a three-hour drive to Hobart, or mail order. Classic modern design Tizio reading lamps or Eames lounge chairs must travel to Melbourne for repair. Daniel obligingly gave us the full tour of the house, its spa with an ocean view, an art library you would die for—and high, bright spaces in tune with the coastal setting.

Shirley and Snow had guests arriving at their homestead, so took us back to pick up Penelope by driving through Port Sorell—and thoughtfully locating Sorlrite for me on the way. The cottage looked exactly the same! After farewelling the Thomases we drove straight back to the caravan park to put The Manor in camping mode for our first 'proper' night of the trip, and to have a more leisurely look at Sorlite, which was really just around the corner from our camp. (I must have subconsciously known.) It was also much closer to the beach than I remembered.

Although most Australians call their weekenders 'the shack', this was a fairly accurate description of Sorlrite—a brown wooden cottage with a green tin roof and a generous open veranda in front, glassed in on both sides to make extra sleeping space. The dunny was out the back in my time and there was a line of huge old pine trees on the front border, but they were now gone. From the front aspect it was astonishingly unchanged. I simply had to take a photograph, and as I did so a woman came out to greet me. Helen Sankey had not long owned Sorlrite (now called The Den) and sensed that we might be able to tell her something of the cottage's history. I spoke of the happy times I'd had there as a kid, and she asked me if I'd like to come inside. For some reason I didn't want to, and I hope she understood. (She did say the dunny had been moved inside.) Helen said that she and her husband wanted to keep the historic character of the place, and I told her that it was a remarkable time warp for me.

In fact, Sorlright had been bought from my uncle Stuart Maslin in the late 1950s by Don Cunningham, whom followers of matters Tasmanian will not be surprised to hear I knew! Don was an apiarist with the State government's Agricultural Department when I was with the ABC in Launceston in 1963. It was early days for television in Tasmania then and—keeping a safe distance from the action—I hired a freelance cameraman, Bob Montgomery, to film bees constructing a honeycomb using a micro-lens and guided by Don. We kept in occasional touch over the years, and I knew that Don and his wife Jess had only recently moved into a retirement village in Hobart. I suppose when you reach ninety that's a fairly reasonable thing to do. So the Sankeys had bought the renamed Sorlrite from Don, whom I was proposing to visit in a few weeks' time. That's Tasmania for you.

One of Don's projects in later life was to publish a list of all the ships that came in to and out of Port Sorell from its heyday in the nineteenth century to the end of the twentieth.[4] Port Sorell has the distinction of being the oldest settlement on the north-west coast. Snow Thomas told me that only the estuary was known as Port Sorell. The town was originally known as Burgess (after the Chief Police magistrate) and was laid out in 1844, when there was a brisk trade in wattle bark, used for tanning, and farm produce—principally potatoes. By the 1850s it was the largest town on the north-west coast, apart from Stanley. But the estuary was handicapped by a rocky entrance unsuitable for ships over 100 tons, unpopular with ship owners and captains. It could not compete with the superior depth and entrance of Devonport and had declined to no more than a fishing village by the 1890s.

Just consider for a moment the early historical dates we have been discussing here. Tasmania was the first place to be settled after Sydney was established in Port Jackson in 1788. The settlement of Hobart was first established at Risdon, on the River Derwent in 1803, and Launceston (first called Paterson) in 1806. By 1810 Launceston, on the Tamar River, was both the capital of the north and the port for the Tamar settlement. Melbourne hadn't even been thought about and, indeed, was discovered and settled from Launceston—a reality that northern Tasmanians, perhaps with some justification, have always felt smug about.

It happened like this. In 1821, John Batman and his brother, Henry, moved to Tasmania from Sydney. John

---

4 DG Cunningham & Bryant Griffiths, 1991, *The Shipping History of the Port Sorell Estuary 1789–1991 and a History of the Griffith Family*, self published

Batman was a government meat contractor and was granted farming land on the slopes of Mt Ben Lomond, south of Launceston. He was a colourful figure. In 1826 he and a band of volunteers captured the notorious bushranger Matthew Brady and in 1830 he won the commendation of Governor Arthur for his wise and humane treatment of Aborigines. John Batman and his fellow graziers needed more land so after reports of good prospects of high quality land at Port Phillip, across Bass Strait, Batman formed a loose association of fourteen members—later named the Port Phillip Association—to explore the new country and perhaps bargain with the local Aborigines for a large tract of land. Batman sailed to the future Victoria in May 1835, and first explored the Geelong area. Ostensibly he purchased from the Dutigalla tribe some 243 000 hectares of land in return for blankets, various other articles and the promise of yearly rent, but the bargain later was disallowed by the Governor of New South Wales, Philip Gidley King.

On 7 June, when returning to their ship *Rebecca*, the party came again to the Yarra River and Batman's diary for the next day reads:

> The boat went up the large river I have spoken of which comes from the east and I am glad to say about 6 miles up found the river all good water and very deep. *This will be the place for a village.* [My italics]

Batman headed back to Launceston with the joyful tidings, and despite the fact that the New South Wales Governor disallowed the land deal with the Dutigalla tribe, a steady stream of squatters began to arrive. (With fine local chutzpah Snow Thomas maintains that Batman actually set off from Port Sorell to locate Melbourne: he had to take shelter there from strong winds after leaving Port Dalrymple at the mouth of the Tamar River—now George Town—before beginning the crossing of Bass Strait on 26 May.)

There is dispute about who should actually get the credit for founding Melbourne because John Pascoe Fawkner, a Launceston businessman who had not been part of Batman's exploring party, had also heard about the favourable land across Bass Strait. In August 1835, Fawkner bought a schooner to carry a party of settlers to Port Phillip. On 11 October 1836 he arrived at the Port Phillip settlement and established a store and a hotel, and in January the following year a newspaper he called the *Melbourne Advertiser*. In any case, he set out from Launceston, so Melburnians should be equally grateful to the two founding fathers from northern Tasmania. (And in the great Australian tradition of de-mystifying our historical figures, I heard John Batman described on ABC Radio National recently as a syphilis-ridden rake and a con man.)

By the way, Lloyd Robson in his *A Short History of Tasmania* says other northern Tasmanian graziers may have gone to Port Phillip even earlier than Messrs Batman and Fawkner. 'James Whyte claims he took rams to the area as early as 1833.'

Things might have been otherwise had the original settlement planned for Port Phillip Bay gone ahead in 1803. Fearful of French territorial ambitions Lord Hobart, Secretary of State for War and Colonies, commissioned Captain David Collins to form a new settlement in the area. The expedition set off from England in two ships, *Ocean* and HMS *Calcutta*, carrying 307 convicts and their families, 22 settlers, and a detachment of 50 Royal Marines with their wives, children and staff—467 people in all. Collins chose an area in Port Phillip he called Sullivan Bay (near Sorrento) but the sandy soil was deemed unsuitable for crops, and the only water available was from inadequate sandy soaks. They landed on 15 October, but the settlement was looking shaky by the end of that year. Collins and his party arrived in Hobart early in 1804 where, under instructions from Governor King, he took over command of Lieutenant Bowen's struggling settlement at Risdon. Collins didn't think much of the Risdon site and moved the settlement further down the Derwent River to Sullivans Cove, the present site of Hobart. (At least the Rt Hon. John Sullivan, Under Secretary at the Colonial Office, finally had his name commemorated in a going concern.) By the end of June 1804 the last remnants of the ill-fated Port Phillip settlement had arrived in Hobart Town.

Melbourne would not be located or settled for another thirty-one years, until Batman and Fawkner set off from Launceston—via Port Sorell. (I continue to harbour a nagging doubt that Victorians are not as appreciative as they should be about their northern Tasmanian origins.)

**Travel Diary Thursday 13 February**

Last night can only be described as bloody cold. A southerly change came in about midnight. We have not brought enough cold weather sleeping gear and bedding. My veteran down sleeping bag is thinner than Ros's and I nearly froze my nipples off. The good news is that the weather stayed fine, with clear bright skies. We were away by 9 am—after a bit of fiddling about filling that pesky empty gas bottle on The Manor—to explore the hinterland behind Devonport, as far as Mole Creek. First, though, we are heading east to the Tamar River valley to have a morning cuppa with Peter Cundall, the ABC's veteran gardening guru, with whom I share a passionate interest unconnected with horticulture. Ros, on the other hand, is looking forward to seeing Peter's garden, not the one used at the Royal Botanical Gardens in Hobart featured in *Gardening Australia*.

Driving east on a lovely sunny morning, with occasional clumps of scattered cloud, we ran through a landscape which presented a patchwork of the blissful and the ravaged. Some areas were unspoiled and idyllic with natural forest, other tracts had been cleared and planted with pine trees for the softwood market, killing all vegetation beneath them as pine trees do. Occasionally, with a shock to the senses, we were confronted with the ugly ravages of clear-felling, where the original bush had been dragged down for wood chips, burnt, and now was waiting to be planted out with a monoculture of pine trees or silvertop gums—a fast growing species originating in New South Wales and used mainly for woodchips.

Within minutes we had crossed the Rubicon—the name of the river that actually flows into Port Sorell. The devil would be encountered later that afternoon. Not many people progress from the devil to paradise—but we were about to manage it.

Actually we came devilishly close to disaster when a back road we were on merged into another highway and I sub-consciously thought we had right of way. We didn't, and I was exceedingly glad I had had The Manor's electric brakes attended to before we left: I stamped hard on the brakes, tyres screaming, as we speared towards the rear of a car that had been driven quite legally along the highway and that I feared I'd barge into. It was a very close call and had it not been for a warning anguished squawk from Ros, we might have brought our Tasmanian trip to a premature end. I made a mental vow to concentrate more on the road and less on the scenery. I don't think Ros realised how close we were to an accident. She will, however, when she reads this.

Tasmania's cool temperate climate attracts high winds, and most of the farms and paddocks are shielded with surprisingly big wind breaks, lines of veteran cyprus, some of them more than a hundred years old, or massive hawthorn hedges which may well be the same age.

Peter Cundall and his wife Tina live on the West Tamar and I had to promise to guard the location of his farm carefully, as you can imagine how many gardening enthusiasts would love to 'drop in'. Peter and I first met in 1990, after I won the Wilkie Medal, awarded by the Anti Football League, for the person who did the least for football in the best and fairest manner in that particular year. The Wilkie Medal is announced in the same week as the Brownlow Medal in Victoria, and is presented on the hallowed turf of the MCG. (The medal is named in honour of Douglas Wilkie, who with columnist Keith Dunstan founded the real AFL in the late 1950s in Melbourne in protest at the complete domination of all conversation and thought in Victoria during the seemingly endless football season.)

I had scored my first Wilkie (I was the first double winner) probably because of the way I had been thundering about the appalling violence of football, and on television in particular, on *Backchat*, the ABC's viewer reaction program which I hosted for eight years from 1986. The following brief excerpt from my Wilkie Medal acceptance speech gives some measure of my indignation:

> I am well aware of the impoverishment of the quality of life in Melbourne by the incessant talk of footbrawl during the season—and even outside it.
>
> But the situation in the thugby states is equally desperate. It's not so much a matter of conversation revolving about teams with ludicrous names like *Bears*, *Crows* and *Crushers*, but the brutality and violence of a so called sport, where beefy buffoons crash into each other, grope and grovel in the mud with their bums in the air, and thump each other with dare I say gay abandon. Eye gouging, bitten off ears, broken limbs and quadriplegia are so common that they are hardly newsworthy. Often the lists of the injuries sustained take more air time than reciting the names of selected players.
>
> Televised thugby is so violent that if the Australian Broadcasting Tribunal's standards were enforced, no child under the age of sixteen would be allowed to watch it. The sheer brutality of thugby is so gross that it makes Australian Rules Footbrawl look positively benign.

It is also the duty of the Wilkie Medal winner to destroy a football in a ritual manner. There are some class acts to follow. Barry Humphries, as Sir Les Patterson, won it several years before me. He coated a football with cream-cake and a camel ate it. Footballs have been exploded, burned and chopped up and eaten as curries, but on this occasion, in more ecologically aware times, it was decided to turn footballs into objects of useful beauty by chopping off the tops of six gleaming new Sherrins and transforming them into pot plants and hanging gardens. Somehow the secretary of the (real) AFL, Keith Dunstan, managed to get permission to bury one of these converted footballs on the centre forward line of the Melbourne Cricket Ground. (All this was in a good cause by the way; the AFL raised money for the St Johns Children's Homes.)

Anyway that is how I met Peter Cundall, who eagerly accepted the invitation to travel from Tasmania to help relieve the barren grass-scape of the MCG with some greenery, and who also turned out to be strongly opposed to 'the unnecessary, meaningless, socially corrupting—and unfortunately encouraged—violence within rugby and Australian rules football'.

As television cameras rolled, Peter was simply marvellous. The smirking groundsmen sliced into the sacred turf with their spades and Peter planted a flourishing grevillea in a decapitated football, recommending a rich potting mix made from 'old footy sweaters, jock straps and under-arm material, rotted down to make a perfect mixture devoid of all aggression'.

We did meet a few times in later years, generally at various 'Save the ABC' rallies in the 1990s. Actually Corporal Cundall and Private Bowden *nearly* met at Brighton Camp, Tasmania, in the late 1950s when I was called up to compulsory National Service. We missed by a few months. Like many of our instructors at the time, Peter was a Korean War veteran. Another common bond between us was bad hearing, his obtained from combat as a machine gunner in Korea, and mine less bravely by firing .303 Lee Enfield rifles in the school cadets, and later in compulsory national service training in Brighton Camp, Tasmania. No one ever thought ear plugs were necessary in the 1950s, either at school or during National Service—and certainly not in Korea!

Peter had said to call in any time we were passing, and that's what we were about to do. Ros, the horticulturalist of the Bowden family, was looking forward to seeing the Cundall garden. His hideaway was fairly cleverly concealed and we drove straight past the gate, but were flagged down by a vigorously waving Peter on our second pass.

It was late summer and his gardens and fruit trees were bursting with produce. Being shown them was like a personally conducted *Gardening Australia* as the unstoppable octogenarian ran up and down the fecund rows of tomatoes, zucchinis, potatoes, capsicums and beans, all the while pulling deliciously ripe plums, peaches, nectarines and early apples off his orchard of fruit trees for us to sample, continuing in full explanation and compere mode. It would have made a wonderful program had it been filmed, but this is Peter and Tina's private world. It's an organic garden, of course, and Peter keeps the loaded branches of some of his bigger fruit trees within reach by hanging baskets of stones off the higher branches—a typical example of Cundallian pragmatism.

Peter is experimenting with several varieties of different coloured tomatoes, burgundy and yellow among others. Perhaps he can see more easily if they are ripe. He is slightly colour blind and can't see red—which is appropriate as he is a peaceable man and very even-tempered. He also picked us some black capsicums.

Foraging possums, famous for eating absolutely anything, and wallabies are kept away from his garden by an ingenious electronic gizmo which emits a high frequency clicking sound the marsupials don't like. It is from the United States and there are settings to repel gophers, raccoons, skunks and bats. But Peter says it works well with wallabies and possums out here. The device operates at night and Peter can't hear it anyway, but he has to be aware that his neighbours might.[5] The device is mains powered, and costs about 50 cents a month to run.

'We left three of them clicking furiously for two months when we went overseas several years ago. They were still clicking away when we returned to our completely unfenced, undamaged garden, surrounded by several thousand circling, but highly frustrated, starving wallabies, possums and inquisitive dogs.'

Over a cuppa in the large, cheerful Cundall kitchen, surrounded by shelves of preserved fruit and vegetables processed by Tina, Peter kept dashing off to pile more fruit and veggies into cardboard cartons for us to take away. We handed over a bottle of my late mother Peg's famous home-made tomato sauce (the recipe appears on the following page)—warning that it might be a back-handed present as Tina would have to make it from then on. (We were right, and after emailing the recipe, we've since heard it has become a Cundall staple.)

Peter doesn't need much sleep, and is an internet junkie for which he blames me! Apparently he started to use a computer to follow the Anti Football League shenanigans and now follows world events on the internet during the small hours, reading the early editions of the international papers like the *New York Times* and *The Guardian*.

We drove away laden with enough potatoes (of various varieties, including my favourite pink-eyes), fruit and veggies to feed an entire camping ground for a month.

---

5  The clicking gadget is called a Heavy Duty Transonic CIX 0600 Pest Repeller, manufactured by Weitech, USA. Their website is: www.weitech.com/products

## PEGGY BOWDEN'S LEGENDARY TOMATO SAUCE

5 kg cooking tomatoes—Roma variety are good if they are cheap

1 kg onions

1 kg green apples

1–2 heads of garlic

1200 ml brown vinegar

30 g whole cloves

30 g whole spice called pimento (can be hard to get)

30 g ground ginger

1 kg sugar

125 g cooking salt

In a large saucepan put the roughly chopped tomatoes and onions, cored apples roughly chopped and peeled garlic, then add the vinegar. Tie the spices into a muslin bag or an old handkerchief and add to the other ingredients.

Boil all the above ingredients for 2 hours, stirring occasionally. Leave overnight and next day pull out the bag of spices and squeeze the juice into the mixture. Process the mixture finely in a food processor. Return to the saucepan and add the sugar and salt and boil for a further hour or until the sauce gets a bit thick. Stir occasionally to stop it sticking to the bottom.

Cool and stir, then bottle. Makes around 9–10 conventional tomato sauce bottles.

Turning off the West Tamar Highway at Exeter, we ran south on a minor but well made bitumen road to join the main north-west coast highway at Deloraine, where we left it to head due west to Mole Creek. There we wanted to meet the faintly marsupially named Androo Kelly, who ran the Trowunna Wildlife Park. Afterwards we would climb out of the Meander Valley and the craggy mountains of the Great Western Tiers and head due north back to Devonport, not forgetting, of course, to pass through Paradise on the way.

We were hungry for honey. The drought in south-eastern Australia had taken its toll on bees and honey had been scarce in New South Wales. I'd been on the lookout for leatherwood honey since arriving in Tasmania, but would almost certainly have to wait till we reached the west coast for that, where the leatherwood trees grow in the rain forests. The little hamlet of Chudleigh, on the way to Mole Creek, has a honey farm in the main street—for honey deprived people a haven of exotic delights. There is a working glass hive on the eastern wall of the honey shop where you can watch the industrious little critters actually making the stuff. The Honey Farm claims to have fifty varieties of honey, even though some of those are blended nonsense like caramel, strawberry or banana and passionfruit. But there's lots of proper honey too, with tasting bars and little wooden paddlepop sticks to sample everything from clover to stringy bark or blue gum blossom nectar. The staff are friendly and helpful and you can eat as much free honey as your system will absorb. As I had recently been diagnosed with late onset Type 2 diabetes I had to be moderate. I couldn't resist a honey ice cream, though. It was fabulous!

A giant, brightly painted sculpture of a snarling Tasmanian devil marks the entrance to the Trowunna Wildlife Park just a few kilometres further on and, as we had already decided on the title of this book, I simply had to be photographed with the devil.

The island's biggest marsupial predator, the Tasmanian tiger, as it used to be called, or more correctly thylacine, is almost certainly extinct. The last one in captivity died in a Hobart private zoo in 1936—although many sightings in the wild have been alleged over the years. Also sometimes called Tasmania's marsupial wolf, the thylacine was an aggressive hunter, pulling down its prey—usually wallabies or emus when Tasmania had them—in open country. Unfortunately for the Tasmanian tiger it also developed a penchant for sheep shortly after European settlement, and a bounty was placed on its head by the government. Recent research has established that the biggest killers and stealers of sheep were probably human beings, but the quite generous bounty on the thylacines gave them little chance.

The smaller Tasmanian devil (*Sarcophilus harrisii*), about the size of a medium sized terrier dog, is a carrion eater and used to dispose of the carcases of the thylacine's kill when it had finished. With its enormous gape, sharp teeth and voracious appetite, it is an impressive carnivorous scavenger. Dr Eric Guiler, a Hobart zoologist who researched the devil's habits for many years, told me that a pair of devils once set up house inside a dead cow and stayed inside their malodorous accommodation until they ate the lot—bones and all.

With a harsh, hissing call—rather like listening to someone vomiting loudly—and exceedingly bad breath because of their eating habits, the devils are bad tempered, even with each other, and don't lend themselves to being patted by tourists. I saw a baby devil being handled for tourists later in our Tasmanian travels, and it grabbed hold of its keeper's wrist with its already fearsome teeth and had to be spoken to very sternly. They are also nocturnal creatures so daylight viewings are likely to be less than satisfactory—just a black backside, or flank, half buried in the straw of the den. The only hope is feeding time, and then the devil's likely to wake up, grab its food, and disappear back into its sanctuary.

I remember Eric Guiler telling me that Tasmanian devil populations tend to rise and fall quite dramatically every decade or so, and no one really knows why. They can certainly exist happily on the fringes of towns, enjoying rubbish dumps and not being fussy about what they eat. Unfortunately the devil population is now in decline because of a terrible, disfiguring virus, or cancer, that is eating away the faces of the devils and killing them. Grotesque tumours on the devils' faces (and elsewhere in their bodies) are thought to have already dropped Tasmania's devil population by one third since a peak in their numbers reached in the mid 1990s. Tens of thousands have died. In some communities only two in ten animals have survived. Only about 100 000 may be left in the wild. This mysterious malady has been called devil facial tumour disease (DFTD), but its origins remain a mystery. Scientists are working on the problem, but there seem to be no quick fixes, either on what is causing this awful scourge or how to combat it. If it isn't overcome, either by natural or scientific means, one worst-case scenario is that the devil population on the island will drop to the point of no return, and there will be yet another extinction.

I was keen to talk to Androo about his devils because I'd been told that his park had once had a devil that was so tame it could be patted and handled by tourists. We found Androo, a lean, fit-looking feller, in the park shop, issuing tickets to visitors who, he told us, might stay an hour or so, or even all day once they realised they could see so many animals and birds in their natural environment. I asked whether the story about the tame devil was true.

'This park does claim to have been the first place to have a friendly or tame Tasmanian devil,' Androo explained. 'That was during the time of Peter and Judy Wright, who first started the park in 1979. Nicky was the original devil. He was still here when I started in 1986, a little shrivelled-up old feller by then. He was considered the first friendly devil in Tasmania, the first devil that people were able to touch.'

Androo took us down to his new education centre, bristling with computers, posters and information booklets. The park specialises in research on Tasmanian devils, and also has a koala breeding program that has been active through eight generations of disease free animals. The park is now able to supply other parks and zoos with breeding stock. Androo Kelly positively vibrated with enthusiasm about how the whole experience of visiting his wildlife park had changed from the 'fast food' approach of sixteen years before. 'People then wanted to be entertained quickly by a kind of show. Now they want to learn something, and tend to stay longer than they thought they would. Some stay until night. At dusk the potoroos are all through this area. You can see goshawks in the trees in the wild, nesting. The night tours are now very popular.'

A more leisurely visit can take in hand-fed Tasmanian devils (naturally) as well as koala and baby wombat cuddling, experiencing the nocturnal house, eagles, snakes, kangaroos, waterfowl and other birds. There is also the magnificent tiger quoll, sometimes called the spotted-tail quoll (*Dasyurus maculatus*). It is a handsome animal with golden brown fur on its back and sandy coloured fur underneath. Its body is covered in different sized spots, including the tail which distinguishes it from the smaller Eastern quoll (*D. viverrinus*), or native cat. I remembered Huon pine getters who worked in the wet rain forests of the upper Gordon River on the west coast telling me when I interviewed them in the 1970s that these 'tiger cats' as they called them would eat your boots if you left them outside the hut or tent. One man, Bob Thomas, told me he thought that if he or any of his timber getters was ever injured and had to lie out in the bush, these animals would be capable of eating them!

Androo was dismissive about that claim. 'Devils are more likely to get that accusation. The tiger quoll is an efficient predator, a silent animal moving through the bush. It is very solitary. A male might have a home range of 100 square kilometres. They are genetically very closely aligned to thylacines. They are vulnerable and threatened on the mainland, and there are thought to be only about 3000 left there. We have that many in Tasmania.'

Unfortunately, Androo said, the tiger quolls weren't doing so well: 'They are one of the animals that are persecuted still. Stories are told like the one you mentioned about the Huon pine getter. The Tasmanian psyche has created a real myth in a lot of things. Call something a tiger, then it's a man eater. So now we have every argument to kill it, to get rid of it. Pay a bounty, get rid of this thing. It's only knee high to a human. Imagine if we really did have leopards and tigers, they would have gone too.'

The worst thing tiger quolls can do to humans, said Androo, is to eat their chickens. And then the humans demonise the quoll. 'It is a five kilo maximum weight animal, yet it could be a fifty kilogram monster the way people talk about it. It is a fierce animal, a top predator, with a big mouth full of big nasty teeth and a huge open gaping jaw designed to take down a pademelon wallaby by closing its jaws over the neck and suffocating them. Of course it has to be fierce. And if they bite you, you know about it. But they are secretive, nocturnal, rarely seen. To be honest, people only encounter them when chicken houses are raided. Unfortunately they are like a fox. The trouble with them is they raid a chicken house and they kill everything. They take the heads off everything. Anything moving they have to stop.'

I suggested that sounded like the behaviour of dingoes indiscriminately killing sheep in a paddock.

'Sure, a dog pack will do that. But we believe here that they are such a treasure of an animal, an animal that Tasmania hasn't yet really pushed. You watch. International tourists just fall for the spotted-tail quoll.'

Androo's mention of foxes reminded me that Tasmania is no longer free of those terrible pests and destroyers of native wild life. In 2003 the body of a pregnant vixen was found as road kill and authorities are keeping a sharp lookout for any more evidence of foxes. It is not known how they got back to Tasmania. Hitching a ride by sea is considered unlikely. One theory is that some red-necked, mindless, gun-loving moron brought them in deliberately as a kind of 'pay back' for the anti-gun laws brought in by the Federal government. We will probably never know. Unfortunately their survival will be helped by the drop in the Tasmanian devil population, as devils are known to be predators of baby foxes.

It was a reminder of Tasmania's dark side, but we banished such thoughts as we began the climb out of the Meander Valley on our way back to Devonport via Paradise.

Paradise is a small farming hamlet on the C137 road between Mole Creek and Sheffield. Unfortunately we passed through it before we knew we had even arrived. Perhaps someone had nicked the sign from the roadside. We did catch a glimpse of Paradise through the rear vision mirror as we left it, because the sign on the northern side was still there. There is probably a moral in this somewhere, along the lines of not knowing you've experienced Paradise until you've left it. Or maybe we were not destined to experience it.

Still, it's not every day that you cross the Rubicon, have an assignation with the devil, and enter—albeit briefly—Paradise.

# two

## A Hard Nut to Crack

**Travel Diary Tuesday 18 February**

We are back in Devonport at the delightfully situated caravan park and camping ground on Mersey Bluff, overlooking the beach on the western side of the harbour where we can see the two *Spirit of Tasmania* ferries come and go, laden with happy campers. We've had another very cold night, but this time warmed with extra blankets unearthed from Penelope's deep storage. On the radio we hear that very cold southerly winds have swept up from Antarctica and there are sheep grazier alerts in the high country and snow showers in the south. And this is February! There is no doubt the north of the state is the best place to be right now even with the strong off shore winds. There are clear skies and sunshine, and Bass Strait is a striking cobalt blue with white caps visible to the horizon.

The small three-way fridge was giving trouble. Either our auxiliary battery was not charging properly or the fridge wasn't working on 12 volts. I dropped Ros off in Devonport's main shopping area (to find some tracksuits to combat this surprisingly cold snap) and sought out an auto electrician. In Sydney they would probably have told me to come back next week, but not in Devonport. Noting we were visitors, the very obliging leckie stopped what he was doing to investigate the problem. With his testing probes and meters he quickly found a faulty lead from the fridge to the car and also improved the earthing to the auxiliary battery—so we were back in business. Not only that, he charged me token lunch-money for the half hour it took him to do the job. I find that trades people in smaller places are almost unfailingly obliging.

(While Ros was locating our tracksuits in K Mart she encountered some fellow grey nomads having a spat over their trolley—this is why I try to leave all shopping to Ros. She said the wife yelled at the husband: 'If you don't shut up, I'll hit you on the head with a brick!' He shut up.)

Fully provisioned, both fridges now working, and with a warmer wardrobe—I did live in Tasmania for the first thirty or so years of my life so I must be a slow learner—we headed west along Highway 1, hugging the north-west coast bound for Stanley.

The new highway is a great improvement on the old, narrow, winding, death trap of a road from Launceston to Burnie I remembered from the 1960s and which used to kill hundreds of people. Tasmanian 'expressways' have 110 kph speed limits and good surfaces, but have the disconcerting practice of changing suddenly from dual carriageway to a one-lane-each-way road with only a dotted line separating oncoming traffic. If you are used to mainland driving you could be tempted to stray into the death lane thinking it was all one way.

Stanley is also known as Circular Head because of the distinctive flat topped hill, surrounded by steep cliffs, looming over its harbour and more colloquially known as 'The Nut'. We planned to bypass Burnie (now the second major city and port for the north-west after Devonport's ferry-led expansion) and nearby Wynyard to investigate a fascinating part of Tasmania's pastoral history—the Van Diemen's Land Company (VDL), still run under a Royal Charter originally granted in 1825 by King George IV and to this day maintaining the tradition of having a Court of Directors, not your common or garden board. Its first head-quarters was established at Circular Head.

We drove through lush country characterised by the rich red volcanic earth which sustains Tasmania's vigorous potato growing industry, as well as grazing and general farming. But most of this 'easy' farming country, including the naturally occurring grasslands near Launceston and the Tamar Valley, had been taken up by the time the Van Diemen's Land Company came to Tasmania in 1825, led by its emissary Edward Curr, to take up the 350 000 acres of land in the north-west granted by far off King George. The world needed wool, and the Napoleonic wars had devastated sheep flocks in Europe. (The hungry Spanish had eaten theirs.) Investors in England were eager to put capital into any proposal concerning wool production, particularly in the new colonies in the southern hemisphere. Curr had migrated to Van Diemen's Land in 1820 and, seeing opportunities, had returned to England and written a book about his experiences, lauding the fertile farming country and pastoral opportunities waiting in the new world. He was rewarded by being made leader of this new enterprise.

The VDL Company had actually drawn the short straw for the land available. Curr's knowledge of the north-west was slight and in fact was largely based on a sketch book (now lost) that Lieutenant Charles Hardwicke, a pioneering early settler, had given him. Curr had put a very positive spin on things to the investors, because Hardwicke had reported, after expeditions on foot and by boat along the coast in 1823, that apart from some land at Circular Head (Stanley) and Cape Grim (on the extreme north-west tip of the island) the 'whole of the interior . . . is quite impenetrable and totally uninhabitable'. This seemed a bleak description of country it was hoped would sustain a fine-wool pastoral venture.

Despite this gloomy first assessment, Curr and his party had been instructed to select their farming land in the far north-west. The first settlers arrived at Circular Head on the brig *Tranmere* in October 1826, and included the company's first indentured servants, livestock, vegetable and pasture seeds, farm machinery and building materials.

Their own surveyors fanned out to try to find suitable land. The chief surveyor, Henry Hellyer, and two other employees headed inland from Circular Head and climbed a 3600 ft mountain to view the surrounding country in search of grasslands. After naming St Valentine's Peak, Hellyer was able to see large areas of apparently clear country that looked suitable for sheep. He named the area Surrey Hills and Hampshire Hills after the lush green fields of England.

But the treeless plains Hellyer had seen from St Valentine's Peak (14 February—St Valentine's Day—1827) were clear because they were above the winter snow line. The low highland scrub of button grass plains and heath provided little feed, and when thousands of pure bred merino sheep were taken there it was an utter disaster. All but a few died in the freezing sub-alpine winters. The company concentrated its efforts on the land grants at Woolnorth, near the sombrely named Cape Grim—so called by Matthew Flinders and George Bass in their sloop, *Norfolk*, in 1798. It was then they discovered that Tasmania was indisputably an island—and for good measure saw and named Circular Head where we planned to camp that night.

The first VDL Company surveyors were a resourceful and rather colourful group of men. The country they traversed was a primeval rain forest, thick with huge ferns and moss-covered myrtle trees (*Nothofagus cunninghamii*) which had grown completely undisturbed for thousands of years. Gullies were choked with Tasmania's unique horizontal scrub whose slender trunks collapse under their own weight, then produce fresh upright stems. The whole mass of interlocked lattice is a formidable barrier like a barbed-wire entanglement and has to be crawled through, or climbed over, with the unseen valley floor often ten to twenty metres below. Some, who attempted to climb through it, were never seen again.

One of the intrepid explorers risking such hazards was the famous—or infamous—Jorgen Jorgenson, who in the course of an adventurous life wrote a book about the Van Diemen's Land Company and became (briefly) the King of Iceland!

For a quick overview of this larger-than-life, tall, blue-eyed Dane, there is no better summary than the following, written by the late northern Tasmanian historian Karl von Stieglitz in *A Short History of Circular Head and Its Pioneers*:

This vagabond genius, this plausible rascal, had seen and done things not often found in the way of men. That he climbed so high and fell so low was entirely due to his amazing courage and lack of scruple. A hasty list of his exploits shows that he had worked with Matthew Flinders, was mate on the famous *Lady Nelson*, was mate on the ship which brought Bowen to found Hobart, and saw the first settlement at Risdon Cove. Returned to Europe, served on a Danish privateer, was taken prisoner by the British (whom he loved). Was sent to Iceland with food supplies for the discontented inhabitants there, took the Danish Governor prisoner, proclaimed himself their ruler and his intention of annexing the whole island for Britain. He ruled Iceland well for a few months, when he was deposed by the British who necessarily explained that the whole affair was, of course, quite illegal, and what he had done was without their knowledge or approval. He returned to England and was sent to the Continent as a British secret agent, returned to England, gambled, stole from his landlady, wrote books and sermons in a simple, flamboyant style. And in the end he was sent out to Van Diemen's Land for theft and being an alien at large. Became a policeman at Oatlands and elsewhere, married a bad lot, who made fun of him and legend says beat him with a pot-stick, and in the end he died of exposure after a drunken brawl in Hobart Town.

Jorgenson seemed to have packed more into his life than most.

Anxious to get to Stanley in time to camp, we drove through Burnie without stopping and paused by the banks of the Cam River at Somerset six kilometres further west, where we had a picnic lunch beside its small estuary. A boy and an elderly man were fishing in bright sunshine with no evident success, but they looked content just holding their rods in such a tranquil place. There was a timelessness about it that took me back to the 1950s.

Somerset is where the Murchison Highway turns off to Rosebery and Queenstown. There was no road for trucks and general transport to the west coast from the north-west until the Murchison Highway was opened in 1961. The new road traversed what was called the 'Missing Link', connecting Guildford Junction (the railway junction to Waratah) with Rosebery. Before that, the only connection between the mining communities on the west coast and the north-west coast was by rail. The Emu Bay Railway Company line ran between Zeehan and Burnie. (The northern section, over forty-eight miles, was initially built by the Van Diemen's Land Company as a horse tramway from Burnie to the tin mine at Mt Bischoff, and was completed in 1878.)

The isolation of Queenstown and Zeehan, the principle mining towns of the west coast, from Hobart or indeed Launceston, meant that west coasters were more closely allied to Victoria than the rest of Tasmania. The first road link with Hobart, the Lyell Highway, was not built until 1935. Most supplies were brought in by sea from Victoria. The residents followed the fortunes of Victorian football teams rather than the competition in their own state. I remember being surprised that even in the 1970s the ABC, on the west coast, didn't broadcast Tasmanian races, but took their coverage—and the footy—from Victoria.

As we had our lunch beside the river I noticed a sign to Hellyer Gorge through which the Murchison Highway passes on its way to Queenstown. It was named after Henry Hellyer, who discovered it while he was desperately trying to find good grazing land in the late 1820s.

Unlike his flamboyant colleague Jorgen Jorgenson, Hellyer did not make himself king of a foreign country but he was, nevertheless, a most interesting man, well liked and able, who explored and named the features in great swathes of extremely difficult country. He was thirty-six years old and a bachelor when he arrived in Tasmania with the VDL Company, and by all accounts was cheerful and humourous, particularly in adversity—and there was plenty of that in the wet, miserably cold gullies and mountains of the wind-swept north-west.

But like Jorgenson, his life ended tragically. After nearly a decade with the VDL Company, Hellyer decided to move to Hobart in 1832. His work with the company was complete and he had been offered the job of Assistant Surveyor General. To the utter astonishment of everyone who knew him, Hellyer shot himself the day before he was due to leave Circular Head for a new life in Hobart. I wondered why, and made a mental note to find out more about this curious affair.

On a whim we turned off the main highway to see Boat Harbour, originally called Jacob's Boat Harbour, a favourite bolt hole of one of the VDL Company's boatmen so my local historian friend, Snow Thomas, believes. In the early days the sea was the 'road'. Transport of people was frequently by open boat, with oarsmen who needed sanctuary where they could find it if sudden storms blew up. Snow said that Boat Harbour is remembered by those who walk the beach for its 'squeaking sand', which we had no time to test out. One guide book I saw described it as a 'beautiful cliché of a bay', which is a bit rough really for such a coastal jewel with its clear turquoise water and vivid white beaches underneath steep cliffs. It has a caravan park and other places to stay, and even a few eateries. It's a bit out of the way and difficult to get to unless you have your own transport, and we were tempted to stay there. But Circular Head and Stanley beckoned—and we had booked a berth in one of the two caravan parks because since the two *Spirit* ferries had started disgorging hordes of fellow travellers, Tasmania's caravan parks were bursting at the seams. Booking ahead, we found during the next six weeks, was essential in popular locations.

Not long after we left Boat Harbour the country changed dramatically from the mid north-west coast's characteristic red fertile red volcanic soil to the thick heath and white quartzite hills typical of the west coast.

One of our aims in the north-west was to see Hydro Tasmania's recently established wind farm, and we were already realising why they chose this area for it. The distinctive circular outline of The Nut loomed ahead as we drove along the promontory towards it, with a screaming southerly behind us. We'd booked a beach-front powered site which sounded just fine in theory, but the southerly was howling straight into the caravan park, situated just under The Nut. The only wind break was a vibrating patch of green shade cloth, which was obviously ineffectual. One of The Manor's weak points is exposure to wind when our canvas walls are wound up and beds extended. I wanted to give it a go, but Ros (who hates wind) was stroppy about the site. The amiable caravan park proprietor, Des, seemed a bit nervous about us and our demands, but did suggest the perfect solution—an unpowered site behind some thick vegetation and beside a cabin. This was a splendid move because we don't need power anyway with our gas supplies for the fridge and auxiliary battery for The Manor's interior 12 volt light.

With Tasmania's long twilight we had time to explore Stanley, a pretty little town, with historic buildings well preserved, weatherboard shops cheek by jowl with old bluestone buildings crafted from dolerite quarried from the volcanic plug of The Nut. Back at the camp I went to have a shower and saw the western flank of The Nut bathed in the last of the brilliant sunshine—it was 8 pm. I dashed back for my camera, but missed the moment.

Safe and snug from the buffeting wind we dined on grilled chops and Peter Cundall's exquisite, organically grown pink-eye potatoes, zucchinis and tomatoes. A glass or two of red seemed appropriate, and I added a measure of Johann Sebastian Bach—a CD well titled *Angels' Voices*.

**Travel Diary Wednesday 19 February**

Ros wasn't all that keen to climb The Nut, so I headed out on another clear, cold morning just before 8 am, drove Penelope to the beginning of the track and headed up. The sign said ten minutes by chair lift and twenty walking. The lift wasn't working yet anyway so I was up the zig-zag track in ten minutes without any drama other than heavy breathing. There were splendid views over Stanley, and to the north, sharply defined by the morning sun, I could see Highfield House, originally built for Edward Curr, the Chief Agent of the Van Diemen's Land Company, and his family, which we planned to visit later in the day. The Nut (no one calls it Circular Head) is a fantastic feature, a volcanic plug with steep cliffs all around and a flat, undulating grass-covered cap. The track runs around the circumference, and the views are spectacular. The signage and lookouts are well done and informative. One, overlooking the Stanley wharf, said that in 1892 they wanted some rock fill for a new breakwater so they put 5000 lbs of gunpowder into the sheer dolerite rock face and set it all off. There was a spectacular explosion, but after the smoke cleared away absolutely nothing had happened! Then twelve years later, 200 000 tons of rock suddenly came crashing down. Fortunately no one was killed.

I found out that Circular Head was known as 'The Nut' from the moment of the failed blast because—wait for it—it was 'a hard nut to crack!'

As I had seen from the top of The Nut, Highfield House and its surrounding buildings stand in splendid isolation on the northern end of the peninsula, with superb views along the coastline and of Circular Head and Stanley. Gradually being restored to its former splendour, Highfield House has the commanding air of a government house of a separate colony—which in a sense it was, to the fury of Tasmania's real governor, George Arthur, in Hobart. The two-storey residence was designed by the multi-talented Henry Hellyer. It needed to be a substantial dwelling to accommodate Curr, his wife Elizabeth and their family of fifteen children—nine boys and six girls.

Curr took a great deal of interest in the design of his house, which avoided the conventional Georgian style that characterised so many early Tasmanian private dwellings and public buildings. Highfield House was smart and avant garde for 1832. The four-panel doors and French windows were advanced for their time, as were the construction techniques. The house has tongue-and-groove floors, fine plasterwork, a bell system and a particularly elegant staircase among its other fine features.

The outbuildings include a handsome stone church for religious worship—but the church was never used because Stanley's first minister insisted on an Anglican church being built in the town. It was later used as a storehouse. About half a kilometre to the east of the homestead and its outbuildings are the stone remnants of the convict barracks, partly demolished early last century as were many such relics of Tasmania's convict past. But you can still get a good impression of what the barracks must have been like. Although Curr was a difficult, prickly man in many ways, he is said to have treated his assigned convicts well, and in 1841 wrote: 'Whenever skill or trustworthiness is required, it is not amongst the free men, but amongst the convicts we are obliged to look'.

I recommend a visit to Highfield House, on North Point, which has been restored in the current conservation vogue of showing you, where possible, how the building was constructed—with holes in some walls showing how the plaster was applied, and fragments of paint and original wallpaper preserved without embellishment. Apart from the fabulous location, we could hardly tear ourselves away from this link with the colonial past which was so well presented and explained.

A funerary monument in the garden marks the spot where, in 1835, the Currs' two-and-a-half-year-old daughter Juliana was killed in a tragic, freak accident. She was being pulled along by a family dog in a little cart when the dog decided to run under a wooden railed fence, smashing her head. She died almost instantly.

During our tour of Highfield House we found out more about Henry Hellyer's death: he probably took his own life because of rumours of homosexuality circulating in the officer's mess and involving a young convict named Harley. The young man had worked with Hellyer on some of his toughest expeditions and had been granted a ticket-of-leave, largely through Hellyer's recommendation.

When I mentioned this story later to my friend Snow Thomas, he reacted indignantly, saying he had heard the same story from a guide recently during a tour of Highfield House and that it was a total fabrication—in his view a slur on the reputation of one of Tasmania's finest pioneering explorers, and skewed history. Snow alerted me to an article by Harold Trethewie in the *Local History Journal of Circular Head*, written in 1986, which presented a scholarly and reliable account of the events leading to Hellyer's suicide.

The 'incident' concerning the convict Harley took place a year before Hellyer took his own life, when the surveyor was in charge of a gang of assigned convicts building a bridge across the Wey River (during the VDL Company's disastrous experiments to run merino sheep in the cold mountainous country Hellyer had named Surrey Hills). Trethewie wrote:

> As one of the men named Harley was felling a tree, a branch struck Hellyer in the groin, causing a wound that became badly infected and required regular dressing . . . Each man was promised a bonus of twenty shillings on completion of the bridge, but Hellyer denied the bonus to two of them, Ward and Harley, on the ground that they had stolen liquor from the Company store. Harley at the time threatened to get even with Hellyer.

Hellyer—in later correspondence and indeed in his suicide note—makes reference to the wound in his groin. Harley, who had fallen foul of Hellyer previously and held a grudge against him, saw him attending to his awkwardly placed injury and conjectured he was masturbating. In any case, Hellyer heard reports that Harley was spreading malicious rumours about him several months later.

Henry Hellyer was a man of deep religious convictions and was exceedingly vulnerable to any remarks which might reflect adversely on his moral character. Five months after he heard of Harley's denigration of him—so sensitive were the mores of the time that he could not bring himself to write down what the slanders were—he wrote to Edward Curr, alleging that 'prejudicial reports' were being circulated about him and had been mentioned in his own military mess at Circular Head. Harold Trethewie went on:

> Hellyer suggested [to Curr] that Ward and Harley were 'the fabricators of the slander, *whatever it is*', and should be 'dealt with' accordingly . . .
>
> Curr wrote back on the following day, telling Hellyer in effect that the whole business was beneath his dignity and best forgotten. Hellyer replied on the same day, agreeing with Curr, and adding, 'Unless I see further occasion I shall take no more trouble about it.'

Three days later Henry Hellyer was dead. His body was discovered on 2 September 1832. He had discharged a horse pistol against his forehead, in his bedroom. A suicide note 'very much underlined and corrected' made a garbled reference to dressing a wound in his groin, presumably, wrote Trethewie,

> . . . a reference which was the source of fanciful stories that he had a homosexual relationship with one of the assigned servants, or was guilty of sexual misconduct. Such stories are no more than scurrilous speculation and totally false.

Another more likely theory is that Henry Hellyer may have suffered from depression, and the rumours of sexual impropriety just added to his increasing mental torment. Whatever the reason it was a sad end to the brilliant career of this sensitive and multi-talented pioneer. I agree with Snow Thomas that the spice of sexual scandal now emanating from Highfield House to visitors is ill-founded and based on poor history.

Edward Curr presided over tough times in the Van Diemen's Land Company's history. After the disaster of the failed Hampshire and Surrey Hills sheep venture, he knew the Tasmanian operation could not be profitable in the foreseeable future. And diplomacy was not his forte. He had consistently failed to acknowledge or cooperate with Governor George Arthur in Hobart, considering that the Royal Charter made him the master of his granted territory. The two men quarrelled the day after Curr arrived in Hobart in 1826, while Curr was being entertained at Government House, and he immediately fell out with the governor over the location and extent of the VDL Company's proposed grants and their differing interpretations of the instructions from the Colonial Secretary Lord Bathurst about where they could settle. As the company's fortunes declined in the following years, the VDL Company would have located to Port Phillip if that option had been available. For five years after the failure of the Hampshire and Surrey Hills operation, Curr and his fellow directors made repeated approaches to colonial officials to exchange their north-west holdings for some of the newly discovered pasture lands at Port Phillip. But New South Wales had declared Port Phillip the exclusive territory of the Australian Agricultural Company, by coincidence founded in the same year as the VDL Company.

By the late 1830s the Court of Directors of the VDL Company was losing patience with Curr over his continuing and acrimonious disputes with the colonial government. In 1834, Curr himself had suggested to his directors that the fine-wool enterprise should be abandoned and that the company concentrate its efforts on breeding stud rams and thoroughbred cattle and horses for sale to the rest of the island and for export to New South Wales and Victoria.

In 1836, Governor Arthur was replaced by Sir John Franklin, who refused to have anything to do with Edward Curr or even correspond with him, and by 1840 his own Court of Directors gave Curr his marching orders.

The VDL Company limped on with their Tasmanian holdings until 1851, when the directors and shareholders had had enough. In twenty-five years their 300 000 pound investment had returned only 50 000 pounds. Over the next three years all livestock was sold—except 2400 cattle at Surrey Hills—all employees were dismissed and land was offered for sale or lease. In 1852 the Woolnorth property on the extreme north-west tip of the island was leased to Dr James Grant, of Launceston, for fourteen years at 300 pounds a year. After that lease expired, the VDL Company revived its interest in farming in Tasmania, and in 1869 appointed JW Norton-Smith as the manager of Woolnorth, with the brief to revitalise the pastoral properties at Circular Head, Woolnorth, and other holdings south of Burnie. Four years later, in 1873, the company established a pure-bred Hereford herd, after buying breeding stock from leading Tasmanian studs.

Direct, although distant, descendants of the original stock still graze at Woolnorth, now Australia's oldest Hereford herd, and Ros and I planned to see them the following day as well as what remained of the Royal Charter property after more than 175 years of continuous occupation. In the meantime, after leaving Highfield House, we set off inland, via Smithton, to drive down to the Julius River Forest Reserve and in a loop via the intriguingly named Milkshakes Hills and back to Stanley. Feeling a bit frisky without The Manor behind us, Penelope seemed to bound over the sealed but narrow roads through timbered hills and lushly pastured valleys to our first stop at the Allendale Gardens ('From roses to a rainforest', claimed the brochure) about twenty-five kilometres south of Stanley.

I found Allendale Gardens unexpectedly charming, a cool temperate garden composed of a bewildering variety of exotics, laid out over five acres. Visitors wander over cleverly laid out paths through themed areas that might include a mix of camellias, rhododendrons, magnolias, azaleas, lupins, delphiniums and roses—the list is long—set among equally diverse and unusual trees from just about every country in the world. Each season has its own delights, of course, and I noticed the winter photographs had the gardens under thick snow! There is even an area specially designed for the blind, with carefully selected scented plants and trees.

Admiring visitors can walk across a stream by any number of 'theme' bridges, including the 'Bridge of the Apple Blossom' or, more romantically, the 'Bridge d'Amour', leading appropriately to the Bridal Walk. And, immediately beside the eclectic mix of imported flora, those who begin to hunger for Australian plants can experience a circular walk in a dinky-di Tasmanian rain forest through huge ferns and towering eucalypts, many more than 300 years old.

The whole complex was created by Lorraine Cross, assisted by her husband Max, not even twenty years ago. I was fascinated to find out how such a magnificent obsession (and Lorraine did not quarrel with that description) had been achieved in such a short time. While she and Max served Devonshire teas to coachloads of visitors, I asked her how Allendale had come to be.

When Lorraine and Max got together in 1986, he was a dairy farmer. She told him she wanted to establish a special garden and Max said she could have a cow paddock and make one. She immediately began planting trees to realise her master plan and grand dream—which has turned out exactly as she visualised it. She was told it would be difficult to organise a circular walk in the natural rain forest, but set off—helped by her grandchildren—and put plastic ties where she felt the track should go. Lorraine has new areas planned for Allendale Gardens and hopes that someone with an equivalent passion for horticulture will take it on in future years when she is no longer able to continue.

We drove on through Edith Creek and Roger River—where I checked my phone messages in New South Wales from a phone box surrounded by curious cows—and on to the Julius River Forest Reserve, another twenty-five miles south from the Allendale Gardens. The contrast between the dairy country we had just left and the Julius River was extreme. We were now in what I call typical west coast territory with roadside scrub so thick you simply could not move through it and rain forest mostly composed of myrtle trees which once grew in a hotter Gondwanaland before Australia drifted off from Antarctica so many million years ago. I had seen the same distinctive dark green, rounded little leaves in Tierra del Fuego on the tip of South America, which once had its own links with a warmer Antarctica. The leatherwood trees were in bloom, covered in their distinctive white flowers, and apiarists had their hives stacked beside the road in small clearings to harvest Tasmania's prized and aromatic leatherwood honey.

We had time to do the twenty-minute rain forest walk before our picnic lunch at the Reserve, and we wandered among the moss-covered trunks of myrtle, sassafras, leatherwood trees and ancient ferns that we were pleased to find well identified with discreetly placed information panels.

The picnic area at Julius Creek is blessed with the most wondrous composting dunny that the world has ever seen. It is a tall timber edifice constructed down the slope of a steep hill. It has a walkway from the high ground leading in to the operational area. At the base there are windows, presumably to let in sunlight and warmth to help with the composting process. Beside the hand basin (its taps supplied with rain water collected from the roof) is a shelf on which is to be found a visitors' book. I can honestly say, being a fairly well-travelled feller, that this is the first dunny I have ever encountered anywhere in the world with a visitors' book. I was happy to write some complimentary remarks about this splendid, ecologically sound crapper. I even took a photograph of it. Ros was equally impressed.

We noticed on a local tourist map that we were too early to visit an attraction still under construction—the Dismal Swamp Maze and Visitors Centre. We had passed the turn-off to Dismal Road earlier in the day (after driving over Welcome Bridge!) and conjectured just how miserable the country it led to might be. I found out later that the Dismal Swamp Maze is a Forestry Tasmania project, mired—as it were—in some controversy over the disruption it might cause to sensitive wetlands. I wondered aloud to Ros whether the name might put visitors off, particularly on wet days when the idea of being lost in the Dismal Swamp Maze might not seem like the ideal family treat.

The road to the Milkshakes Hills Forest Reserve was gravel and fairly rough, but this is what Landcruisers are designed for—and more. The greater danger was from marauding log trucks, roaring around the narrow bends laden with logs almost certainly destined to be turned into woodchips for export rather than saw logs for local mills. This was our first encounter with the rampaging Tasmanian logging industry that is causing so much heartburn to conservationists, green groups and even saw-millers who fear a sustainable local timber industry is vanishing before their eyes.

I hadn't been able to find out any useful information about Milkshakes Hills in any of the literature available. Were they mountains shaped like old-fashioned milkshake containers? (Snow Thomas has since derided my ignorance and 'innocence'. In local dairying parlance, the milkshakes refer to hills shaped like women's breasts.) In any case I was never able to make the connection, because when we turned off to visit them we reached another thickly timbered reserve with yet another rain forest walk, and we literally couldn't see the hills for the trees. As we were a bit 'rain-forest-walked-out' by this time we set sail for Smithton and Stanley to prepare for our tour of Woolnorth the following day.

**Travel Diary Thursday 20 February**

There has been a wind change in the night. It is now screaming in
from the east! The prevailing wind here is almost invariably
from the west. No wonder Tasmanians spend a lot of time
talking about the weather, it changes so often and so dramatically.
We are beginning to understand why this area was chosen for an
electricity-generating wind farm. I wonder if some crusading
surveyor from Hydro Tasmania (a modern-day Henry Hellyer)
stood on the cliffs near Cape Grim, buffeted by the Roaring
Forties, and intoned John Batman-like, 'This will be the place for
a wind farm'.

We were up early to drive to Woolnorth, right on the north-
west tip of Tasmania and sixty-six kilometres west from
Stanley. Woolnorth runs tours of the historic property, which
also includes the Hydro Tasmania wind farm. It was a bit of
a scramble to get to the impressive gates by 10 am but we
made it with twenty minutes to spare, and boarded the
small Woolnorth tour bus driven by Cynthia, our guide for
the day. There were six of us—an elderly Scottish couple,
Ian and Kathleen, and a younger pair from Sydney, Adam
and Diane.

It was not hard to spot the first six operational, sixty-
metre tall towers stretching along the skyline as our bus
rolled along a farm road recently sealed by 'the Hydro', as
Tasmanians still call Hydro Tasmania. On top of each
tower is a nacelle (as big as our small bus) containing the
generator and the revolving hub from which sprout three
carbon fibre turbine blades, each one as long as a telegraph
pole—thirty-three metres. Their smooth, tapered, white
towers rise from a four-metre diameter at the base and I

thought them quite aesthetically pleasing in a futuristic kind of way.

They are difficult to photograph because they are so tall, and widely spaced. We drove to the base of the six working towers that have been operating since early 2003. Seventy-nine will eventually be built, pulling 138 megawatts of electricity out of thin air, enough to power a city of 56 000 households. Each turbine produces 1.75 megawatts—if the wind is blowing at more then 25 kph, which happens most of the time at Woolnorth, day and night. The wind turbines had taken the easterly wind in their stride, swinging around 180 degrees, their finely sculptured blades making a steady, vibrant whoosh whooshing sound. If the wind picks up to more than 90 kph (and during the storms that devastated the Sydney to Hobart race yachts in 1998 the wind speeds at Cape Grim were 176 kph) computers turn them off.

Hydro Tasmania bought the land from Woolnorth (and the VDL Company) and then obligingly leased it back so that cattle and sheep graze placidly while above them the great turbine blades revolve in seeming slow motion. It's difficult to comprehend the scale of these white behemoths. The Hydro literature (appropriately local) has provided an artist's impression showing that each tower is as tall as the Wrest Point Casino in Hobart or, for mainlanders, equivalent in height to the lighting towers at the Melbourne Cricket Ground.

Once reviled by conservationists for its seemingly unstoppable zest for damming every free-flowing river in the island, Hydro Tasmania is now fashionably clean and green, boasting that Tasmania produces 60 per cent of all of Australia's renewable energy. It is Forestry Tasmania and its support of woodchipping and clear-felling of old growth forests that now cops the kind of opprobrium dumped on 'the Hydro' by conservationists when it planned to dam the Franklin River in the 1980s, until stopped from so doing by national and international outrage. Concerns remain, though, about the hazards posed to local and migrating birds by the massive, whirling carbon fibre blades.

The wind farm's statistics are impressive. The power generated just by the six wind turbines we were looking at will be the equivalent of what otherwise would have contributed 44 000 tonnes of carbon emissions—the exhaust gases spewed from more than 11 000 cars. When the Woolnorth Wind Farm cranks up its 79 turbines, 530 000 tonnes of carbon emissions will be saved from entering the atmosphere, helping to reduce Australia's contribution to the greenhouse effect and global warming.

And, of course, when the Basslink cable under Bass Strait is operational and connects Tasmania to the mainland Australian electricity grid in 2005, excess renewable energy can be piped benevolently to the mainland, which will have to pay for it during peak demand periods. The cable is capable of shifting about ten per cent of Hydro Tasmania's installed capacity. It is a further testament to my belief that Tasmania is the testicle of Australia—suffusing the mainland with strength and vigour. Not only in human terms, but electricity as well.

The Scottish couple on our tour, Ian and Kathleen, were staying at Woolnorth in what must be one of Tasmania's swishest B & Bs, the big house on the hill. This is not the manager's house but the Director's Lodge, built fairly recently for on-site meetings of the VDL Company Court, with commanding views of Woolnorth's grazing lands to the distant coastline. At other times it provides upmarket and spacious accommodation for visitors. As we had signed up for the full day tour, rather than a half, Cynthia told us we would have lunch there.

We had our morning cuppa and home-made fruit cake in Woolnorth's big new shearing shed, constructed only a few years ago. The nearby buildings were much older and one looked like a child's drawing of a house, a single-storey dwelling with two square windows on either side of a door with a brick chimney plumb in the middle of the roof. It is Cookhouse Cottage, built in 1831, the oldest private home in north-west Tasmania.

The first settlement at Woolnorth dates back to 1826, the year the VDL Company's brig *Tranmere* first arrived at Circular Head. Early settlers built a jetty, six cottages, a blacksmith's shop and a store for twenty-five free men and their families and a similar number of convicts. In 1831 the main settlement moved to the site where we had morning tea. Nothing remains of the original settlement but a few piles of stones and broken bricks.

By the end of the nineteenth century the VDL Company's fortunes had improved, despite the depletion of its sheep numbers by Tasmanian tigers, Aborigines and renegade whites. The company diversified into timber and building wooden horse-drawn tramways—later a narrow-gauge steel railway—through the company's land, to take advantage of a mining boom sparked by the discovery of tin at Mt Bischoff, on the west coast. Things went so well, in fact, that in 1883 the Tasmanian government offered to buy the company's assets, but the Court of Directors advised shareholders against it. In 1954 the VDL Company broke with tradition and installed its first resident Tasmanian manager to take charge of its island operations instead of importing an Englishman. To this day, Woolnorth remains the VDL Company's greatest asset and is still quaintly operated under its original Royal Charter. I was curious about this and hoped to find out more at lunchtime when the manager's wife (and architect of the delicious fruit cake at morning tea), Stephanie Porteous-Else, would join us. Presumably Betty Windsor at Buckingham Palace still has to be paid an annual emolument to continue this arrangement.

Over thick and tender 'American cut' grilled steaks and glasses of chateau cardboard red in the Directors' Dining Room (I'm sure the members of the Court do themselves better than that), I asked Stephanie why she thought the VDL Company kept the Charter going into the twenty-first century. She wasn't absolutely sure but knew that one reason was it enabled more control of the land. Woolnorth is on a peninsula and under the Charter has jurisdiction right down to the high tide mark. Stephanie said the VDL Company once owned down to the low tide mark, but this had changed over the years. (Most Crown grants of land in Tasmania from 1830 and onwards only go to within one chain of the high water mark—32.48 metres—which ensures public access to the coast.) I wondered whether there might also be some taxation advantages under the Charter, but Stephanie could not confirm that.

After lunch Cynthia drove us to the north-westernmost point of Tasmania, where the Southern Ocean meets Bass Strait. On getting out of the bus we stayed upright with difficulty, leaning into the screaming easterly wind and looking out towards the offshore islands. The nearest to us was Trefoil, just offshore to the north-west, and the larger bulk of Robbins Island could be seen to the east. At our feet were steep cliffs and a view over the sombrely named

Suicide Bay. Its history relates more to murder than suicide as it was here in 1828 that four convict shepherds from the Van Diemen's Land Company were alleged to have murdered some thirty Tasmanian Aborigines in retaliation for the blacks having driven a flock of sheep over sheer cliffs into the sea several weeks earlier. The Aborigines were angry because the shepherds had tried to entice some of their women into a hut. In the fracas that followed one shepherd was speared in the thigh and one Aboriginal man shot dead.[1]

This massacre is one of many challenged by the controversial writer Keith Windschuttle in his book *The Fabrication of Aboriginal History, Volume One: Van Diemen's Land 1803–1847*, although Windschuttle does believe six blacks were killed. A contemporary diary, by a woman in Van Diemen's Land at the time, Rosalie Hare, but not quoted by Windschuttle as a source for his book, does make reference to the Cape Grim massacre:

> We have to lament that our own countrymen consider the massacre of people an honour. While we remained at Circular Head there were several accounts of considerable numbers of natives having been shot . . . The master of the Company's Cutter *Fanny*, assisted by four shepherds and his crew, surprised a party and killed 12.

It is not clear whether the Aborigines were killed on the high ground above the bay or on the rocky shore below. If sailors were involved, the blacks may well have been

---

1 Kerry Pink, 1986, 'The Woolnorth Massacre', article in *Local History Journal*, ISSN 0814-8708, Vol. 2, No. 4, Circular Head History Project

trapped on the beach, under the cliff. This seems likely in the light of historian Henry Reynold's mention of the incident in his 1995 book *Fate of a Free People*, where he discusses the great difficulties faced by Europeans who wanted to shoot blacks for 'coming up with them', as it was described in contemporary accounts. The wary Tasmanian Aborigines did not hang about to be shot at, and were often warned by their dogs of whites approaching their camps, or bivouacs, and were able to escape. Reynolds says:

> Yet another danger for the Tasmanians was to be trapped by some geographical feature which made escape difficult—a situation which apparently occurred in the case of the infamous Cape Grim massacre in the far north-west of the colony. After tit-for-tat skirmishing between the local clans and servants of the Van Diemen's Land Company, four shepherds trapped a group of men, women and children at the edge of the sea and were able to fire down on them from above.

Windschuttle might dispute the numbers, but there is little doubt that Tasmanian Aborigines were murdered at Cape Grim. As we looked over towards that rocky beach at Suicide Bay, under the looming sandstone cliff from which the convict shepherds are said to have gunned down their trapped victims, I felt a sudden shiver. It looked a sinister, forbidding place and it is no wonder that the Tasmanian Aboriginal Land Council has included Cape Grim in the list of places designated as areas of spiritual significance.

It was with a feeling of relief that we drove down to the eastern side of the peninsula, to the scant remains of where the first white settlement at Woolnorth was established in

1826. Cynthia volunteered that Woolnorth employed the services of 'a full time flagellator' to keep the assigned convicts in order. This conjured up unworthy thoughts about the joys of promotion for the man concerned. I could imagine his mother in the Old Dart, in conversation with a friend who'd asked how her boy was getting on, 'We've just had wonderful news from Van Diemen's Land— Matthew is doing so well that he's been appointed a full-time flagellator at Woolnorth!'

Although Woolnorth still operates under its Royal Charter it has not been controlled from Great Britain since the 1950s, when control of the company passed through the hands of several private owners. In 1993 a New Zealand company, Tasmanian Agriculture Limited (there seems a contradiction in terms here), acquired 85.7 per cent of the shares for $18.6 million. Since then TasAg has invested millions more to bring nearly 5000 hectares of scrub and heathland to pasture, to support one of the biggest dairying operations in the southern hemisphere. Today TasAg milks about 9000 Friesian cows daily in ten rotary dairies operated by share farmers. The oldest part of the property still carries about 1200 breeding cattle, including the descendants of the Hereford herd introduced to Woolnorth in 1873.

Cynthia drove us to one of these automatic milking roundabouts to see some of the daily quota of milk go gurgling from the teats of the obliging Friesians into the holding tanks. As we watched from a viewing gallery the placid cows, doubtless anxious to discharge their swollen udders, walked without any directions onto the slowly turning circular automatic milking merry-go-round. The only human involvement was a couple of rubber-aproned workers, slipping the softly pulsating clusters of suction cups onto each newly arriving cow's teats—and disengaging them at the end of the cycle. Otherwise the whole shebang was automatic, with the cows obligingly stepping in and out of their individual stalls as they arrived at the start and finish point.

So that's what modern dairy farmers do: just stand there and watch the cows wander onto the merry-go-round while the milk splashes into the tanks and the dollars into the bank. Edward Curr, eat your heart out.

**Travel Diary Thursday 20 February**

Full marks to the Stanley Visitor's Centre. Got back from Woolnorth by 5 pm and, with little hope, took my laptop to the centre to see if I could importune my way onto a phone line to check my email. Internet cafes don't let you do this. You have to use their computers. To my delight the nice woman behind the counter let me plug in to one of their lines, and charged an exceedingly modest fee to do so. A welcome contrast to importuning motel owners in remote places to hire me a room for ten minutes, 'Just to check my email.' 'Oh yes?' the proprietor would say with a leer? 'Are you sure ten minutes will be long enough?'

We passed the turnoff advertising the siren joys of Dismal Road yet again, this time with The Manor in tow, and headed away from the partially cracked Nut to the remote north-western town of Marrawah, where we were to turn south to drive down the remote and mountainous west coast—or as close to the coast as we could get with the limited roads and tracks available. We planned to camp for a couple of days by the Arthur River, where we would meet up with Brian Mansell from the Tasmanian Aboriginal Land Council, who had promised to show us some rock carvings and other evidence of ancient Aboriginal presence on the west coast.

Anyone who has read our last book in the Penelope series, *Penelope Bungles to Broome*, will know that I am utterly fascinated by Aboriginal rock art. I have seen engravings and etchings in diverse locations in the Kimberley, the Burrup Peninsula and the Pilbara. Rock engravings are immensely old and were created many thousands of years ago in contrast to painted rock art, which is more recent—except, of course, for the marvellous Bradshaw paintings in the Kimberley, possibly up to and beyond 30 000 years old, where the brown pigment has fused into the rock. These are unthinkable periods of continuous culture when measured against our own two-centuries-and-a-bit European presence in Australia.

I was aware that Aboriginal rock engravings had been found at Mt Cameron West early last century—now called Preminghana by the Tasmanian Aboriginal Land Council, which has custody of the site. Before we left Sydney I wanted to arrange to see them if possible, and asked advice from a Tasmanian contact, Joe King, who lives just north of the Arthur River and who, among other activities, runs a tourist operation where people can see Tasmanian devils feeding at night. Joe said, 'Why don't you just ring Brian Mansell at the Tasmanian Land Council in Hobart and ask him?' Simple really, and I used to be a reporter! I have to admit, though, that I did so with some trepidation. Joe told me Brian was Michael Mansell's brother. I was well aware that Michael—a lawyer—had a reputation of not only being a fierce fighter for Aboriginal rights, but one of the stroppiest of the activists, who didn't suffer fools gladly. I had no way of knowing whether Brian was similarly inclined.

When I rang the TALC I was put straight through to Brian. I drew a deep breath, told him I was a former Tasmanian, that I was planning to write a travel book on the island, quickly sketched out my interest in ancient Aboriginal rock art and asked if it would be possible to visit Mt Cameron West.

Brian, who hadn't had a chance to get a word in edgewise while I rattled on, replied politely that he couldn't see any problem with that. 'If you tell me when you are coming down,' he said, 'I'll come over to the west coast and show you around myself. There are a few other sites south of the Arthur River that you may be interested to see as well.' I certainly was! And so we arranged to meet Brian Mansell near the ranger's station at Arthur River. Before that we thought we'd make camp and do a bit of general touring in the area.

There were heavy road works from Marrawah to the Arthur River as the road is being prepared for sealing, mainly because of the increasing tourist influx, and it is now possible to continue driving down to Zeehan since a controversial road was pushed through the Tarkine wilderness—against the wishes of conservationists—in 1995 and 1996. It's a fairly rough drive through wonderfully wild heathland and mixed forest, winding through some spectacular mountain peaks. Visitors then have to cross the Pieman River on a vehicular ferry to link up with a gravel road from the Savage River at Corinna and on to Zeehan. Travellers are well advised to make sure the ferry is actually operating before committing to the trip.

The road to the Arthur River traverses undulating, fairly open country with trademark patches of thick melaleuca scrub so typical of the west coast. The road works continued right to the river, the approaches to the narrow bridge being kerbed and guttered, no less.

We called in at the ranger station to get some information (there wasn't much in the way of pamphlets or maps to take away, but there were large scale maps on the wall to look at). The camping is self regulated—you pay your fee and choose your own spot. It's just bush camping, with no power and a few long-drop loos. There was a shower and flushing toilet block near the gate, but we gave it a wide berth as there was a camper and caravan rally spread out around it. Otherwise the camping ground was lightly occupied, and we found a top location in a small clearing which was surrounded by thick scrub and was utterly private. It even had a small fireplace and we had brought firewood in on Penelope's roof rack—which is becoming common and sensible practice now in national parks and reserves to preserve the natural bush in areas of heavy usage.

After getting The Manor ship-shape we drove across the Arthur River to see what was on the other side. There are only twenty-six permanent residents at Arthur River and two operators conducting river cruises up the river, promising various scenic and wild life delights. We called in to a shop to buy a few supplies, but mostly to get some information. A rather dour looking fellow appeared and after the usual pleasantries I mentioned that there wasn't much in the way of printed information available for tourists. This prompted a mega-whinge about how that should be a National Parks and Wildlife Service responsibility and they did nothing. 'It's all gone bad since the

Arthur River was made a conservation area. Before that people used to come here with their kids and bring in horses, trail bikes, four-wheel-drives. They could bring in their guns for hunting and really have fun. Now there are so many rules and regulations about what you can and can't do that the locals don't bother to come here any more.'

I happened to know that conservation areas were a lot more relaxed in the way they were run than national parks. Thank God there weren't a lot of hoons roaring around on trail bikes, quads and four-wheel-drives any more shooting anything that moved. It sounded like a great improvement to me. I confess I didn't have the courage to put that point of view to the shopkeeper.

The uncharacteristic easterly was still blowing strongly as we drove down to the shore, beside the mouth of the Arthur River. This is harsh dolerite country, with rocky spurs and gulches and occasional small beaches sandwiched in between the rocks. To the south of the river mouth was a very strange sight—a profusion of dead tree trunks that had either been washed down the river, or brought in by winds and tides to festoon the rocks and beaches. They were big trees, too, hundreds of them. This was driftwood on a giant scale.

The weather was balmy and as we'd been on the run fairly intensively since we arrived on *Spirit II*, we thought a lazy afternoon at our nicely secluded camp was a good idea. An afternoon nap seemed more attractive the more we thought of it, and I needed to prepare the fire for our evening barbecue. It's becoming increasingly difficult to light fires when camping, due to bushfire dangers, national park policies and scarcity of firewood. Yet there is surely no greater delight at the end of the day than to sit around the glowing embers of even a small campfire with a libation of red under a canopy of stars. All of which came to pass.

Only one incident marred my enjoyment. During the night I awoke, slipped on my thongs and left The Manor for a nocturnal pee. I had not taken more than three steps before I felt a stabbing pain on my foot, as though someone had jabbed the end of a burning stick into it. Hopping and cursing (and waking Ros up in the process), I switched on my torch and saw I'd been fanged by a wandering ant—one of Tasmania's belligerent jack jumpers. Unlike most other ants, which tend to follow established trails, jack jumpers are freelancers which just wander around looking for food. They are particularly pugnacious and their name comes from a habit of jumping around frenetically when disturbed in a kind of mad antly rage. My assailant was understandably cross about being trodden on, and had given me the full treatment by using its jaws to grab on to my foot and inject its venom from an abdominal sting. Jack jumpers are endemic to Tasmania and are difficult to avoid because of their wandering habits. I'd been stung many times as a kid. Fortunately I had not—as happens to 1 to 2 per cent of the population—developed an allergy to its poison. If I had, I would have been in serious trouble. I swore an oath (silently in deference to my drowsy partner) that I would not venture out in the night again with thongs, but always put on proper shoes.

In his best-selling travel book on Australia, *Down Under*, Bill Bryson made much of the many unexpected ways travellers can be killed by Australia's dangerous creatures ranging from crocodiles and snakes to the tiny blue-ringed octopus and even a small jellyfish colloquially called a 'snottie'. He terrified an American travelling companion, quoting from the apocryphal book *Things That Will Kill You Horridly In Australia (Vol. 19)*. I've checked, and he did not mention the Tasmanian jack jumper. I'm sure he would have if he'd had access to recent research on this savage little 10–12 mm ant (*Myrmecia pilosula*).

To those who are allergic to jack jumpers and who have a severe heart condition, just one bite could be fatal. Here's what can happen. About thirty minutes after a bite there is facial flushing and itching and rashes break out else-where on the body. Nausea, vomiting and abdominal pains are next, accompanied by swelling of the lips, face and—understandably—feelings of severe anxiety. There may be difficulty in speaking or swallowing. Then comes breath-lessness and wheezing, impaired vision and a drop in blood pressure leading to collapse and unconsciousness.

Only in the last few years has a Tasmanian research team, led by Dr Simon Brown at the Royal Hobart Hospital, developed a preparation made from the venom of the jack jumper which can be used in a technique known as venom immunotherapy (VIT) to reduce a patient's allergenic response to the sting. Before that, no treatment other than palliative care was available.

Fortunately I am not allergic and returned, cursing, to bed knowing that my foot would itch and hurt for the next few hours but that I would not wake up dead.

# three

## The Wild West

**Travel Diary Saturday 22 February**

We woke to the insistent and loud buzzing of bees that had Ros worrying that The Manor might be becoming a hive. This particular species of stinging insect was harmlessly harvesting the nectar from eucalyptus blossoms on the gum tree overhead. The weather was still warm, the wind—still unusually from the east—had eased, and we breakfasted under our leafy bower, as warm sunshine filtered through.

Brian Mansell was waiting at the ranger's station at 9.30 am and we returned to camp for a mug of tea and to work out what we'd do that day. Brian, a stocky, quietly spoken man in his early fifties—he told me later he didn't actually know how old he was but thought he was about fifty-three—did not look in any way Aboriginal to me. This is the case for most of the 16 000 people in the state who currently identify themselves as Aboriginal Tasmanians. Brian explained to me later that this was only one of many difficult and complex issues of identity for a people who, until recently, had been deemed to be an extinct race.

As manager of the Tasmanian Aboriginal Land Council in Hobart, Brian surely had more important things to do than show a couple of travellers around this part of the west coast, so we felt very privileged indeed to have his company. On the other hand, he said with a laugh that the prospect of visiting some of his favourite Aboriginal sites on the west coast wasn't too onerous when he might otherwise have been sitting at a desk. He suggested we all travel in the Land Council's Landcruiser, rather than in convoy, so he could explain things as we went along.

The plan was to drive about thirty kilometres south to Sundown Point—where he planned to show us some rock carvings—and then work our way back to the Arthur River visiting some Aboriginal middens he said had only recently been located, and some other sites which he said he'd keep as a surprise. After lunch we would drive north to Mt Cameron West, now known as Preminghana, where the Tasmanian Aboriginal Land Council controlled the site of the extensive rock carvings first located in the late 1930s. Brian said he had a surprise to show us there too.

Sundown Point is a public reserve run by the Parks and Wildlife Service. There is no way we would have known where to look for the Aboriginal petroglyphs if Brian had not been with us. They are on a small sloping belt of sedimentary rock between the beach and a sheltered estuary. Like petroglyphs I had seen on the Burrup Peninsula in the north of Western Australia, the designs were etched into the rock by the artist striking repeatedly with a pointed, stone tool harder than the rock being worked on.

I thought the Sundown Point gallery was stunning. Most of the designs were concentric circles—similar to photographs of the carvings I had seen from the Mt Cameron West site. Those, however, are on a much larger scale and more deeply inscribed into the softer sandstone. At Sundown Point, the sedimentary rock is hard and layered. Some of the rings had a bar drawn across low down on a circle. Not all the circles were regular or concentric. There were some irregular designs on darker rock but not obviously representing any animal or plant shapes. Due to their great age, their ceremonial significance can only be guessed at now. As we walked along the lower edge of the gallery, the sun broke through scattered cloud, the stronger light putting into relief and giving us new aspects of some of the less obvious etchings.

The site is not identified by a sign because, sadly, some of these priceless carvings have already been vandalised and stolen. Brian showed me several places where art thieves (or just idiots) had chiselled off slabs of the layered stone, desecrating this priceless stone age gallery.

It is clear that Sundown Point was a tribal meeting point where ceremonies were conducted in a sheltered bay. Fish and shellfish were plentiful, and fresh water—seldom a problem in Tasmania—abounded. Having searched in the Kimberley for unmarked Aboriginal rock art sites, I know you can often find them intuitively by looking at the landscape, noting the nearness of a river, or waterhole, and by then looking for a spectacular rock or cliff formation you feel might have been the kind of place where people could have gathered. To me, Sundown Point had that kind of ambience.

It was a great start, and there were more joys ahead. Brian was keen to try to find some recently located shell middens on the coast that a Parks and Wildlife ranger had shown him a few weeks before. But he wasn't doing the driving at the time and couldn't remember exactly where he had been. I'm a fairly cautious four-wheel-drive person, which is just as well because I have never done any formal training and have not driven much in sand. Brian, on the other hand, had done an advanced 4WD course and tackled situations I would never have attempted myself. The combination of soft sand and extremely brutal water-sculptured spikes of dolerite rock made our exploration an adventure.

Churning around the base of a sand dune on a promontory, Brian found he had the choice of a rocky, metre high rock face on the seaward side, and deep soft sand on the other. He chose the base of the sand dune, but the soft sand skewed us down the slope on top of a trunk of driftwood which inconveniently wedged itself under the centre of the Landcruiser amidships. The effect of this was that we were balanced on the log and had no traction on the front and rear driver's side wheels. Interesting, I thought to myself. No one knows we are here. We're not on any recognised 4WD track, and we have no shovels or jacks to help sort this out. It was possible we might be in deep schtuck.

I was pleased that Brian seemed cheerful enough, although maybe he was putting a brave face on things. I did know that Ros had that look on her face that translates as, 'O God, boys doing silly things'.

Brian and I dug some sand out from under the front and back wheels with the only tools available to us, our hands, and lifted the biggest rocks we could carry to put under them. Then Brian spreadeagled himself and began digging out sand under and behind the log that had stranded us so inconveniently. His only concern was that the log, with the weight of the Landcruiser on it, might suddenly shift and crush his arm.

There are more ways of killing a cat than stuffing its fundamental orifice with desiccated coconut, as my old father used to say, and after about ten minutes of digging the log slowly slid into the cavity Brian had created. We hopped aboard, the wheels connected with the rocks we'd stacked under them, and we were mobile again. I was glad Brian had done the advanced 4WD driving course. He said he thought we should get back to known tracks, and Ros agreed. There is a network of 4WD tracks along this part of the coast, linking rocky gulches and small beaches behind which are a collection of fishing shacks thrown together with a mix of timber and corrugated iron. At a more established place, like Couta Rocks, professional fishermen go out when they can to fish and harvest crayfish. There is no harbour and the westerly winds more often than not make getting out hazardous, if not impossible. Some of the biggest swells in the world crash in on the exposed west coast from the vast Southern Ocean. To safeguard their boats, the fishermen have constructed what I called 'cradles to nowhere'—steel rails supported by wooden legs that rise up from the shoreline and come to an abrupt stop, leaving the fishing boat high and dry, sometimes six or eight metres up in the air.

The surprise Brian planned for us was, again, something we could never have found even had we known about it. He showed us a large midden, a circular mound formed over hundreds, perhaps thousands, of years by Aboriginal people discarding shells of cockles, oysters, mussels or abalone. This midden was about ten metres high and had an indented crown, which Brian said had once been used as a shelter, with a roof constructed probably of branches and animal skins. Brian said that anthropologists were right to say that these middens occurred because they were near a reliable food source and fresh water. But it should also not be forgotten, he said, that these sites were important because they were also ceremonial meeting places where Aboriginal people honoured their ancestors, while the middens slowly grew higher and higher.

Recent rain had exposed small stone tools, flakes of flinty rock, probably used as scrapers. Brian said one of the biggest problems was to stop the culture of souveniring these artefacts, and try to prevent 4WD vehicles from being driven over Aboriginal middens, something no one had worried about in the past. But times and attitudes were changing. 'These sites are very significant to Aboriginal people and we are now trying to protect them.'

We returned to camp for a quick lunch, and the chance to talk to Brian about his own life and some of the difficulties faced by those people in Tasmania who claimed Aboriginal ancestry. As we sat down under the shade of the trees overhanging our enviable camping spot, Brian told me a revealing and rather depressing story about the racism Aboriginal people have come to expect from white Australians. As a young man he left Tasmania and joined the army. He remembers the first time his name was called out by his platoon commander as 'ManSELL'—with the emphasis on the second syllable. In Tasmania this recognisably Aboriginal name is always pronounced 'MANsell'. He realised with a sense of relief that no one knew anything about him. For the first time in his life he wasn't being 'badged' by being a MANsell. This, to him unique, state of affairs continued for ten years. By then he had achieved the rank of corporal. But one day he was called into the office of his new commanding officer, a colonel.

'As I marched in to present myself to my new commanding officer, I halted in front of him, saluted, and said, "Good morning Sir, Corporal ManSELL reporting for duty". The regimental sergeant major was standing beside the colonel. "Ahh, MANsell," the colonel said, "you must be from Flinders Island!" The manner in which he said those words made me feel dirty again but I was not going to give in easily. "No sir," I said, "I am not from Flinders Island."

'"Well, I say you are from Flinders Island and I should know as I formerly lived at Scottsdale, and Flinders Island is where all your kind comes from."

'My mind was in turmoil. On one hand I could not afford to tell a colonel he was wrong, as that was insubordination. Secondly, he had the regimental sergeant major as a witness and that would make it very bad for me if on my first day at my new posting I start off on the wrong side of the two most senior people in the camp.

'"Bugger it," I thought, "this bloke has it in for me anyway so I may as well let him have it." I said, "Well sir, if you originally lived at Scottsdale you must have been a potato farmer."

'To his credit the colonel told me to get out of his office rather than have me charged with insubordination to a senior officer and behaviour unbecoming a soldier serving in the Australian Army. I unfortunately encountered other ex-Tasmanians who all outranked me. One was a female captain who constantly made me double count my pay and salute her twice each payday. It is a requirement based on respect that one salutes an officer and that the officer returns the salute. That bitch never ever returned the compliment I paid her. She was later to deny me an additional five minutes to complete an examination paper to qualify me for promotion to sergeant.

'Anyway, after the first day at my new camp, things went progressively downhill. Senior officers would make snide remarks about "abos or darkies" whenever I was in earshot. Whenever I attended training briefings on behalf of my "boss", the major in charge would sneer as if he was full of hatred for me. It was difficult to take as I had no recourse whatsoever. Had I said anything back to this particular major I knew he would use all of his powers to have me demoted and probably placed in prison. The power that officers have over their subordinates borders on the dictatorial.

'I should say that some time later the colonel came to my rescue in a civilian court where I was charged with assault and gave me an excellent character report. Despite not having touched the alleged victim I was found guilty. However my time was running out in the army, as the "news" about my Aboriginality had finally reached my Head of Corps in Canberra. When I had reason to telephone the Canberra office all I received were snide and offensive comments.

'The next slip up I made was all my enemies were waiting for. I was discharged within three months. I was sad to leave the army as I had had such a great time just being treated like a "normal" person. I had attained my Army Education Certificate Class 1 (Grade Ten equivalent) because I was not treated any differently from any of the other "students". I found a new enthusiasm for learning and had supportive instructors during all my promotional training. This experience was vastly different to the racism and discrimination that I encountered on a daily basis during my primary and secondary schooling in Tasmania.'

Later I asked Brian to talk about growing up in Tasmania as an Aborigine:

BRIAN: Well, Tim, I remembered being called a whole range of names—nigger, black bastard, abo, quarter-caste sixteenth—which was the lowest I got down to—and so you grow up being called a whole range of names.

TIM: This despite the fact that looking at you in the playground there is no outward reason to say that you are Aboriginal.

BRIAN: Yeah, that's what I thought too! (Laughs.)

TIM: So how come you were getting this stuff?

BRIAN: It seemed at that time if you had a name like Mansell, Maynard, Brown, Everett or Thomas you were an 'abo' or something of that nature. And so you grow up really not knowing who you are because when you sought advice from your parents or your family, they'd just say, 'Don't worry about it'. Later on in life I realised that their lives must have been even more traumatised and they weren't able to deal with the situation, so they couldn't then help me. So you grow up not knowing who you actually are. You have a name, but the name seems pretty dirty and you long to be separated from it.

TIM: Which is a very sad thing.

BRIAN: It's sad if you don't get over it. (Laughs.) It is sad because it torments you so much, and when you are young and growing up you want to be with your mates and you want to be with the pack, the group, your friends. But sometimes your best friends were your worst enemies because they knew your family more intimately than other people did. At times your best mates called you the worst names—but perhaps only in the heat of an argument or something. But as you got into your teenage years and you formed an identity, sometimes that was even more difficult.

You leave school and then you start work and the name, the tainted name of Mansell, haunts you all the way. Your mates and the people in the workforce say things to you. And so in my experience, I went on to get experience in a sport where I wanted to be part of the group, nothing more nor less. I got involved in cycling. I remember the very first training session I had on the York Park Velodrome, in Launceston, it would have been about 1966 I think, one bloke came up beside me—I was riding around the track very nervously, it was a completely new world—and this bloke came up beside me and said, 'Move over half-caste'. But fortunately he was just one of the few silly people who I never befriended after that.

The most unfortunate thing that happened to me in my cycling career was that I went from a nobody to being a champion! So I went from the bottom of the ladder to the top of the ladder without even trying to, or even wanting to. At one stage I was being called a dirty name, and given an identity, and three or four months later I was given a new identity which I didn't want. All of a sudden I'm not 'abo' or a 'half-caste', the next thing I'm a champion! I couldn't deal with either of those descriptions.

TIM: What was wrong with being a champion?

BRIAN: I didn't want to be a champion. I didn't want to be any better or any worse than anyone else—just part of the group. I wanted to have friends, I wanted to have people I could socialise with. All of a sudden I went from feeling I wasn't as good as them, to being better than them. I didn't want to be better than them! It's a difficult situation when you are young and dealing with issues of identity, with self-esteem, self-confidence and all that stuff.

TIM: You said earlier you were working with an Aboriginal organisation, and I take it you would rather be doing that than some other kind of job?

BRIAN: I'd much prefer to work within an Aboriginal environment, especially an environment which allows you to have contact with the land and different land types around the state. But even if it wasn't involved with land management and that kind of stuff, working within an Aboriginal organisation—despite all its political infighting and the really deep personal arguments you get involved in—you know each other so well, so at least your identity isn't attacked. You can deal with all sorts of issues without people saying to you, 'Well, you're not a real Aboriginal person'. And that's the really troubling position when someone says to you that you are not a real person.

So you say, 'Well, what does a real person look like?' It really attacks your very soul. And so I've moved from being 'a person of Aboriginal descent' or whatever, half-caste and so on, to an Aboriginal person, and I've moved from that to being a person. And so if someone says to me, 'Who are you?' I say, 'Well I'm just me. I'm just Brian Mansell, I'm just a person. And I recognise you as a person.' I don't want to know what your identity is 'cause I'm not going to tell you mine until we find some common ground, some common understanding, and then we can talk to each other. And then you can tell me that you're Chinese and I'll tell you that I'm an Aboriginal. And I'll say, 'Oh, Chinese, I've got no problems with that.' And you might say to me, 'Well you don't look Aboriginal to me, but that's OK.' So that's a thing you build up, and then you build on that. But first to meet each other and say, 'Look I'm proudly Aboriginal whether you like it or not', you might think, 'Well shit! I know what an Aboriginal person looks like and that doesn't look like you.' So therefore we have problems in communication, we have problems in understanding, we have problems in our minds. It's something the Yolngu people call *mardhubarlyon*—'confusion of the mind'. To move away from this confusion, we must see each other as people.

After lunch we headed north towards Marrawah, but Brian took off down to the coast again to show us some more indented middens that had been used as shelters by Aboriginal people long ago. The concave tops to the middens were hard to see because, Brian said, the Parks and Wildlife Service had planted a coarse kind of dark green reed in them, perhaps to discourage people from making use of them in any way. People crouching down in the shallow basins could not be seen from below and Brian said that holiday makers had been crapping in them. Perhaps the reed plantations were a better option. Such behaviour seemed an awful metaphor for the way some white Tasmanians were treating Aboriginal heritage aspirations. A little further along the coast Brian showed us where there had been Aboriginal seal 'hides' (shallow saucer-like depressions in the sea-rounded stones where seal hunters lay in wait) that had been clearly visible until a few years ago, but had been destroyed by four-wheel-drivers churning past on the loose scree.

'I'd like to recreate an Aboriginal shelter on top of one of the middens with branches and bark to show visitors what it might have been like,' said Brian as we headed back to the highway again on our way to Preminghana—Mt Cameron West, on the coast just north of Marrawah.

I remembered having seen photographs of the large rock carvings that were discovered at Mt Cameron West in 1933 by a Devonport schoolteacher, A L Meston, after having been tipped off by locals. Some of the carvings were later removed and taken to the Queen Victoria Museum and Art Gallery in Launceston.

'I'm really looking forward to seeing them,' I said to Brian as we drove along.

'I'm sorry that I can't show them to you,' said Brian.
'Why not?'

'I'd like to, but they are buried under the sand and haven't been visible for half a century or more. In a way that's a good thing because it has stopped people damaging them or trying to souvenir them.'

Brian explained that the 524 hectare site at Preminghana had been under Aboriginal control since the mid 1990s when twelve parcels of land in Tasmania of significance to indigenous people were returned to the Tasmanian Aboriginal people under the Aboriginal Land Act of 1995. Before that Mt Cameron West was a reserve under the control of the Parks and Wildlife Service.

'But there was no presence here by Parks and Wildlife officers so any one who had a four-wheel-drive could please themselves where they drove over the land and of course a lot of people wanted to drive down to the beach and along the beach, in the process damaging the sand dunes and also Aboriginal midden sites. All of those things happened up to 1995 and now we have to say, "Look we can no longer tolerate people damaging these special sites". So to preserve the land and what it contained, we now ask people to leave their cars in the car park and walk down a few hundred metres to the beach.'

The Tasmanian Aboriginal Land Council now has a caretaker living on site, and anyone can visit Preminghana providing they ask permission first. I wasn't surprised to hear that most of the locals were incensed they couldn't drive their 4WD vehicles down to the beach and over the dunes as they had done in years past. The local Circular Head council wants to construct a road right down to the beach through Aboriginal land and that issue is still unresolved. Only the Tasmanian Aboriginal Relics Act stands in the way, described by Brian as 'The weakest bit of legislation in the world in terms of protecting Aboriginal heritage . . . We don't think it is unreasonable to ask people to park their vehicles in the car park and walk a few hundred metres to the beach. But there is a culture among people who have four-wheel-drives that they must be able to drive wherever they want at all times.'

There was no point in walking to the cliffs at the base of Mt Cameron West if we couldn't see the carvings but Brian had a surprise up his sleeve. Dashing into the tussocks behind the beach he pulled some branches away from something I couldn't see, and asked Ros and me to come and have a look. To our astonishment he was holding a piece of white sandstone, tilted on its edge, with two concentric circles deeply etched into it. He said it had been washed up onto the beach about eighteen months earlier. It had been discovered by a tourist who recognised its significance and not only notified the Tasmanian Aboriginal Land Council, but stood guard over it until it could be secured. Brian keeps it carefully hidden to show selected people. But how could such a thing happen?

'The Preminghana lands contain the greatest collection of Aboriginal rock engravings in Tasmania,' Brian explained. 'I think there are in the vicinity of 400 individual engravings here, but we must remember that 10 000 years ago and beyond, the sea level was much lower than it currently is. And so we have to go back 10 000 to 12 000 years or more to when the coastline was further out. People then would have been putting their engravings on the sandstone which is now covered by sea. From time to time these engravings break loose from wherever they are out there and get washed up by the heavy west coast seas as this one has been. It's about twenty kilograms in weight, almost a metre square and it has two circular engravings on it. So we must deduct from that situation that further out there under the water there may be another massive gallery of engravings that people just don't know about.'

Brian also produced from another hiding place a superb Aboriginal grinding stone and pestle found in the vicinity, with red ochre still visible in the crevices of the oval-shaped granite hand piece.

We drove out past the caretaker's cottage with the Aboriginal flag flying proudly above its roof. It was already 5 pm and Brian had to drive back to Hobart that night, a journey of some five hours, so we had to stop exploring. We weren't complaining, having experienced the A1 Preminghana tour, as well as our morning adventures at Sundown Point and four-wheel-driving on the extreme fringe of the well named 'wild west' coast.

**Travel Diary Sunday 23 February**

We have become fond of our Arthur River camp site, secluded in our own tunnel of bush, but it's time to head further down the west coast to Strahan, where every serious tourist to Tasmania must go, to experience the famous Gordon River cruise and travel on the recently restored Abt system steam railway that runs from Queenstown to Macquarie Harbour, puffing up—and down—impossible gradients by means of the engine locking on to an ingenious system of metal cogs in the centre of the track. We will continue down the coast using a rather controversial road that was pushed through what is known as the Tarkine wilderness in 1995 and 1996. It's a narrow, rather basic road, but can be used by conventional vehicles as well as four-wheel-drives. I want to see it for two reasons—because it is said to reveal some spectacular country and because my youngest brother Philip built it! Well his company was responsible for the construction, and he managed the project on the ground.

The road's northern section that we began to drive that morning was called, by locals, 'the road to nowhere', because it ran as far as the Lindsay River and then just stopped. At least that was the case until some fifty-four kilometres of the Tarkine road (for want of an official name) was constructed down to Corinna and the Pieman River. Travellers have to cross the river by a small vehicular ferry, before negotiating another ten kilometres of gravel road to join the highway that continues on to Zeehan—and eventually Strahan, on the shores of Macquarie Harbour about halfway down Tasmania's west coast. And that is as far as you can go because there are no roads into the World Heritage listed South West National Park.

Crossing the Arthur River yet again on its narrow bridge we drove down the coast where we'd been with Brian Mansell the previous day, noting the turnoff to Sundown Point where we'd seen the petroglyphs, and headed inland for about twenty kilometres before turning south again towards the Lindsay River. The gravel road (we were still on 'the road to nowhere') was well formed and ran through fairly open country alternating with button grass plains and stands of melaleucas and eucalypts. The road my brother built headed into more challenging territory, winding over hills and through gullies, and demanded a good deal of driver attention. I'd have liked to pull over and stop to better admire the great sweep of mountains and pristine wilderness opening up ahead, but there were no bays or even verges big enough to do so and I'd have had to pause in the middle of the road.

Brother Philip told me later that this was deliberate. They didn't want tourists stopping in this sensitive area with the possibility of leaving litter or a cigarette butt which could start a fire. We didn't reach a designated stopping point until the bridge over the Donaldson River, about halfway along the new road, but the parking area was so crammed with campers and other vehicles that we couldn't fit in. We did find a place a few kilometres on, however, where we could pull off near a small bridge over a rivulet to enjoy our thermos coffee and biscuits.

On the map the road skirts a huge area—350 000 hectares—of pristine wilderness between the Arthur and the Pieman Rivers, officially designated the Arthur Pieman Conservation Area, which encompasses a great range of habitats including beaches, dune systems, rocky headlands, coastal heath, mountains, rain forests and open plains. It receives the full fury of the Roaring Forties straight from the Southern Ocean, and its average rainfall is an astonishing three metres. It also contains some of the world's tallest hardwood forests, some 200 000 hectares of myrtle, celery-top pine, sassafras, leatherwood, horizontal and blackwood trees, under which flourish a lush array of shrubs, ferns, lichen and fungi. The Tasmanian Wilderness Society and the conservation movement have called it the 'the Tarkine', a name not recognised by the Tasmanian government.

The conservation movement opposed the building of the link road because they did not want the Tarkine wilderness area compromised. In June 2003 Tasmania's then deputy premier (and now premier) Paul Lennon, a hard-nosed pro-development politician, announced that red myrtle would be logged in the Tarkine (although he didn't call it that) along the 'pipe line corridor' that takes crushed iron ore from the Savage River mine some 80 kilometres across country to Port Latta just to the east of Stanley on the north-west coast. Together with opposition to clear-felling Tasmania's old growth forests, the exploitation of the Tarkine promises to be a monumental and savage battle between conservationists and the seemingly unstoppable timber industry.

There was a vigorous campaign organised to try to stop the Tarkine road being built in the first place. My brother's attitude was essentially apolitical—that someone had to build the road and it might as well be his company. (Incidentally I can say with fraternal pride that when the project was finished his firm won a national environmental award for best practice in construction.) Philip is a very diplomatic fellow, but this job tested him to the utmost. I talked to him about what happened.

PHILIP: The protest action started on a day I remember very clearly. They'd walked in for a considerable distance and some of them were quite elderly. They were peaceful protesters and initially they used to just sit down around the machinery. Our policy was never to confront them or react in any way—one of my biggest battles in a way was to convince our fellows that a conflict wasn't going to get us anywhere. Essentially we were paid to stop—the agreement we had was that we would be paid for delays caused by protest action. And then the police would come in and because of the isolation it all took a bit of time but that's what happened. The police would deal with the protesters, arrest them if need be, and take them away.

TIM: What were some of the more extreme protest actions?

PHILIP: Later when they became better organised there was a group known as the Tarkine Tigers who were more militant. They would attach themselves to machines by various mechanisms. One was a steel cylinder they used to slide their hands into with a bit of a dog chain inside so you could put your hands in but not out. Now once they were latched on it was a hell of a business for the police to get them out. In many respects it was just like a military exercise, us and the enemy if you like.

TIM: As the manager of this job how did you handle that?

PHILIP: I don't like conflict, but it was a continuous battle. We developed a protest policy—that we would not have any conflict and once a protest action started we would stop the machines and insist the operators just walk away. In ninety-nine per cent of the cases my colleague Tim Payne and I were able to handle things in that way, but the Australian working man and particularly 'the west coasties' wanted to work and they didn't agree with the 'greenies', or Tarkine Tigers, call them what you will. It was very hard for them, they would want to resist. But we were pretty fortunate. We had a terrific bunch of fellas. Our policy paid off and at the end we got the road through.

TIM: Was it a clean fight?

PHILIP: Pretty much. I must say that they never tried to put water in our fuel, or cut engine hoses which they could have done. They only tried to stop us with their own bodies, as it were, by chaining themselves to our equipment. But a couple of incidents I thought were well below the belt. We had put out emergency supplies for the drivers in the lead machines, well out in the bush, who could only be serviced by helicopters with fuel and equipment. In the event of the helicopter not being able to get to them we made up some emergency supply kits—a barrel full of tents and food, water and safety equipment. Now this is what I really thought was awful: the protesters raided these bins and took what they wanted. I didn't find this out until some time later. It would have been terrible for the operators to have had to have stayed the night out there with no gear because it had been stolen by the protesters.

TIM: Were there any dangerous situations during the protests?

PHILIP: There were a few. In one a young lass chose to chain herself with one of those steel cylinders I mentioned underneath the hard bar of a very large dozer, a D7. It happened twice, actually, and the first time I remember the operator just about dry retched because he nearly started working, not knowing she was there. The second occasion it was rather sad for the young woman concerned. The machine had actually broken down and was going to be out of action for some days. She had chained herself to it and other protesters chained themselves to excavators and other machinery, but we had no need to remove her because the dozer she was attached to wasn't going to work that day. I remember explaining to her that there was no need to remove her because the machine had broken down and I felt terribly sorry for her because she actually burst into tears. The act of attaching yourself to a machine took some courage, because it was likely you would eventually be arrested. It was a big decision that she had made and it was just kind of washed away. The police did remove her, of course, and she was arrested but it was very sad for her that she had picked the wrong machine.

TIM: When do you think they realised that the cause was lost?

PHILIP: The middle of the job for the southern gang moving north and the northern gang moving south was the Donaldson River. The protesters had a fall-back position and they were determined to stop the project before we reached that river. That required a bridge construction and it was quite a difficult logistical exercise to get that built in quick time despite the protest action. We had a huge police presence and also security because they had to look after our gear at night. They all did a terrific job. They kept the protesters at bay and stayed long enough for the bridge to get built, and at that point the protesters realised they couldn't win.

As a matter of fact they had a bit of a ceremony at that stage—I think they called it a funeral—and they all jumped in the river. It was rather odd. I remember several of them picked up stones from the river and cut their flesh and drew blood and rubbed it on each other. After that it was really a *fait accompli* that the road would be finished and they quietly moved out.

The southern end of brother Philip's road was the most tricky, I thought, particularly the descent down to the Savage River. Where the grades of the road were really steep, the surface had been sealed. Admittedly there were signs indicating steep grades, but I was caught unawares in third gear, and had to rely on my brakes alone rather than using the engine to help slow us down in first or second as I should have done. Once I was committed to the descent I couldn't stop, nor could I risk changing down in case I lost control. I honestly don't think I *could* have stopped with the weight of The Manor behind us. I was not happy as the brakes began to heat and fade, and we reached the bottom with beads of sweat breaking out on my upper lip. I didn't let on to Ros at the time, although she knew I was tense.

It was a most spectacular drive, and well worth doing. Now that the road is there, it gives a glimpse of the Tarkine that could not be obtained any other way. Perhaps it will help, in the long run, if visitors become aware that the pristine wilderness it borders is to be despoiled by logging.

Most of the moss-covered myrtle trees are many hundreds of years old. Unfortunately you can't tell which have the prized red-coloured wood until you cut them down, and in many cases the logs are unusable because of hollow interiors and sections of rot. Worse, the gaps in the rain forest canopy caused by even selective logging bring in sunlight and destroy other flora. Conservationists fear that myrtle wilt fungus and other plant diseases will inevitably follow.

We were pleased to see the small vehicular ferry waiting in mid-stream on the tea-coloured waters of the Pieman River, and we squeezed on, our wheels just fitting inside the two raised ramps that connect the ferry with the bank. The operator asked me not to turn my front wheels until both car and camper were completely off the ferry, because of the low tide and steep angle onto the southern bank.

Leatherwood trees were in bloom with their distinctive white flowers as we climbed up the hill from the river and they were interspersed with the gnarled trunks of ancient myrtles with their distinctive small, rounded dark green leaves. Apiarists had left clusters of hives at every available siding beside the road to harvest the distinctive, aromatic west coast leatherwood honey I intended to buy as soon as we got to Strahan.

It is a reminder of the size of Tasmania (small but perfectly formed) that it was only lunch time despite having left the Arthur River that morning, traversed brother Philip's road, crossed the Pieman River by ferry and emerged on the bitumen highway that would lead us to the old mining town of Zeehan, and then to Strahan. But we turned left, not right, and drove east about eight kilometres to see the Reece Dam, which has tamed the waters of the upper Pieman

River and created an enormous artificial lake named after the long-serving and ruthlessly development minded premier, 'Electric Eric' Reece, who hailed from the west coast himself. We drove across the dam wall and picnicked beside the lake before retracing our route and heading down to Zeehan.

There's not a lot left of Zeehan, once a city of more than 10 000 people in the 1890s and known as Silver City because of its proximity to the rich silver-lead mines that sustained it. There's an excellent museum in the old School of Mines building, with an array of steam locomotives and carriages once used on early west coast railways. When I last saw it about thirty years ago it had some of the old nineteenth century puffers that used to haul ore-laden trains over the Abt railway system between Queenstown and the port of Strahan. Some of these have been refurbished to ply this route again, pulling tourists instead of rocks. The *pièce de résistance* of Zeehan architecture, though, is the Gaiety Theatre. The old girl is a bit run down these days, but is gradually being tarted up as funds become available. Opened in 1899, the theatre is conveniently part of the same building complex as the Grand Hotel. There was even a connecting door between the two establishments. I wanted to photograph its impressive facade but the light was not good so we kept on towards Strahan because we weren't sure where we were going to camp that night. We'd heard that in high season Strahan caravan parks and even hotels and B & Bs were as full as the family po. Although we'd booked ahead, we were a day early.

Despite the west coast being the most mountainous section of Tasmania, the road from Zeehan to Strahan is surprisingly open and easy going—the valleys conveniently running north and south. This is not the case with the Strahan to Queenstown road we would travel on our way out. That is certainly mountainous with a continuous series of snaking bends and is entirely devoid of any straight stretches at all.

Queenstown was once the hub of west coast activity—for mining and for tourism. But the decline in the Mt Lyell Company's ore body—and fortunes—coupled with a shift of tourism focus to Macquarie Harbour have transformed Strahan, which I remembered as a sleepy backwater, into a smart, bustling hub of tourist activities. These are mainly centred around the Gordon River cruises and, more recently, the revival of the Abt railway. Salmon and trout farming has also contributed to the economy and added another dimension to the tourist experience—not only on the plate, but through visiting the circular floating pens now dotted around Macquarie Harbour at feeding time.

Macquarie Harbour is a singular stretch of water and a haven for shipping once the ships have gained access through the infamous Hell's Gates, a narrow rocky entrance continually swirling with strong tides, and a treacherous sand bar thrown in for good measure. In the early nineteenth century sailing ships would sometimes have to wait for weeks at a time for calm seas and a favourable wind to get in. But once inside it, this remarkable inland waterway is found to be bigger than six Sydney Harbours (as tour guides delight in telling you) and, although sheltered from the great swells of the Southern Ocean by its narrow entrance, is big enough to generate sharp, short seas quickly whipped up by gales spawned by the Roaring Forties—seas that have sunk many a small craft. The waterway has a tidal range of only 5.1 metres but that can vary through barometric pressures, sudden rainfall in the upper catchment areas, and the amount of water released from Hydro Tasmania dams in the interior of the island. Because the tides are governed more by atmospheric pressure than the moon's gravity, there was once an outgoing tide that lasted for eight days!

Brother Philip, who knows this area well, told me of a camping ground at Macquarie Heads, about fifteen kilometres south of Strahan, where Ocean Beach reaches Hell's Gates. Great swells that build up unimpeded in the Southern Ocean all the way from Antarctica crash in on this beach which runs in an unbroken stretch for thirty-three kilometres north to Trial Harbour—which isn't much of a harbour actually. (There is an automatic wave rider anchored off the coast near Hell's Gates to measure the size of the swells. In 1998 it broke away shortly after recording a swell 23 metres high.) Strahanites go to Macquarie Heads to fish from the inner beach, and the camping ground is nearby. We decided to explore the town of Strahan the next day and headed straight down a gravel road, through softwood pine plantations, with the dark, peat-stained waters of Macquarie Harbour on our left, hoping we could find a camp site.

We stopped at the caretaker's cottage to pay our $5 camping fee and pick up some drinking water as advertised, but some idiot had left the hose running from his rain water tank and driven off, leaving the caretaker and everyone else without fresh water. You don't expect to have problems finding water in Tasmania, but fortunately The Manor's sixty litre tank was full so we weren't in trouble. The caretaker drove ahead of us to where a collection of shitty fishing shacks made from scrap timber and corrugated iron, plus rusting unloved caravans, littered an otherwise pleasant place, and said we could camp where we liked. I began to realise why the camping fees were so low, and why there was not a queue of campers waiting to get in. I asked about the toilet block. There wasn't one. The malodorous long-drop dunny was not an inviting prospect and Ros and I instinctively and correctly divined that there would be no toilet paper in it.

It was a deeply depressing environment in what should have been a delightful haven. The fishing beach was only metres away, behind the sand dunes, where happy locals, with their four-wheel-drives parked beside them, were pulling quite decent sized fish out of the harbour mouth with monotonous regularity. The contrast between the natural beauty of the beach and the squalor of the camping area behind was profound. It seemed crazy, with caravan parks and camping grounds bursting at the seams in Strahan, and people camping in the public car parks because there was nowhere else to go, that the local council didn't have Macquarie Heads spruced up as an alternative.

Normally we prefer camping grounds to caravan parks, but we managed to tear ourselves away from this shambles quite quickly the next morning, claimed our booked site in one of Strahan's two caravan parks and headed straight for the showers.

Strahan is booming, its waterfront location sprouting new restaurants and smart hotels seemingly by the minute. But it has some fine old buildings too, dating from the days when it was a bustling port for the Mt Lyell Company's copper and silver ore that was hauled over the mountains between Queenstown and Macquarie Harbour by the engineering marvel of the Abt railway system—now recreated for tourists. Since the 1920s, as most of the mines were worked out and the Lyell Highway connected Queenstown with the east of the state in the 1930s, Strahan declined in importance. The Huon pine timber getting industry kept it ticking over to some extent, but when I first went there as a schoolboy in the 1950s it was a forlorn collection of decaying, rain-sodden, mostly timber buildings.

Curiously enough it was the environmental protest movement in the early 1980s that kick started Strahan's renaissance. Crusading conservationists used Strahan as the base for a flotilla of canoes and rubber boats to voyage to the headwaters of Macquarie Harbour to try to prevent the then all powerful HEC—the Hydro Electric Commission— of Tasmania from building a series of dams which would have contained the flow of the west coast's last major free flowing river, the Franklin, and on the lower Gordon River. Despite the fact that the south-west of Tasmania was accorded a World Heritage listing, the Tasmanian government pressed ahead with its dam proposals. The government fell over the issue, and the Franklin River then became a major issue in the 1983 federal election. In the summer of 1982–83, the Strahan-based protests reached their peak with 1400 people being arrested for 'trespassing' on the Gordon River dam site. A new Labor federal government moved to implement the World Heritage principles and the Franklin River still runs free. It was a major victory for conservationists and signalled a change of policy for the HEC (now re-badged as Hydro Tasmania), which is currently exploring other forms of 'clean' electricity generation like the wind power we had just seen at Woolnorth.

So these days seaplanes and helicopters buzz about on sight-seeing excursions and big catamarans glide in and out of Strahan harbour taking tourists first to Hell's Gates, and then—via the circular salmon and ocean trout pens—up the lower Gordon River. There primeval rain forest still lines the dark waters which create extraordinarily vivid reflections that have boosted the fortunes of Messrs Kodak, Fuji and their ilk over the years. Busy tenders head out into the tea-coloured water of the harbour carrying pellets of processed food to feed the sleek salmon contained in their mesh pens. Sometimes the nets are damaged, perhaps by seals, or just wear through and tear, and there are mass escapes. Sad for the companies concerned, but the locals wear grins from ear to ear as they harvest the unexpected and succulent bounty in their nets.

The big catamarans' last port of call before they return to Strahan is Sarah Island, or Settlement Island, where the worst and most recalcitrant of Van Diemen's Land convicts were sent from 1821, to labour in chains harvesting the unique Huon pine and hardwoods that flourished not only on the shores of Macquarie Harbour but in the upper reaches of the great Gordon River. Huon pine was particularly prized, because the slow growing, easily worked timber was impregnated with an oil that made it impervious to rot and to the destructive teredo worm that ate into ships' hardwood planks. Between 1821 and 1834, half-starved and ferociously flogged convicts—punishments of 100 lashes with a cat 'o nine tails were regularly, almost casually, prescribed—worked even through the snow and intense wet cold of winter to harvest the logs of Huon pine and tow them in open rowing boats to the saw pits on Sarah Island, where they sustained a ship-building industry that for a time actually made the Macquarie Island penal settlement profitable for the colonial government. And while you might think that banishment to a cold and wet island isolated at the farthest end of the earth was extreme enough, there was worse in store than floggings and working in chains for malcontents on Sarah Island. A last resort punishment was to be sent to a wind-swept speck of rock nearby, Grummet Island, with barely any shelter and starvation rations—also known, with some accuracy, as the Isle for the Condemned.

Macquarie Harbour was thought to be escape proof, but that wasn't so. The most notorious escapee—who in the process became the first European to cross Tasmania from west to east in 1822—was an Irish convict, Alexander Pearce, who survived in the mountainous rain forests through cannibalism. He was one of eight escapees who first planned to steal a boat to sail away from their terrible situation, but before they could do so their escape was discovered and they had to flee into the mountains and rain forest. There was absolutely nothing to eat in the dark understorey—or nothing they could catch anyway. Seven days into their escape, the topic of cannibalism was broached—at first half in jest. But the idea festered in their minds. The self-appointed leader of the group, Robert Greenhill, was a seaman who would have been essential to their escape had they secured a ship. He was the only one who could navigate—which was simply to head east, but that was hard enough when confronted with precipitous mountains and often impenetrable scrub. As a sailor, Greenhill would have been aware of the seventeenth century 'custom of the sea' which condoned cannibalism under certain circumstances, usually in a lifeboat after a shipwreck, so that the majority had a chance of survival. Sometimes such a selection was by mutual agreement, or drawing lots, but this did not happen. Greenhill, Pearce and two others selected a man named Dalton, and killed him with an axe while he slept. Two of the party could not bring themselves to eat their companion, and slipped away into the bush, actually making it back to Sarah Island. But they were so starved, injured and debilitated that they died shortly afterwards.

The five remaining men continued on through Tasmania's roughest mountainous terrain, constantly wet, cold and, of course, hungry. They were nourished only by human flesh, and murdered and butchered luckless comrades one by one until Pearce was the last man standing. (His remaining companion, Greenhill, sensibly hung on to the only axe, which he put under his head when he slept. But Pearce stayed awake the longest and did Greenhill in.) After roaming around the fringes of the Hobart settlement with other absconded convicts for some months, Pearce was captured and interrogated. He confessed to cannibalism, but corroborative evidence was difficult to obtain in the circumstances.

Pearce was sentenced to Sarah Island yet again and, incredibly, in November the following year, he escaped once more, stealing a rowing boat this time with the aim of heading north up the coast rather than west. He figured the going couldn't be worse, and might be better. He only had one companion, Thomas Cox, but old habits died hard, as it were. Even though he still had some flour, salt pork and some fish, he killed and ate his mate two days after they landed on the northern shore of Macquarie Harbour. Pearce (who then abandoned his escape and gave himself up) told those who found him that he preferred human flesh to the other food he had, and was carrying a 'piece of flesh' from the unfortunate Mr Cox of about half a pound in weight.

This time Alexander Pearce did not escape the gallows and was executed at Hobart Town in 1824, having made a full confession.

As you can imagine, this story lost nothing in the telling over the years, and the slavering, bestial convict cannibal, Gabbett, created by the author Marcus Clarke in his book *For the Term of His Natural Life*, is based on the Pearce story.

Other convicts got away in the boats they were helping to build. In 1824 Matthew Brady and some companions escaped from Sarah Island, and sailed through Hell's Gates and around the south of the island to South Arm, near Hobart. Brady then became Tasmania's most notorious—and famous—bushranger, ranging as far afield as Launceston for the next three years. Although most of Brady's original fellow Sarah Island escapees were captured by 1825, there was no shortage of eager convict recruits to his gang. His most daring escapade was to storm the township of Sorell, to the east of Hobart, locking up all the police, soldiers and prominent citizens in the town jail! Although not as brutal as many of Tasmania's bushrangers, Brady was eventually betrayed for a reward and hanged in April 1826.

But perhaps the most cheeky escape from Sarah Island, this most miserable of prisons, was in what has become known as the 'ship that never was'. A playwright and actor, Richard Davey, who now lives in Strahan, dramatised this story and regular performances are staged at the theatre attached to the visitors' centre on the Strahan waterfront. It is an exciting and dynamic dramatic experience, not to be missed. In 1834 the Hobart colonial government decided to close down the Macquarie Harbour operation—not only because of the obvious operational difficulties of the location, but because the 'model' prison at Port Arthur on the Tasman Peninsula was deemed a safer option for containing intractable convicts in solitary confinement. For more than ten years a very competent ship-building industry had been carried out on Sarah Island, but the edict came from afar that no more ships were to be built. However, work had already begun on one last 'special purpose' project, the 100-ton brig *Frederick*.

Ten convict shipwrights who built *Frederick* seized her and got away from Macquarie Harbour after putting ashore the captain, crew and soldiers guarding them. Newly constructed wooden ships, even of Huon pine, always leak and the escapees spent most of their time on the pumps, but they did succeed in reaching South America, battling some ferocious storms during the voyage. When they saw land they scuttled their leaking brig—which would have given them away—and arrived at Valparaiso, Chile, in a launch. The authorities were suspicious and after a more thorough interrogation, quickly realised the shipwrecked mariners were escaped convicts.

This escape story from Sarah Island has a happier ending than others because all ten men won their freedom, although four were sent back to Hobart for trial for mutiny and piracy on the high seas. Both these offences were punishable by death. Surprisingly the original convictions were overturned after appeal judges became bogged down in some knotty legal issues. Piracy has to take place on the high seas, and the ship was taken over in the sheltered waters of Macquarie Harbour. As far as the mutiny was concerned, was the brig a proper ship? It wasn't finished, had no papers, and was on its way to Hobart to be completed and registered. Could it even be described as a vessel? As *The Tasmanian* newspaper reported on 5 May 1857:

> Did the floating bundle of materials in this case so consist? The very opposite would seem to be the fact . . . That which the accused took away was, in fact, as far as the legal offence goes, a mere bundle of materials of various descriptions . . . What then is the nature of the offence which, at the very utmost these men *could* have been legally charged with—the stealing of a bundle of materials for the purpose of making their escape from slavery!

It all got too hard, and the learned judges were unable to agree. A rare win for the underdog in nineteenth century colonial justice.

All this talk of nineteenth century deprivation turned our footsteps towards one of Strahan's finest eateries, the Risby Cove Restaurant at the head of the bay. We scored a window seat looking out at a small dock where some of the salmon farming tenders were moored and where the harbour was still clearly visible at 8 pm with the combination of Tasmania's longer twilight and summer daylight saving. The menu was impressive, with local salmon featured as you would expect.

I reminded Ros that the last time I'd been to Strahan was in 1975, recording interviews for an ABC documentary I did on the south-west of Tasmania. At that time there were still men alive who remembered mining and timber-getting in the area almost back to the beginning of the twentieth century. One of the younger pine loggers was Bob 'Cowboy' Crane who, as a horse boy, worked in the Pine Creek area behind Macquarie Harbour in the 1930s with his father. Like many of the timber men he had a deep love of the bush and the Huon pine timber they were harvesting, knowing full well that some of the bigger trees were 2000 years old, and some even more ancient than that. Huon pines are slow growing and with their unique aromatic oil are impervious to rot, so even large logs that have been dead for nearly 200 years are still able to be used.

Back in the 1970s Bob Crane took me into the Pine Creek area where he'd worked as a boy. He was in his fifties then and I recorded an interview with him as we walked among the stumps and 'headers' of the Huon pines that had been logged forty years before when he was there in 1936.

BOB: There's no timber in the world just like Huon pine, it's so easy to work and such a beautiful timber to look at. When you're working in the Huon pine bush you never ever seem to end up with any aches or pains or get crook with flu or anything. I don't know what it is, whether it's the pine or the smell of the oil you get. When you cut a tree down with a chainsaw the fumes are so strong and the sawdust is thrown back all over you, and the fumes will nearly choke you, they are that strong! Whether that keeps the germs away from you or what, I don't know, but God, it's powerful. After a while it loses all that real strong smell, but it never ever loses it altogether. Huon pine's a wonderful timber. They haven't got anything in the world *anywhere* to match it.

You know just being here reminds me of when I was working in the bush as a boy. I can just picture it in my mind. Dad would have a big team of horses—five horses hooked onto a big Huon pine log just going up the hill. They'd be scrambling up, sendin' the stones flying from their feet. You could hear the jingle of the chains and everything . . . Gee it was wonderful to see that. I can just picture it now, five beautiful big draught horses, with their coats all shiny and this great big Huon pine log behind 'em.

TIM: We're standing in an area that's been logged—how many years ago was that?

BOB: At least forty years ago, probably a little bit over that, 'cause when I worked here as a boy this area had been cut even before that.

TIM: This one here just looks like an old decaying stump you wouldn't look twice at, if you didn't know what you were looking at.

BOB: That's right, yes. You see where they've cut it off there, with a cross-cut saw? Now that's as solid as the day they did that.

TIM: Just about half an inch in, it's just beautiful yellow wood . . . sweet smelling Huon pine. Will you make use of this one?

BOB: Oh, yeah sure! That's got a beautiful log in it—there's fifteen to sixteen feet. See, the old fellers only took the best, just the straight barrel of the log. They wouldn't touch anything like the one we're looking at because they had to pull it so far with horses and they just wanted the heart of the tree. But we can take all this sort of stuff now, because so much wood turning goes on. That's beautiful timber for wood turning and for furniture.

TIM: People are always saying that Huon pine's gone, that its days are numbered. Now you're in here commercially milling Huon pine, moving into areas that have been logged fifty or sixty years ago.

BOB: As you can see yourself, there are hundreds of trees that've been left behind, poked away in corners and that. You hear a lot of people say, 'It'll be extinct in a few years time, there'll be no more of it left'. But look at all those young pines growing up here where it's been logged over so many years ago.

TIM: Accepting that the new ones will take hundreds of years to grow, because that's how they grow, how long could you keep on working this area, do you think?

BOB: Oh . . . twenty years at least, logging it like this. Taking these old heads and one thing and another, as well as trees left standing. But even then, there'll be hundreds of trees, a foot to two feet in diameter. You've seen some of the big old fellows that they didn't even bother with. They'll all be still here as well as the little fellows growing up all the time.

Well, it's nearly thirty years since I recorded that interview, and Bob's still milling Huon pine out of the same area! Bob Crane is now eighty-one, and works in one of Strahan's two sawmills processing Huon pine. The following morning we drove out to say hello. He was driving a fork-lift truck and eventually I caught his eye. He remembered me and we sat down on a log—Huon pine of course—for a yarn, while his son kept working. Bob said he'd go mad if he retired. 'Besides I can still tell my son the best place to put the saw blade through a log.' Ros took a photograph of us together and we left him to niggle the next log over towards the saw-pit.

There are two companies running cruises on Macquarie Harbour and we booked with Federal Hotels' Gordon River Cruises on their big white catamaran, *Lady Jane Franklin*. Feeling indulgent, we chose the upper deck alternative, and were plied with fine Tasmanian wines and cheeses while we sped towards Hell's Gates to experience an uncharacteristically calm exit through the narrow entrance to nose briefly into the Southern Ocean just to say we'd been there. Back in the harbour, we went past the circular salmon farm pens right to the eastern end of the harbour and up the smooth dark waters of the lower Gordon River. It is said that it can rain

300 days out of 365 in this part of the world, so we appreciated the fine day we'd been blessed with, as well as calm conditions. The river winds through pristine rain forest, and we learned to recognise the various timbers—first the ubiquitous Huon pine (*Lagarostrobos franklinii*) with its dark green rather shaggy fronds, as well as celery-top pine, leatherwood, blackwood, sassafras and myrtle.

The reflections were perfect, mirroring the forest in the still waters of the river so accurately that it was difficult to see where reality and reflection began and ended. Then as *Lady Jane Franklin* voyaged slowly up river, the reflections curved in the serpentine wake as if in a fairground distorting mirror.

There is a rain forest walk at the turning point where we walked around a circuit on a graded timber walkway for a closer look at the primeval rain forest, including the feared horizontal scrub which isn't really scrub but an intermeshing, intertwining hardwood tree which grows sideways as its name suggests, throwing up branches in all directions. It is feared because it is diabolical stuff to try to get through. A slight shudder ran down my spine when I saw it again, because in the 1950s I was once lost in an area called the Arve Valley, in southern Tasmania, on a bushwalking trip with two friends, and we could well have died after three days without food, wet, cold and hopelessly lost in—yes—horizontal scrub. Had we died, it is unlikely our bodies would ever have been found.

It seemed a more agreeable alternative to sip a chilled Tasmanian sauvignon blanc as we headed west again to our last stop, the fabled Sarah Island. On a fine day like we were enjoying this little island looked positively benign. The original rain forest was cleared off to make room for ship-building workshops and accommodation for convicts and guards, but is now re-establishing itself. The usual mania for destroying convict relics last century has completely devastated even the substantial stone buildings that were once there, but there are foundations, some walls and features like brick ovens and even some roofless cells to see.

The indefatigable Richard Davey (creator of the drama 'The Ship That Never Was') was on hand to put some historical flesh on the stone skeletons with one of the best bravura commentaries and the most entertaining inter-action with visitors that I have ever experienced as a tourist, anywhere in the world. First rate social history. He even walked on the water—well, almost—by venturing out on the original Huon pine logs just below the surface of the harbour waters where the old slipways were built. Being Huon pine, of course, the logs are as good as new, and will almost certainly be there in the twenty-second century and beyond. Richard wore gumboots for this demonstration, but sometimes he wears a wetsuit under his garb and dis-appears unexpectedly off the end of the slipway to the appreciative cheers and laughter of his audience.

And so back to Strahan. Due to the speed of the fast, modern catamarans in Macquarie Harbour, it is possible to have two cruises each day. The Sarah Island visit topped things off splendidly.

Even considering the commercial advantage of Huon pine and other rain forest timbers available to the colonial government in 1821, I still find it extraordinary that they would have bothered to send convicts to Macquarie Harbour. Surely just being in Tasmania (or van Diemen's Land as it was then) made it escape proof! When you are actually in Macquarie Harbour, and see its remoteness and the difficulty of getting there—to say nothing of feeding and guarding the convicts—it seems an unimaginable thing to have done.

I am indebted to my former ABC colleague, Father Paul Collins, for enlightening me about this period of Tasmanian colonial history. I should say Dr Paul Collins, for Paul is no longer a priest, having resigned from the church after a book of his, *Papal Power* (1997), was 'delated' (reported) to the Vatican's Congregation for the Doctrine of the Faith, formerly the Roman Inquisition. While critical of the papacy, the book was really advancing a more co-operative and collegial way of dealing with papal authority. After being accused of various 'doctrinal deviations' by the Vatican and refusing to be dealt with by a secret tribunal, he decided to resign from the priesthood after thirty-three years in the ministry. He is now writing books for a living, including a re-examination of the extraordinary saga of Alexander Pearce titled *Hell's Gates*.[1]

Although you might think that being transported to Van Diemen's Land was drastic enough for most of the convicts who had come from desperately poor conditions in England and Ireland, it wasn't a bad deal. It at least gave them the prospect of a new life on the other side of the world, and even a prosperous future if they worked hard enough. It was made clear to the convicts when they arrived in Hobart Town that providing they did their time without causing trouble, they would be granted a ticket of leave (some were pardoned), granted some land, permitted to marry (if they could find a wife because the population

---

1 Paul Collins, 2002, *Hell's Gates: The Terrible Journey of Alexander Pearce, Van Diemen's Land Cannibal*, Hardie Grant Books, Melbourne

was chronically male dominated) and have children. Indeed many of Hobart's impeccably respectable families have convict ancestors. I know because I have convict fore-bears myself.[2]

But as Paul Collins points out in *Hell's Gates*, some of the convicts simply could not tread the straight and narrow. They got drunk, stole or forged promissory notes, escaped into the countryside near Hobart, became bushrangers and, as their numbers built up, became a security problem. In 1821 the resources of Governor William Sorell were spread exceedingly thin, particularly trained personnel to police the colony:

> Constables were usually ex-convicts themselves, largely untrained, and their only pay was their keep. They were often unreliable. Sorell had very few troops at his disposal and would not have been in a position to deal with a serious revolt, and a convict rebellion was always a lurking fear for the governments of New South Wales and Van Diemen's Land.

The authorities in Sydney had other options for their recalcitrants by sending them to what were known as 'places of secondary punishment'. Newcastle was the preferred option. But Sorell couldn't send his hard cases to Newcastle from Van Diemen's Land.

---

2  My paternal grandmother was descended from Edward Garth and Suzannah Goff (or Gough, because spelling varies), who were First Fleeters. Both were convicts so I scored a double there. Immediately after their arrival in Port Jackson in 1788, they elected to go to Norfolk Island for the first settlement there, and married on the ship *Supply* which took them to the island. After gaining their freedom they farmed a small property and later moved to Hobart in 1808 to take up a land grant there before the first Norfolk Island settlement closed down in 1814.

In Hobart Town in 1821 eighty per cent of the population were either convicts or ex-convicts. They were kept in control through assigning them to farmers as labourers and the threat of floggings—and there were plenty of those, far more than in England or Ireland where sentences of 50 or 100 lashes were rare. But not in Van Diemen's Land or Port Jackson.

With growing numbers of absconded convicts roaming around the countryside near Hobart causing mayhem, Governor Sorell sought permission from Governor Macquarie, in Sydney, to have a 'local place of secondary punishment', which is how Macquarie Harbour and Sarah Island came to be chosen. But a convict revolt was a possibility even in the 'secondary place of punishment' and was only prevented by the routine of grinding work and brutal punishment.

And Sarah Island looked so benign on that lovely sunny Macquarie Island morning.

# four

## To the North-east

**Travel Diary Wednesday 26 February**

Yet another fine west coast morning. A leisurely start as our West Coast Wilderness Railway journey did not begin until 10.15 am from Regatta Point on the southern side of Strahan Harbour. It was a journey I was looking forward to as I remembered when the Abt railway closed down in 1963. I was working with the ABC in Hobart at the time. Television had just started there, and a colleague, John Roberts, managed (with some difficulty) to organise an ABC film crew to record one of its last journeys for posterity. There was talk then of keeping it going as a tourist venture, but it didn't happen.

Ros and I were a bit too leisurely getting to the train and discovered all the forward facing seats were occupied, and so were nearly all the other seats as well. We had relied too much on having 'First Class tickets'. Well it turned out that everyone else on board had them too! They covered everything from the one plush Pullman carriage with padded seats to the other more basic wooden bench seats in what might be considered Second Class. Still, Australia is a classless society is it not? A diesel engine is used in the flatter, early stages of the journey to Queenstown. The steam locomotive is used on the climb over the King River gorge (using the Abt system) and on into Queenstown. We squeaked and rattled into action almost bang on time with a diesel loco pulling us along the shores of Macquarie Harbour towards the entrance to the King River.

At the end of the nineteenth century, the Mt Lyell Mining and Railway Company had one hell of a transport problem. It had discovered a hugely rich and extensive copper and silver field near Queenstown in some of the roughest terrain you could possibly imagine. They had to find—and quickly—some way of getting their raw ore, and later smelted copper, to Macquarie Harbour and thence to wherever its markets were after running the hazardous gauntlet of Hell's Gates. The Abt railway first started hauling the Mt Lyell Company's copper and silver ore from its mines in Queenstown to Macquarie Harbour in 1896, and was extended to Regatta Point in 1899. Various alternatives were discussed at the time, including a tunnel and a bucket and cable system, because the mountains, valleys, rivers and gorges and the insanely steep grades required seemed to rule out a railway. Enter the ingenious German inventor Dr Roman Abt, who invented the rack-and-pinion system in the 1880s to enable trains to climb into the Hartz mountains where conventional locomotives could not go. His Abt railway can (and still does) climb and descend grades of from 1 in 16 to 1 in 20, unimaginable to those then designing and building railway systems elsewhere in Australia which could only climb elevations of 1 in 40!

The rebirth of this historic railway is a great tribute to the members of the Mt Lyell Abt Railway Society, who took it on themselves to begin clearing vegetation, rebuilding some of the bridges and digging out old drainage ditches in the hope they might one day get enough funding to reconstruct the railway. Due credit must be given to Launceston businessman Roger Smith, who supported the Abt revival not only by investing in it himself, but by canvassing other investors. In 1998 the Abt Railway Association scored a twenty million dollar grant from the Commonwealth government's Federation Fund, and by the end of 2000 had the first eleven kilometres from Queenstown to Rinadeena (the highest point on the railway) operating, using two of the five original nineteenth century locomotives refurbished and rescued from the Zeehan Pioneers Memorial Museum and from a display in Queenstown. In August 2002 Federal Hotels & Resorts Tasmania took over the project, and in December of that year the line became fully operational from Queenstown, over the top of the King River Gorge, and on down to Macquarie Harbour and Regatta Point at Strahan. It had only just begun operations when Ros and I reached Strahan.

The one-way journey between Strahan and Queenstown takes just over four hours, with several sight-seeing stops and a meal break. It's only thirty-five kilometres long, but what spectacular kilometres they are through some of the west coast's wildest country, clattering over forty bridges spanning valleys, creeks and rivers. Then the *pièce de résistance*, climbing up 200 metres on the Abt system with fabulous views of the mighty King River Gorge. The King River, no longer mighty, alas, is still showing the strain of acting as a waste disposal system for the tailings of the Mt Lyell copper and silver processing. One of our first landmarks was the siding at Teepookana on the King River, which was Tasmania's fourth busiest port when the railway opened. Today the river is a sad sight, clogged and silted up by grey mine tailings dumped into it for more than half a century. Teepookana shows little sign of ever being able to accommodate ships of any size again. Another landmark is the 240-metre long railway bridge along and across the King, which was terribly difficult to build and expensive to maintain. In fact it was the main reason why the railway closed in the early 1960s.

My pulse quickened as we rolled into Dubbil Barril station, where our steam locomotive waited to take on the Abt system climb up over the King River Gorge. I'd previously read an article by a journalist who had travelled in the cab of the steam engine, so I asked Graham Cook, who managed the Federal Hotels operation in Strahan then, whether I could do the same. To my great delight permission was granted. On our Strahan to Queenstown trip Dubbil Barril was a lunch stop, and as we snacked we could see our little steam locomotive—so small in fact that you wondered how it could possibly pull our train up the hill— being revolved on a turntable so it could take us back to Queenstown after having delivered its passengers to Dubbil Barrel the previous afternoon. Eventually with a shrill toot and puffs of photogenic steam, the brightly painted green and black Abt No. 3 locomotive (with a snazzy red front buffer bar) backed in from the turntable to begin the steep climb to Teepookana.

The all-important rack-and-pinion strip was clearly visible in the middle of the three-foot-six-inches wide track (metric measurements are irrelevant in this context). This middle rail or rack is the crux of the Abt system, and supports two parallel rows of overlapping 'teeth'. The steam in the rack cylinder of the locomotive turns a toothed pinion wheel, which hauls the train up the slope by the teeth. There is a double advantage here. The steam engine continues to deliver power to the wheels on the rails as well, giving a firm grip of slippery rails in wet weather. And the west coast has plenty of that—rainfall in this area can be as high as 150 inches (3.81 metres).

When his engine was safely coupled up with our train I made myself known to the engine driver, Mark, who looked every inch the part with his denim cap, trim black beard and blue overalls. I was pleased to see he even had a Gladstone bag, of which he was inordinately proud. His fireman, Caroline, was an attractive young woman, also in blue overalls, with her long blonde hair safely secured in a ponytail. (She prefers to be described traditionally as a fireman rather than a firewoman, or the politically correct 'fireperson'.) I wondered where I was going to stand, because there seemed only room enough for the two crew. Had Abt No. 3 still been burning coal for fuel, there was no way I could have travelled with them as Caroline would have had to shovel coal from a tender into the centrally situated furnace door. But the locomotive is now oil fired and I was able to stand directly in front of the furnace between them, so it was just as well I was wearing long trousers. Had I turned up in shorts I simply could not have travelled in the cab!

At this time on the Abt railway (early 2003) there were only two locomotives available, 1 and 3, which were at least close by in Zeehan and Queenstown when they were needed. In fact, it is asking a lot of one engine to pull a train load of tourists over the hump by itself. Two loco-motives, front and rear, were generally used to move the ore and passenger train combination in the line's opera-tional era. There are four of the five original Abt locos notionally available. No. 2 is at the Tasmanian Transport Museum in Glenorchy, a northern Hobart suburb No. 4 was scrapped, and No. 5 was at the Puffing Billy display in Victoria but by mid 2004 was in Hobart being restored and likely to resume its duties some time in 2005. If tourist numbers continue to build (and why wouldn't they so as to experience one of the great railway journeys of the world?), a bit of extra puff might be needed as I was about to find out.

The Abt locomotive's distinctive shrill 'toot' sounded as we began steadily grinding our way forward at slightly more than walking pace. The rack-and-pinion system was already engaged as we headed away from Dubbil Barril to begin our climb up beside the King River Gorge. There wasn't any time for chit chat as Mark and Caroline juggled their various nineteenth century brass levers and wheels, some of which spat little spurts of boiling water at them. As it happened, No. 3 was misbehaving itself. I sensed Mark was a bit preoccupied and asked him if there was a problem. He said that although the boiler had just been serviced, it was producing dirty water which caused bubbles to rise up in a glass column, positioned about halfway along the boiler outside the cabin in front of the driver. This was nineteenth century instrumentation and the water level, calibrated to the boiler's innards, had to be kept about halfway up the glass. The bubbles in the murky water told him that all was not exactly as it should be. It would be embarrassing if No. 3 didn't produce enough power to get up the hill. I gathered that if we stopped on the 1 in 20 grade, it would be an 'interesting' exercise getting going again.

Caroline asked me to stand aside while she opened the furnace and shovelled in some sand. This makes a hotter fire, and I noticed that the furnace door started to glow red. I could see why shorts were a no-no, and was glad of my thick cotton pants. Nevertheless I developed hot knees and began to wonder about fried gonads—fortunately my baby-making days were well behind me anyway.

The glass tube beside the boiler began to bubble more ominously, Mark was winding wheels and pulling levers and was clearly too preoccupied to consider idiotic questions from me. Turning around and looking through the rear open window of the cab, I could catch tantalising glimpses of the King River Gorge through breaks in the trees and saw my fellow passengers photographing furiously. I did have a small digital camera and managed to get some action shots of Mark and Caroline hard at it. Eventually we made it to Teepookana, and stopped while Mark organised some more water for his over-active boiler. Although they said I was welcome to stay in the cabin with them for the descent and on into Queenstown, I had one quite pressing personal reason to decline their invitation. In any case, Mark said, the descent was even steeper—1 in 16—and he would therefore have less time for talk on the way down but I was happy to return to my seat in our carriage.

As we left the mountain behind us and started to see the beginnings of civilisation on the outskirts of Queenstown, our young steward told a charming if rather indiscreet story about working on this section of the revived railway. He pointed out a small gold mine with its poppet head and mullock heap. 'Our boss at the time told us to build this. It's a fake, actually. When we finished digging it one of my mates found a dinkum one in the bush only a few hundred metres away!'

Fortunately the old Rack and Pinion Railway Station had not been redeveloped, although it was in the heart of Queenstown. By the time we had bought some souvenirs and a soft drink, driver Mark had swivelled Abt No. 3 on the turntable and was choofing back in to the station to be ready for the next run.

The centre of Queenstown always reminds me of the set of a western. You almost expect to see horses tethered to the veranda posts of the weatherboard pubs, which sensibly build their second stories over the pavement for extra shelter from the omnipresent rain. To the east are the denuded hills around the Mt Lyell open cut and underground workings. The hills were originally stripped of their rain forest timber to make charcoal to fuel the furnaces to smelt the copper ore. In 1896 the brilliant American metallurgist Robert Carl Sticht pioneered the revolutionary process of pyritic smelting at Mt Lyell. The pyritic ore is fed straight into the furnace where the iron and sulphur ore itself combusts, helping to fuel the furnace and dispensing with large quantities of expensive coke. This was wondrously efficient in smelting huge quantities of copper cheaply, but it was ruinous for the environment. The billowing clouds of sulphur killed all the vegetation for miles around. In summer, raging bushfires consumed what was left of the logged rain forest (and many houses) and then Queenstown's torrential rainfall did the rest, washing the topsoil off the hills and mountains around the city. In his history of the Mt Lyell Mining and Railway Company, *The Peaks of Lyell*, first published in 1954, historian Geoffrey Blainey said that the early surrounds of Queenstown resembled '. . . a cemetery of black stumps. Two beautiful valleys had become as ugly as battlefields'.[1]

When I first saw them in the early 1950s they looked more like the mountains of the moon, utterly without vegetation, the charred stumps of the bigger trees like rotting teeth against a chemically stained wasteland of obscene orange and yellow hues offset by patches of white quartz and bare clay.

In the early 1970s I returned to the west coast to record interviews with miners and Huon pine timber getters (like Bob Crane in Strahan), and also spoke with Geoffrey Blainey in Melbourne who believed then that the devastation was so gross it should be preserved for all time:

Things do grow and the vegetation is creeping back onto the hills. It's piffling scrub but it's beginning to cover the area around the old smelters. I think there's a strong case for using defoliant in the area and perhaps keeping a square mile or two square miles of land in its denuded state. This would show what an unregulated industrial process can do to the landscape.

Also, in certain lights, when the sun comes out at Mt Lyell especially in late afternoon, and it shines on those hills, it really is a strange, sombre, beautiful sight and I think there's a very strong case for trying to stop the vegetation from returning to parts of those hills.

1 Geoffrey Blainey, 1967, *The Peaks of Lyell*, Melbourne University Press, London & New York

Well, Geoffrey Blainey's suggestion has not been taken up and thirty years after our conversation the stricken hills are even more clothed with 'piffling scrub', but they are still a depressing sight. *The Peaks of Lyell* was written from Blainey's PhD thesis on the history of the Mt Lyell Company and started him on his career as a historian. When he was there in the early 1950s some of the original prospectors were still alive, including Jimmy Elliott, whose pick had chanced on the quartz reef at Lynch's Creek in 1880 that yielded the first good gold on the west coast. It was as a result of discovering that gold at Lynch's Creek that other prospectors came in and pushed on to Mt Lyell.

TIM: Jimmy Elliott was certainly a primary source!

GEOFFREY BLAINEY: I was very lucky. Some of the early prospectors were still around, men with good memories. When I first met Jimmy he'd have been about 83 or 84. I used to roll him cigarettes when he came around to where I lived. He was so stooped that as I opened the door, I'd instinctively look out at the wrong height, because he'd come in so low. He always wore an overcoat. He was a man of very little education but was extremely well spoken and had a good vocabulary. He had very wide interests. He'd been a miner or billiard room keeper or publican most of his life. He always wanted to become a member of the stock exchange. Well, he never really achieved that ambition, but perhaps he was better off, because he'd had a full and an interesting life.

I'd come straight from university and I had the mistaken idea that educated people probably had the most reliable memory; and it took me a long while to realise that a person of little education relies more on his memory and if he's actually seen an event taking place, he remembers what he's seen very accurately . . . he had a much better memory, you know, than a university professor, lawyers or doctors or members of the learned professions.

Jimmy Elliott lived in Bowers Hotel. Bowers were very good to him—I suppose he paid them part of his old age pension. He slept on a balcony and most of the time he'd sit in front of the fire in the lounge—every hotel had a fire or two going—and he'd poke the fire and talk. He was a great one for the 'king size whisper'. I'd be sitting there beside the fire talking to him and somebody would come into the room and he'd put his hand beside his mouth and say to me, 'See that fellow who's just come in there?' and I'd say, 'Yeah, yeah . . . I can see him'. 'He's old Scotty, he's just run away with somebody else's wife . . .' Of course these king size whispers could be heard, very clearly.

Jimmy was a miner and a prospector, and was very interested in share speculation. Once in the late 1880s he became very interested in a silver mine at Zeehan and believed that the shares were going to rise and he walked overland to Hobart . . . there was just a single track . . .

TIM: That would be about a 300 kilometre round trip . . .

GEOFFREY: . . . and he walked to Hobart, bought the shares and came back. And that was the last time he left the west coast—in 1888. He used to come around to my place with some tobacco and I'd roll him cigarettes. Once I was away, I went down to Hobart for just three or four days and when I came back he said, 'Oh, where have you been, I've been looking everywhere for you?'

'Oh!' I said, 'I've been to Hobart.'

'Hobart! Hobart! [said Jimmy.] You certainly get around!'

Although the Mt Lyell mine is still operating in a limited way, Queenstown has a rather dejected air in comparison to Strahan's tourist-fuelled rebirth. You had the feeling that most passengers on the Abt did what we did and headed straight back either on the train, or if another four-and-a-half hours on the train seemed a bit much then took a bus back to Strahan. I remember hearing a few years ago that you could pick up a miner's two-bedroom or three-bedroom cottage in Queens-town for $7000—about the size of the then first home owner's grant from the federal government. So if it was your first home, you got it for nothing! But not today. Real estate is booming in Tasmania after decades of doldrums. The same cottage today might cost you from $40 000 to $80 000. Still cheap as chips compared with the mainland, if you don't mind an annual rainfall of 2.5 metres and a gravel lawn. When I first came to the west coast in the 1950s, I noted that the Queenstown football oval had nary a blade of grass and was surfaced with quartz gravel. A nurse from the local hospital said that three-quarters of the casualties they had to cope with came not from the mines or traffic accidents, but from the Aussie Rules footy on this brutal surface.

Our bus left at 3 pm from the station to return to Strahan, over forty-one kilometres of extremely hilly and bendy road; essentially over the same country we had puffed through on our train, but with extra kilometres because of the serpentine nature of the road. Given the way we travel, I don't experience buses very often. Perhaps it is just as well.

**Travel Diary Wednesday 26 February**

The bus driver yakked at us incessantly as we left Queenstown for what seemed like an eternity, but was probably only fifteen minutes, giving us his version of the history of Queenstown and the Mt Lyell Company. Then he triumphantly announced that he would stop talking and, 'Play youse some music'. This was too much and I yelped that some silence would be much better. He was resistant to this challenge to his authority at first. I said perhaps we could have a show of hands. It didn't quite come to that, although he didn't give up easily, saying that he would put it on quietly. I yelled loudly, 'No music!' The driver was obviously deeply pissed off, but spared us. I suppose I should have taken more account of what the other people on the bus thought about this, but I think (well I hope) everyone was quietly pleased. These bus drivers are real tyrants. They think you have to be besieged by sound for the entire trip with either their commentary or blaring music. The bloody bus was equipped with a video as well, but the winding road would have made everyone sick if they'd looked at that, so mercifully it was not an option.

Having visited the north-west of Tasmania and now the west coast (where at last we were able to stock up on the region's unique leatherwood honey), we decided to head towards Launceston to explore the north-east before heading south down the east coast to Hobart. The sensible way to get to Launceston is to avoid the tricky Lyell Highway between Strahan and Queenstown (that we had experienced in the bus) and head back the way we came as far as Zeehan, then across the Reece Dam and on to Rosebery, Tullah, Guildford—through the Hellyer Gorge—and through to Somerset (just to the west of Burnie, where we had lunched on our way to Stanley and Woolnorth). Then you drive Highway One back to Devonport and eventually to Launceston. That is the way my brother Philip *thought* we would go, although we never discussed it.

But I wanted to drive the Lyell Highway out of Queenstown and up onto the highlands plateau to Derwent Bridge, then take what looked like a major road (but which actually turned out to be an unsealed goat's track) on the western side of the Great Lake and on to Deloraine, to rejoin Highway One for the final leg into Launceston. There were sentimental reasons for this. While still a schoolboy, but with a recently acquired driver's licence, I used to make a few pounds delivering brand new Holden cars from Hobart to Queenstown, and then returning in whatever car was 'traded in' on the new one. The Lyell Highway was unsealed in the 1950s, and it was an exciting drive. The return trip could be even more exciting as the traded in cars were sometimes barely roadworthy. One nearly shed a wheel on a steep mountain descent. All the nuts save one had departed from the studs on the left front wheel when I fortunately sensed all was not well and pulled over. I had to borrow some nuts from the other wheels to get home. There were bushwalking ventures as well in the National Park, called the Cradle Mountain-Lake St Clair reserve in my day, also accessed by the Lyell Highway. In any case we wanted to return to the north by a different route just for variety.

The Lyell Highway winds out of Queenstown up those cruelly denuded, barren hills and then descends into another valley where the once flourishing mining town of Gormanston used to challenge Queenstown for relevance and supremacy. It lost. The highway then skirts the shores of Lake Burbury, a huge Hydro Tasmania impoundment which I had not seen before. To the south-east we could see the great jagged peak of Frenchman's Cap (1443 metres), which I once climbed with a few mates many moons ago. It was a day's walk to get there, and we slept in a hut about halfway up the mountain hoping for fine weather the following day. We woke to thick mist but set off anyway, hoping it would clear. It did, and we reached the summit in warm sunshine, with the tops of nearby peaks poking through the mist before it gradually lifted. It was a simply fabulous view, and an utterly memorable moment. We carried up an outsize can of Foster's beer which we placed in a snowdrift to cool before toasting our climb. It reminded me of that wonderful scene in Mike Todd's *Around the World in 80 Days* where David Niven reached out with a champagne bucket from the basket of a balloon and secured some snow as they literally scrape over the top of the Alps.

After Lake Burbury, the Lyell Highway begins to climb up towards the central Tasmanian plateau through typically west coast dense vegetation—blackwood, tea tree, melaleuca and small leatherwood trees smothered in their distinctive white flowers. Clusters of roadside hives were evidence of commercial interest in the west coast's trademark leatherwood honey. That also reminded me of my schoolboy journeys to Queenstown along this road. A local identity we only knew as 'Taffy the Bee Man' had a little hut beside the road on the western side of Mt Arrowsmith and would sell you some honey at bargain rates. One day my father was driving to Queenstown and he stopped at Taffy's hut. He noticed another car already there, but didn't take particular notice of it. Taffy was talking to a bloke in a suit and tie when my father knocked at the door.

'Can I buy some honey, Taffy?'

My father was taken aback when Taffy poured out a terrible tale of woe. No, he didn't have any leatherwood honey, the flowers hadn't bloomed, his bees had died and it had rained so much he couldn't harvest the little bit of honey he'd been able to produce. 'Poor old Taffy,' thought Father.

On his way back to Hobart, on impulse, he thought he'd have another try. Taffy was on his own this time. 'Have you got any honey, Taffy?'

'Yeah mate, how much do you want?'

It turned out Taffy's other visitor was the tax man and Father had arrived just at the right moment for the wily apiarist to pour out his woes for his benefit. 'It was a wonder the tax man didn't pull out his handkerchief and burst into tears it was such a virtuoso performance,' recalled Father.

Taffy was brutally murdered in his little hut not long afterwards. Someone probably thought the old man had a hoard of cash there that the tax man had never seen. I remember Father said he thought Taffy wouldn't have had all that much.

Taffy's hut used to be beside the Lyell Highway as it climbs up towards Mt Arrowsmith, with fantastic views to the south down wild, rain forested valleys. This mountain has twin peaks, and a shaft of sunlight broke through the cloud and illuminated the smaller of the two. The effect was subtle and captivating, picking out fluted dolerite columns of lichen-stained rock, which rise up from olive-green high country heath, and offering a glimpse of gnarled, wind-stunted snow gums, their sculptured boughs briefly illuminated for our pleasure. I thought of a passage my friend Christopher Koch wrote recently in a travel memoir, *The Many-Coloured Land*.[2] Chris was travelling by bus in the

---

2 Christopher Koch, 2002, *The Many-Coloured Land: A Return to Ireland*, Picador, Pan Macmillan, Sydney

west of Ireland when he was struck by the similarity of what he saw and the subtlety of the quality of light in Tasmania's cool temperate landscape:

> The rain comes and goes, and the sky remains steely. But there's a strange yellow light on the horizon, leaking through the grey: the sun's huge presence behind. I don't tire of studying this Midlands country, which is never dramatic, but infinitely various and delicate. Nor do I mind the weather, which also recalls Tasmania, where neither sun nor rain can ever be relied on for long, and sometimes coexist in the landscape. The frail, tantalising light is the product of such weather, picking out features on distant knolls or slopes so that they light up in a way that makes them revelations.

I had read this passage only the night before and it 'flashed upon that inward eye' just before the transient shaft of sunlight ceased to define Mt Arrowsmith's lesser peak, and matched it again with its sombre partner.

Mt Arrowsmith marks the western border of the high country of the central Tasmanian plateau. It's almost like throwing a switch. The dense vegetation and white quartzite rock, so typical of the west coast, give way to rolling plains and open woodlands of widely spaced eucalypts with stocky trunks, growing from stony ground to only modest heights in order to cope better with fierce winds and winter snow. We made good time to the turnoff to Lake St Clair, the southern end of the now world-renowned 100-kilometre walking track from Cradle Mountain. I've walked this only once, as a ten year old. My parents deserve full marks for inflicting me on their adult friends during this demanding trek. I must have been a pain in the arse to them all at times, but it was a fantastic experience and no doubt influenced me in my later love of bushwalking and camping. I wanted to have a quick look at the lake (which can shorten the journey by one day if you take a boat to its northern end) for old time's sake. There is a big Parks and Wildlife visitor centre these days, with interpreted displays and posters about the wild life, cautioning visitors about snakes and how to minimise human impacts on the much-trod landscape.

We walked down to the shores of Lake St Clair, which has the distinction of being completely natural and not created by the Hydro, and drove back to the Lyell Highway. I remembered a previous trip when the highway was gravel, and caused much grief. I must have been nineteen or twenty, I suppose, when five of us went on an expedition to a most remarkable area, north-west of Lake St Clair, called the Labyrinth. It was well named, because my parents and their party tried to find it during my bush walk as a ten year old and got lost. It was worth finding, though, because it is a small plateau studded with little tarns, King Billy pines, pincushion moss, and surrounded by spectacular mountains. We camped for several days, swam in the tarns (that's probably discouraged in these more ecologically aware days) and fluked warm sunny weather. It was a splendid holiday and thirsty work. My friend 'Spike' Bryden had borrowed his father's Morris Oxford utility for the trip, and we paused at the Derwent Bridge Hotel for a few cold beers. Perhaps more than a few. These were the days before the breathalyser.

Spike was driving and I was in the passenger seat. The other three were in the back of the ute. I remember we were singing loudly as we reached the first major bend that signalled we were about to descend from the plateau.

Unfortunately Spike hadn't had his licence all that long, nor was he used to driving under the influence of a few sherberts. He hit the bend far too fast, and lost the back wheels on the gravel. We began to skid sideways along the road, which might have been a safer option. All Spike had to do was nothing. But he manfully wrenched the wheel to 'correct' the skid, and we headed over the bank and down into the bush, studded with dolerite rocks and dead logs. We were lucky not to roll over. One of the blokes in the back tried to abandon ship, failed, and gave himself a nasty bang in the groin which didn't improve his sense of well-being or his temper. We crunched to a halt on top of a low rock, and felt happy we were all still alive.

Before we had a chance to find out what had happened to the ute, a battered Public Works Department truck with a couple of local road workers happened to come by. They stopped and asked if we were OK. Then, without being asked, they backed their truck up and winched us back on the road. That kind of thing happens in the bush. The Morris ute was a bit battered, but looked driveable. That was until we looked underneath to see where all the oil was coming from. The alloy sump had been bashed in and holed by a chunk of bluestone rock it had come to rest on. We couldn't see ourselves getting home that night!

But the bushies had other ideas. 'Just run it down the road for a cuppla miles to Alvin's place. It's downhill all the way. He'll fix ya up.'

We thought Alvin would have to be a miracle worker but did as we were told, and finished up at a place that looked like a set for a Ma and Pa Kettle film. A vertical weatherboard house was surrounded by rusting machinery and car bodies and snotty-nosed kids running about in the chaos. Alvin came out to greet us, and he looked smarter than his surrounds in some useful looking blue overalls. Again, without asking us why we were there—I suppose it was fairly obvious—he asked us to briefly start the motor to see if it worked and switch it off quickly. It did. He got us to help him push the utility up on some timber tracks over a pit, so he could inspect the underneath of the vehicle.

Alvin looked up at the sump for about a minute, and wandered into a nearby shed. 'I wonder if that bit of King Billy pine is where I think it is,' he muttered to no one in particular. He then pulled out a pocket knife and started to whittle a wooden plug for the sump! Every now and then he'd hold it up to the ruptured sump, and shave off a bit more. Eventually he tapped it in with a hammer, and then banged it in as firmly as he could.

'Right,' he said. 'Let's see if she can hold the pressure.' He found a can of oil, and filled up the sump. Spike started the engine, and—believe it or not—the King Billy plug held. It was dribbling a bit of oil, but Alvin said that with luck it would get us home, but to check the oil fairly regularly.

He wouldn't take any money, wouldn't consider it. 'You might do me a favour some time.' I wasn't sure when this might be. I think we did give him a few bottles of beer, which he seemed pleased about. Within an hour of our accident, and busted sump, we were on our way. It was unbelievable.

We were losing oil though, and when we got to the first garage at a town called Westerway, we asked the mechanic there to have a look at our sump. He did so and said: 'I want to pretend that I didn't see that. That's impossible. If I were you I'd keep driving and keep pouring the oil in like the man said!'

We got back to Hobart that night.

I kept an eye out for Alvin's 'farm', if you could call it that, but it had either been tarted up or disappeared off the face of the earth. About twenty-five kilometres past Lake St Clair we turned off the Lyell Highway to the left, on the rather grandly named Marlborough Highway. Its quality did not match its thick red line on the map or its ducal overtones, and it turned into a mediocre gravel road very quickly and then a rutted, pot-hole-dotted track which hadn't seen a grader in living memory. This was more an irritation than a problem, because Penelope and The Manor could take worse than that in their stride.

Our next turnoff was at the southern end of the Great Lake, which also failed to live up to its name. In fact it looked like a half-empty bath. Perhaps half-empty was a generous estimate, with sad looking exposed flanks leading down to the reduced waters of the once great lake. The Hydro scheme was begun in the 1930s and finished in the 1960s. Before its impoundment the Great Lake was the headwaters of the Derwent River, which runs south-east to Hobart. After a series of hydro-electric dams on that river was exploited, the Great Lake was diverted north-east down through pipes and tunnels to Poatina at the foot of the Western Tiers, only about fifty kilometres from the 'capital of the north', Launceston. The hydro action then moved to the north-west and west of the state (the Pieman River and the controversial upper Gordon scheme which flooded the wonderful Lake Pedder in the south-west), which dwarfed the older Great Lakes-related schemes. The Great Lake catchment was in drought when we saw it, but locals told me it never fills to capacity any more. Launceston, in fact, was the site of the first hydro-electric scheme in Australia when the City Council built its Duck River generating station on the South Esk River in 1895.

We continued on the Marlborough 'highway', banging over pot holes and corrugations, up the western side of the lake. The turnoff was shortly before what is left of the town of Miena, near the main impoundment dam. In its heyday, Miena was a drawcard for those who practised the arcane art of fly fishing, as the Hydro's dams were always stocked with rainbow and brown trout. My father, John Bowden, a keen trout fisherman himself, was sometimes given the not-too-onerous job of entertaining visiting American bigwigs from General Motors at the Miena chalet. On one of these occasions his boss, Len Nettlefold, helped out by lending his precious Hardy fly rod—the Rolex of rods for anglers. This was used by the wife of the executive being given the VIP treatment. Father was amused one morning when she came down to breakfast and asked in her broad Southern drawl: 'Has anyone seen mah fishin' pole?'

The country we were driving through was fairly bleak with low high country heath, the gnarled gum trees somehow extracting enough nourishment from the relentlessly rocky ground to survive, and areas of what bushwalkers called 'ploughed fields' which have nothing to do with agriculture, although they give this impression from a distance. They are stretches of tumbled dolerite boulders, a relic of the passing of ancient glaciers, on which nothing grows. I couldn't look about much because I was too busy dodging pot holes. My brother Philip later said he thought I was mad coming that way, but I wanted to see that part of Tasmania again.

After a quick picnic lunch under a low containment dam wall—to seek some shelter from the cold winds which sweep unimpeded over the highlands—we found the bitumen again and came down from the plateau in quite spectacular fashion beside the distinctive peak of Quamby Bluff, descending 1200 metres in twenty minutes! Quite suddenly we were back in fertile farming country on the outskirts of Deloraine, where we rejoined Highway One for an easy run into Launceston.

This charming city is built around the head of the Tamar estuary, at the confluence of the North and South Esk rivers, sixty-four kilometres inland from Bass Strait. Bass and Flinders discovered the estuary as early as 1798, and the region might well have been settled before Hobart had Governor King in Port Jackson been aware of what Colonial Secretary Lord Bathurst had in mind. Bathurst decided to send Captain David Collins to the southern regions of the continent to establish a British presence in case the French got in first. In the meantime, as mentioned earlier, Governor King, also worried about the French, had sent Lieutenant Bowen and a party to the Derwent River in 1803 to begin a settlement there. David Collins (who first tried to establish a settlement at Port Phillip and was then asked to take over Bowen's enterprise at Risdon on the Derwent River) had sailed into the Tamar estuary in January 1804. He liked what he saw and the following year Governor King sent his lieutenant governor, William Paterson, to found a colony at Port Dalrymple at the head of the Tamar estuary. However in 1806 Paterson moved the settlement to the present site of Launceston (originally called Patersonia by Governor King). There he ruled his domain benignly for several years until the Rum Rebellion in New South Wales and the arrest of Governor Bligh caused him to be called back to Port Jackson to take over the administration in January 1809.

When Paterson first arrived in Launceston, Governor King in New South Wales gave him jurisdiction over half of the island down to 42° south. That marked the border between the north and the southern territory controlled by David Collins. The history of all this is important because latitude 42° south looms large in the minds of all northerners, well aware that they have the larger population, more industry and in recent years have become Tasmania's gateway for the roll-on-roll-off shipping trade in cargo and people. 'What has the south got going for it?' they ask rhetorically. 'A scenic but basically useless harbour, the state parliament and public service departments, the main campus of the University of Tasmania and bugger all else except a collective determination to ignore or screw the north where all the action really is.'

There has always been a virulent north-south rivalry in Tasmania that makes the even longer-running stoush between the Irish Republic and Northern Ireland look like a minor skirmish.

There is a small town in the middle of Tasmania, nearest to latitude 42° south, called Oatlands. Now, as luck would have it, I have a bit of street cred in the north, because although born in the hated south my mother was born in Launceston and I started my career in the ABC there in the early 1960s. During that time, my late friend Robin Wyly, a rabid northerner, would often fix me with a steely gaze and say belligerently, 'Bowden—there's not a

good man born south of Oatlands'. After the terrible bushfires that devastated the south in 1967, Robin swore on a
stack of bibles that he saw a placard in a Launceston shop
window three weeks after the disaster: 'WANTED 167
GOOD MEN AND TRUE. LET'S MARCH ON THE SOUTH WHILE
THEY'RE STILL WEAK'.

An amalgamation of the Launceston and Hobart
Savings Banks foundered many years ago on the rocks of
north-south rivalry and there has even been heart-burning
about the name of the wider reach of tertiary institutions—
the very name 'University of Tasmania' being associated by
northerners with Hobart and the unspeakable south.

Or, depending on your regional view, paranoia from the
south. The idea of colleges of advanced education was
conceived in the John Gorton years, and implemented in
Gough Whitlam's time. My northern historian friend, Snow
Thomas, reminded me there was a push for a change of
name for the Newnham campus in Launceston to something
like the Royal Melbourne Institute of Technology across
the water. The Tasmanian Institute of Technology (TIT)
was briefly considered, but became instead the Tasmanian
State Institute of Technology (TSIT). Eventually, after
considerable northern heart-burning, the original name—
the University of Tasmania—became the umbrella under
which every new tertiary extension sheltered.

This debate actually goes back to before the turn of
the twentieth century, when some Launceston politicians
campaigned on a platform to abolish the Hobart-based
university if they were elected. The University of Tasmania,
on the other hand, was doing back-flips to keep the north
happy, even arranging extension lectures there as far back as
1884. But the northerners remained exceedingly ungrateful

and often failed to turn up to lectures. On one cold winter's night in Launceston, a visiting Hobart lecturer found himself addressing an audience of two—a lady and a reporter. 'So far as Launceston is concerned,' he was reported as saying, 'we seem to be casting pearls before swine. The people are desperately ignorant and desperately contented with their ignorance.'

I only have the courage to write about this deeply entrenched split because I now live safely on 'the mainland'.

My brother Philip and his wife Angie (their three daughters have grown up and left, as kids do) live on rural land at Relbia, on the southern fringe of Launceston, with a wonderful vista north-east to Mt Barrow and Ben Lomond. The block next door has recently been converted to a vineyard. This is fine visually, but the family golden retriever, Ted, was experiencing a nervous breakdown because of the vineyard owner's practice of firing off what seem to be intermittent gunshots to scare away marauding birds from his ripening grapes. The birds didn't seem to take much notice of the simulated shots, but poor Ted had been deeply traumatised. (He remained a highly disturbed and neurotic dog until Philip managed to get this ineffective bird-scaring method stopped some weeks later.)

We parked The Manor beside Philip and Angie's sprawling farmhouse, which was considerably more manorial than our camper, and spent a couple of days with them, relaxing and visiting friends in and around Launceston. Philip has a small dam which he has stocked with trout. Occasionally he takes his fly rod down there and catches one—then gently unhooks it and puts it back. Fly fishing encourages odd behaviour.

Being in Launceston was a welcome opportunity to catch up with a much loved aunt, Dottie Jowett. The ranks are thinning among my mother Peggy Lovett's seven siblings and Dottie is now in her early eighties. Her husband Wilf died not so long ago, aged ninety-seven. He lost his sight in his last years and Dottie appropriated one of his white walking sticks when she went to town. Over dinner she told us how gratified and surprised she was to find people coming up to her at traffic lights and escorting her across the road. One of her good Samaritans, she said, was a bit surprised to see her toss her white stick into the back seat of her car and drive away!

The morning we left, Philip came out to watch me back up Penelope and hitch The Manor up again. I had the feeling he thought I couldn't do it all by myself. He has always had a low opinion of the practical abilities of his elder brother. (We get on rather well, actually.)

We drove through the centre of Launceston to the Tamar Highway, on the eastern side of the estuary, which would lead us on some lesser roads to Piper's River and then to the coastal town of Bridport where we planned to stay a night with my aunt Judy Diprose (my mother's youngest sister) and her husband Dak. As we drove down towards the confluence of the North and South Esk rivers, I was reminded of how gracious a city Launceston is, with parks, churches and some fine public buildings. The older wooden houses are particularly charming, their verandas, windows and facades decorated with timber ornamentation in what seems to me a uniquely Launcestonian style. Mercifully they weren't torn down as 'old hat' and have now been beautifully painted and kept in mint condition.

**Travel Diary Sunday 2 March**

The weather is cold, but fine and sunny. We heard on the radio that there is a sheep grazier's alert, and snow showers on Hobart's Mt Wellington. Fortunately, we are in the best quadrant of the state for good weather. Tasmanians talk about the weather more than other Australians because there is so much of it, and it is always changing. We are in rampant tourist mode today, thumbing through the brochures and planning our day.

Because we had already seen it on a previous Tasmanian visit, we did not drive over the Batman Bridge (which crosses the Tamar estuary over its lower reaches) to Beauty Point on the western side in order to see Seahorse World, where the improbable looking creatures are successfully bred for export, mainly to China where they are in high demand in the Chinese medicine market. Seahorse World performs two useful functions—it creates a wonderful tourist attraction and also helps to limit the over-harvesting of seahorses in the wild, for jewellery as well as for aphrodisiac and other potions. The seahorse has long held a peculiar attraction for mankind; the Roman god of the sea, Neptune, is usually pictured in a chariot drawn by seahorses. Scientists recognised the horse-like attributes of these fish, so officially designated them *Hippocampus* (Greek: *hippos*, horse; *kampos*, sea monster). The pot-bellied seahorse (*Hippocampus abdominalis*) is bred at Seahorse World, and on our last visit we watched fascinated as a (pregnant?) male seahorse popped microscopic-sized little seahorses out of its swollen belly in a virtuoso display of gender bending. There are also display aquariums where the main attraction is surely the brightly coloured weedy sea dragon, which is more like a surrealist fantasy than a living creature.

Although it seemed a little early in the day for wine tasting, I could not resist calling in to Providence Vineyards, near the hamlet of Lalla, near Lilydale. The Tamar Valley and further east is one of Tasmania's finest wine producing regions. It is also one of the earliest, and although I never met the pioneering winemaker Jean Miguet, who established La Provence—as it was then called—in 1956, he was influential in making me a wine grower briefly when I worked for the ABC in Launceston in 1963. The current owners of Providence Vineyards, Stuart and Brenda Bryce, welcomed us warmly to their tasting bar and had to put up with my reminiscences about the influence of their founder on the brief existence of Windermere Vineyards.

Seven good men and true got together in 1963—having heard of Monsieur Miguet's success in making superb wine in the Tamar Valley—and bought a quarter acre block near Rosevears on the west bank of the Tamar River. We consisted of four lawyers, two journalists and a brewer. I figured the most useful member of the syndicate was Robin Wyly, the brewer, because if we ever succeeded in growing any grapes he might even be able to make some halfway reasonable joy juice. Having four lawyers on board meant they registered a proper business name—Windermere Vineyards—and we had the block properly fitted out with posts and wires. Vines were somehow obtained—perhaps from M. Miguet, I can't recall now—and a variety of reds and whites were planted on our eastern-facing block, including pinot noir, chardonnay and riesling which go particularly well in Tasmania. In fact, the acclaimed St Mattias Vineyard today is not all that far away from our block. Ah, what might have been . . .

The problem was the tyranny of distance. Two of our members lived in Hobart and not long after we started our little vineyard, I was moved to Hobart by the ABC. This put a lot of strain on the Launceston members of the syndicate. But we did our best and made pilgrimages to the block whenever we could to do some weeding and tending of the vines, in company with wives and girlfriends. It must be admitted that drinking tended to start too early in the day and the vines near the bottom gate received the earliest and most attention. Those at the top of the block gradually succumbed to blackberries and a cornucopia of local weeds. One particularly luxuriant vine conveniently near the entrance was nicknamed Lorenzo. It was said carnal acts took place under Lorenzo's leafy bower, but I can't vouch for the accuracy of that.

A few bottles of wine were actually made, not by Robin the brewer, but in Guy Green's kitchen cupboard. I heard they were of indifferent quality. We did have an annual dinner, sometimes better attended than the diminishing weeding sessions. Because we had been registered, Windermere Vineyards even made it into one of Len Evans's early wine books: 'A small experimental plot on the west bank of the Tamar River of which not much is known . . .'

Alas, as our careers moved on and more of us moved away from Launceston, Windermere Vineyards withered and was eventually sold ingloriously as a building block. The posts, wires and what remained of the vines were all grubbed out. I'd like to think that the new owners preserved Lorenzo, but I never went back to look. Some of our alumni went on to great distinction. Windermere could boast two chief justices, two governors of Tasmania and a premier no less. (Sir Guy Green went on to become governor after having been chief justice and was succeeded by his former Windermere colleague, Bill Cox. In November 2004 Bill also made the transition from chief justice to government house.) In 1981 former journalist Harry Holgate became the Labor premier of Tasmania—for six months—but the rest of us failed to reach such stellar heights. The Windermere Seven collectively blew our opportunity to join the pioneers of the Tasmanian wine industry.

At least Jean Miguet made some wine that he and his friends could drink, but he had a hard time nevertheless. A fifth generation winemaker from Provence, Miguet went to Tasmania to work on Hydro Electric Commission projects in the mid 1950s. At first all he wanted to do was develop his plot of land and grow grapes to make some wine. That was hard enough, given the natural hazards arrayed against his vines. As well, various sectarian groups protested at the growing of grapes to produce—shock horror—alcohol! Australia's multicultural society was far in the future, and Miguet (who spoke very little English) was treated abominably by some of the locals, who even went as far as to spray lethal herbicides on his vines. When he did succeed in producing a commercial quantity of wine, the bureaucracy refused to give him a licence to sell it. In 1975 he contracted leukaemia and went home to France to die.

It's not a pretty story, but Providence Vineyards remains as his legacy. Stuart and Brenda told us that the bloke they bought the vineyard from had raised capital with an ingenious scam by offering to sell single vines to individual investors for, say, $10 with the promise (and a handsome certificate) they would get two bottles of wine a year from then on. The trouble for the new owners was that this 'contract' was open ended! The duped investors got not a drop. Eventually, Stuart told me, he had to grub out the Grenache vines that his predecessor had planted, and keep them stored. If any investors turned up at Providence to ask about the progress of 'their' vine, Stuart was sometimes able to offer one of the vines he had pulled out in token compensation. Fortunately there was no legal liability to honour the dodgy fund-raising of the previous owner and when Stuart ran out of his stock of Grenache vines, he had to tell the hopeful investor that, sadly, their particular vine had carked. Which was true. Providence Vineyards is now a splendid example of small holdings that not only produce great cool climate wines, but offer friendly personalised greetings to passing travellers like us.

Our next port of call, Pipers Brook Vineyard, was at the top end of the market with an architect-designed winery and tasting complex and tourists coming by the busload. We arrived at an 'interesting' time for the vineyard, established by the brothers David and Andrew Pirie in the early 1970s and expanded to become the biggest single producer and exporter of Tasmanian wines by the end of the twentieth century. In 2001, Dr Andrew Pirie encouraged a takeover bid by Kreglinger Australia Pty Ltd. In early 2003, a week before Penelope and The Manor drove in to sample Dr Pirie's wares, the general manager and chief winemaker was given his marching orders by Kreglinger.

When we were there the vast tasting bar was staffed with courteous young people uniformly dressed in power black with matching aprons. Pipers Brook wines are top of the range with prices to match. We asked after their Ninth Island product, clearly visible on the shelves and more moderately priced, and found to our surprise there was a policy that they could be purchased but not tasted. Why so? I asked. Because the Ninth Island wines came from a different vineyard. 'But the same company, surely?' Yes, but we would have to go to that particular vineyard to taste them. With so many boutique vineyards awaiting our custom throughout the island we decided not to buy Pipers Brook's undoubtedly good, but expensive, bottled sunshine and headed off to our next (non-alcoholic) destination, the Bridestowe Lavender Farm at Nabowla.

I have to say that I wasn't succumbing to a long-held, deep-seated desire to experience the joys of a lavender farm, and in fact I didn't know there were such things. Ros, the horticulturalist, was quite keen to see it, however, and I must admit I found it an interesting experience. (Speaking of mild expectations, I am reliably informed that there was a television program in New Zealand in the 1960s titled *That's Fairly Interesting*.)

The Bridestowe operation happens to be the biggest lavender farm in the southern hemisphere, with 120 acres of the purple blooms under cultivation. Unfortunately we had missed harvest time so there wasn't any point getting our cameras out—the mechanically farmed bushes were cropped and flower-less. The farm is quite old, with experimental plantings having begun in 1924. The main purpose is to provide lavender oil for the perfume industry, but that's not all. I found a visit to the farm shop almost compensated for not seeing a horizon-to-horizon purple vista.

You wouldn't believe how many products can be associated with lavender. Flowery postcards of course, but also soap, fridge magnets, dried lavender-scented bags, candles—even honey and cheese although these last two mercifully are not lavender flavoured. Ros bought some purple votive candles, and I asked her why. Was she thinking of attending any church services any time soon? A bit nettled, Ros said they were just ordinary candles. 'No they're not, they're votive candles. It says so.'

'How do you know "votive" means they are religious candles?' (Ros knows that my interest in the minutiae of religious ritual is minimal.)

'I just know. Do you want to put money on it?'

'OK,' said Ros, convinced I was having her on. 'Five bucks then.'

The young woman behind the counter obligingly rustled up a dictionary, and I scored a rare win.

Whenever possible on our journey around Tasmania we tried to stay as close as we could to the coast. The south-west of the island is completely closed off because of the mountainous terrain and its World Heritage status national park. In its own way the north-east coast is wild and unspoiled and quite difficult to get to. The main road from Launceston to the biggest town in the north-east, Scottsdale, is well inland. The road nearest the coast, B82, starts from George Town and Bell Bay (near the mouth of the Tamar estuary) and runs parallel to the coast about twenty kilometres inland, until Bridport, a holiday and fishing town about sixty kilometres to the east. There are minor roads up to the coast along the way, but not all that many of them. We did run up twelve kilometres from Pipers Brook to the coast, and had our picnic lunch at Bellingham, across a small estuary from Weymouth.

You couldn't call them towns, just clusters of fishing shacks and a few houses.

Bridport is only eighty-five kilometres from Launceston and is a popular holiday spot, with a permanent population of some 1200 people—swelling to 5000 or so in holiday periods. My aunt Judy Diprose and Dak divide their time between their apartment in Launceston and their beach house at Bridport. Dak is a keen fisherman and I'm sure would like to stay at Bridport for most of his waking moments, but Judy (who is fond of Bridport too) has her main interests in Launceston, so compromises are made—as in all enduring relationships.

We quickly located their house overlooking the deep blue but windswept waters of Anderson Bay. I thought fishing might be off the agenda and I was right. That's Tasmania for you. That's why they have wind farms there. Being campers and travellers themselves until a few years ago, Judy and Dak understood that we were happy to sleep in our camper—we needed to keep the fridge going anyway—and guided us to a sheltered and level spot in their back yard.

Dak and Judy met in the north-east. The Diprose family had dairy farms in the Ringarooma area, a small timber and farming town to the south-east of Scottsdale. Judy was a schoolie at the local area secondary school, having not long graduated from teacher's college. (The Diprose family were heavily addicted to nicknames. Dak—Harold—is not sure why he was called Dak, but none of his siblings used their given names, and were happily known all their lives by short, sharp, pet names like Ink, Budge, Wak and Biz.) The slim, dark-haired schoolteacher and the big, easy-going farmer fell instantly in love and stayed that way for the rest of their lives. Dak, at eighty-two, still carries the muscle and bulk of the timber getter I remember meeting when I went to Ringarooma to stay with them during a school holiday. I must have been about ten, so it was the late 1940s.

Over a glass or three of excellent Tasmanian pinot noir and fish that Dak had caught and was magnificently prepared and presented by Judy (the Lovett sisters have gourmet cooking in their genes), I checked out some of my memories of that visit.

At that time bullock teams were still being used to haul hardwood logs out of the forests. As a small boy I was fascinated by this, and Dak took me out into the bush while they were working. The bullocks were yoked in pairs, and the bullock driver controlled them by yelling strange (to my ear) commands, and occasionally flicking individual bullocks in the team with a fearsomely long rawhide whip. The verbals were also sprinkled with a fair amount of profanity, as was the way of bullock drivers wherever they worked. I'd heard worse at school.

One morning Judy came out with me to see the action. But there was a problem. Deprived of his salty language, in deference to Judy's presence, the driver couldn't get the bullock team to do anything. They just stood there. Eventually the problem was explained to Judy and she retired to a point where the bullocky could yell at his charges in the way they understood, away from delicate feminine ears. I asked Dak if my memory of that was accurate, and he said it was. 'Old Reg Lewis was the driver, and he couldn't talk to the bullocks in the way they understood while Jude was there.'

I asked Dak if the bullocks really needed to be sworn at to understand what they were supposed to do. 'You taught the instructions with the whip and they knew. You didn't use the whip until you had to use it, and that's where you became a little bit annoyed and the adjectives started to flow. And then the bullocks would react.'

I didn't know it at the time, but I was seeing the last of an era that had begun in the very early days of European settlement in Australia. Dak told me that only a few years after my visit, the bullock teams were replaced by tractors. It won't be long before living memory of that era will be gone.

I asked Dak if he would mind recording his memories of how bullock teams were worked before we left the following morning.

TIM: How was a bullock team organised?
DAK: You had your leaders, two intelligent bullocks—it's like human beings, some were a little more pliable and intelligent than the others. You could teach them what they had to do. It's as though they were born to different jobs. You had your leaders first in the team and the ordinary bullocks in the middle. If you had fourteen that was seven pairs—that was about the normal team. Towards the end you had what you called the 'clamp' bullocks and they would be two bigger animals—probably de-sexed bulls or something a bit solid. Say you had your team in a straight line and you came to a bend, you would keep these big fellows over-hanging to make a semi-circle and keep a bend in the team. Right on the end there were two small bullocks, stocky little fellows, called the 'shoe' bullocks, near the head of the log. They were the ones that first copped the weight. You had the big clamp bullocks next to prop when the power was on from the front—on a gradual turn, or something like that. Then they could hold the log straight on a big heavy pull.

The leaders were your main animals because they guided the team. They would walk out wide coming to a turn. If you were in open country they would come out wide to keep the weight off the back. Then the big fellows at the back would 'prop' in so they could hold the log from going into a corner, or into an obstruction.

TIM: Can you remember the basic working commands for the bullock team?

DAK: 'Come hither' was to bring them to you, and the other command was 'Gee off'. In a way it was like boating—port left and starboard right. 'Come hither' was to go to port, and 'Gee off' was to go to starboard. 'Whoa' was to stop. 'Get up' was just to go.

Each bullock knew its own name, of course. You'd call for 'Sharper' and 'Spanker'—they were the two leaders. You'd say, 'Gee off, Sharper' or something like that and they would turn to go the way you wanted. Or, 'Come hither Spanker'. They knew.

TIM: After a while there would be a track to follow anyway . . .

DAK: They would follow the track but they learnt where the weight came on—you'd see their legs prop if there was a snag or an obstacle, a stump or whatever. They would tend to pull towards that—well they would only have to be rubbed on it once. Of course the driver had to be awake because if you didn't pull off the whole weight of the team you could kill them and this happened in a few cases. If a log 'shot' and they didn't have time to get out of the way, they could be maimed or killed. But they soon learned. They weren't idiots.

TIM: Bullock teams could pull pretty big loads couldn't they?

DAK: More than you would realise. A 1000 foot log, which is not all that big—1000 super feet in the round—well that's only 12 feet long and 2 feet six 6 inches through. That weighs about 3 tons. Well, six bullocks could handle that anywhere.

TIM: So with a team of fourteen what kind of loads could they pull?

DAK: I have pulled logs with 2500 super feet in them. That would be about seven or eight tons—about half a ton per bullock.

There was another memory I wanted to check out. I remembered seeing Dak cutting a huge felled log in half with a cross-cut saw, by himself, with no one on the other handle. I thought he was doing it alone because there was no one else around, but he later explained to me that their biggest cross-cut saws were eight feet long. Sometimes the diameter of the log was the same as the saw. In that case they had to axe a V-shaped cut called a 'scarf' into the log a foot deep on both sides of the log to enable the saw to be moved backwards and forwards. Sometimes, in those circumstances, there simply wasn't room for a second man on the saw because one end had to be pulled right into the cut, and it could take one man a whole day to saw through such a large log.

DAK: I've got a photograph somewhere of the biggest tree we ever felled. It took us all day to fall that tree—it was just before we broke up at Christmas time. We started at 8 o'clock in the morning and it hit the ground at 4 o'clock in the afternoon. But we had to chop in what we called the front scarf, and we cut that out with axes. That tree was big enough for us to cut left and right handed. You didn't want to cut through the widest part of the tree right at the base so you would go up to the point where the tree began its natural roundness, up above the spurs. This tree was eight feet in diameter, whichever way you looked at it.

The scarf was like a big wedge, and you'd cut it nearly halfway through the tree and then come in from the other side with a cross-cut saw if you had one long enough.

We were two days falling it and taking the first two logs off. It had 14 700 super feet in it—a magnificent tree. That was the best cut the mill ever had. That particular tree was about seventy feet tall. Not a really high tree but plenty of bulk in him. It was a mountain ash— beautiful clean timber.

TIM: What was the timber used for?

DAK: Oddly enough it was used for coffin boards. It went into Finneys, the undertakers in Launceston. Finneys also used to make furniture which was quite hard to come by in those days—in fact the furniture for our first marital home at Legerwood near Ringarooma was made by Finneys from that particular magnificent mountain ash!

I asked Dak and Judy whether they still had any of the furniture milled from the huge mountain ash, but they didn't. Judy's tastes had shifted to antique furniture and there was no place for the simple minimalism of 1950s timber wardrobes or book cases in their lives in the early twenty-first century.

# five

## Searching for Merle

Our coastal route was taking us into sparsely inhabited grazing country—we left the bitumen half an hour out of Bridport, but it was good gravel that enabled us to cruise comfortably at 80 kph. I noted the turnoff to Cape Portland, on the extreme north-east tip of Tasmania, and remembered a story about Ernie Mills, who ran a property up there and flew a light plane to reach not only remote parts of his own property, but offshore islands, landing on beaches or improvised airstrips. In the 1960s Ernie had the reputation of being a daring pilot who had also carried out some emergency medical evacuations from very difficult locations. One of the problems of his home airstrip was to make sure it was clear of wandering stock. Ernie used to buzz the strip to clear it, before coming in to land. As I heard the story, he did this, and was coming in to land unaware that a horse was galloping down the strip directly underneath him. Ernie landed on the horse, which didn't do the horse, the aircraft or Ernie much good. He managed to walk away from this unusual landing, but the horse wasn't so lucky. Ernie Mills was in the air again as soon as he and his aircraft were patched up.

Perhaps because of the gravel road we didn't pass any other touring campers, which is unusual in a Tasmanian summer, particularly since the two *Spirit*s have been running day and night voyages from Melbourne to Devonport. The main highway to the east coast and the coastal town of St Helens was through Scottsdale, further south. The lesser road we were driving was fringed with the usual collection of dead marsupials, ranging from bandicoots, through Tasmanian devils to Forester kangaroos—a very good reason for not travelling at night when these vulnerable creatures are dazzled by headlights and struck down.

Seeing the results of the night's slaughter reminded me of a conversation I had with the remarkable Don Cunningham a few years ago. Don, formerly an apiarist with the Department of Agriculture, out of the blue, in the late 1980s, sent me a cassette tape on which he had recorded some of his reminiscences about growing up on a subsistence farm at a farming hamlet called Kamona, near Scottsdale on the north-east coast. In that era every animal or bird that moved was considered fair game and, to be honest, anything that could be caught was needed for the pot in those tough times. It was driving along the carcase-strewn road not far from where Don lived as a boy that brought him to mind. I thought his tape contained wonderful oral history and when I returned to Tasmania in 1989 I sought Don out—he was then living in retirement in Devonport—to record him more thoroughly. I was looking forward to meeting him when we got to Hobart.

When I began to write this book I listened again to the tape I had recorded with Don, and realised how well he had described a vanished era, not only in the north-east of Tasmania but throughout Australia, when people had to survive through their ingenuity and raw courage on their small plots of land with only the most basic farming and domestic equipment and without any social service safety net.

Here is part of the conversation I had with Don in 1989.

DON: My very earliest recollection was when I was only three years old, of the Presbyterian minister coming into our house and my mother, with two of her brothers at the war, saying, 'Which one?' And it was one of them, and of course she was very upset that her brother had just been reported killed. It must have made a big impression on me, too, because it is the very first thing I remember.

About three years later, we moved out from Scottsdale to a little district called Kamona. In those days it was pretty basic. There was bracken fern everywhere and nobody had any superphosphate, so there wasn't much grass growing, and nobody had any money. Everybody milked a few cows of pretty low efficiency and struggled along. They didn't starve, though. There were rabbits to be caught and kangaroos and things like that.

TIM: What were your family circumstances?

DON: I was the only child. Life was pretty grim in that we had no mechanical aids. We milked about twenty cows. You got up a bit after daylight and put them in the cow yard which would be anywhere up to knee deep in mud—we had no gumboots of course. We used to put big heavy planks out into the mud and you walked to the end of the plank and waved your arms at the cow and hoped she'd respond and walk in to the bail. The milk had to be carried by hand from the bails across to where the dairy was where the hand separator was turned. So you produced the cream and the milk, and the milk you carried by hand again, mixed pollard with the milk and took it down to the pig sty and fed the pigs. The cream was kept, and about twice a week a lorry came around from the Legerwood area and collected it for butter making.

TIM: Dairying is a terribly constant labour isn't it, it just never stops . . .

DON: The only way to stop dairying is to leave it, because the cows have to be milked. They won't wait—you can't leave them to miss a milking. So even if you arrived home late from school, or late from somewhere and it was dark, the cows still had to be milked. A terrible bind. You were up on a frosty morning and the cows were brought in and so you milked away in the cold. My father actually saw this happen at a farm where there were a number of kids and it was pretty grim. These little kids were bare-footed milking these cows on a frosty morning. So they put their muddy feet down in the bucket of milk, so they had nice warm feet!

TIM: I'd heard about bare feet in the fresh cow pats, but not in the milk.

DON: I don't think they put them in the pats first. I hope not anyway.

TIM: So it was mostly subsistence farming was it?

DON: Pretty much, yeah. We had, I think, 120 acres. That, if it were in good country, would be a very good farm, but the land there was pretty poor. My father was the only one who could afford someone to come and cut the bracken a couple of times a year. This meant that the grass had a chance to grow and we could run a few more head of stock.

TIM: What about augmenting the pot with local game and so on?

DON: Well, kangaroos were not terribly plentiful in our area but we did get one occasionally, and he went into the pot all right. Periodically my father would kill some pigs and that was quite a business. I had to help hold the pig down while its throat was cut—all very gory. That was a bit of a harvest for us because we had pig's liver and pig's head for making brawn—we did quite well. But the rest of the carcase was sold.

I can vividly recall the transporting of those carcases from our farm. We would be up about daylight with a hurricane lamp, down to the slaughterhouse, where my father would have four or five carcases put into chaff bags, into the cart with the old horse, and he had about a four mile trip to make, up steep hills to the railway at the Kamona Railway Station. And the goods train came through about half-past five in the morning on its way through to Launceston. So the pigs would go there to the market and be sold. The returns would be fairly small. We thought that city people got pretty cheap pork at our expense.

TIM: I suppose if it moved you shot it, didn't you?

DON: Yes—very Australian. If it grows, burn it, if it moves, shoot it! As a kid I look back and think of the destructive times I had. We had bows and arrows, we had shanghais, we had air guns and we used to hunt in the bush for the parrots—the green lorikeets, black jays, and there were quite a lot of the wood pigeons around then. These, of course, weren't wasted. We would pluck them and clean them and my mother would make a pie of them, and they were delicious. Parrot pie is a bit of a joke today I suppose, but it was by far better than pigeon pie and the birds were plentiful then.

TIM: Did you knock down birds with a shanghai?

DON: I've shot as many with the shanghai as the air gun, I'd say. We became quite adept. When one first started with shanghais—realising that we were well out in the bush—you had to have rubber for the shanghai bands. Anything in this nature was like gold dust to us. One glorious day a motorist had a blow-out in his car right opposite where we lived and the next day he came back to retrieve it and he gave me this whole inner tube and I had shanghais for ever more. It was probably one of the golden days of my life.

TIM: While we're talking about food . . . what equipment did your mother have in the kitchen?

DON: We had what was called a colonial oven—they were about the first thing that supplanted the old open fireplace. It was simply a square cast-iron box with a door on the front of it that was set on a couple of bricks, so you lit a little fire underneath and had an ordinary open fire up on the top of it, used as an open fireplace. In that oven Mother baked our bread and roasted meat. I remember my father once had some damp cartridges and decided that was the best place to dry them out. But when they dried out they started going off and he wasn't game to open the door, so most of the box discharged inside the oven. I well remember that!

TIM: I suppose shooting wasn't always for the pot, you could make some money as well.

DON: Yes, very much so. Because even with the rabbits you shot, skins were worth quite a bit of money. I suppose rabbit skins were probably worth a shilling a piece in those days, or more. Kangaroo skins had value, but the most sought after skins were from ringtail and brushtail possums. Ringtail possums were then fairly plentiful and there was a season for the shooting. My father had been quite a hunter in his younger days so when the season came, we used to go ringtailing on suitable nights. We had bush all around us, of course, and we used carbide lights.

This was an essential part of the operation. You had a carbide generator similar to what went on a motorbike and a length of flexible tubing and you made your own lamp section. The thing to do was to buy a billycan, and a big concave reflector which you screwed in the back of it, put a burner in front of this, then hooked the gas tube to it. When you set the water going on the carbide, you had a light. A very good one too—they would beam probably a quarter of a mile or more.

This form of lighting was important, because carbide lights weren't harsh like electric lights, so that when you shone the light up in the trees and there was a ringtail up there, he would look at it. If it was an electric light it would tend to be too bright, and he would look away. So you'd see this pair of eyes like red buttons 120 feet up in a gum tree. Really good shots used pea rifles and they could bring them down with that, even at night. But my father didn't ever come up into that category. He used a twelve bore gun. You'd hold the lamp up with your left hand, and raise the gun over the top of the lamp along the top of it and fire nearly straight up in the air, and a big healthy cartridge would nearly knock you off your feet at that angle. If you were fortunate, the possum, the ringtail, just left the tree and came down—wallop—on to the ground and if he wasn't killed by the fall, he'd probably scramble away.

Sometimes the possum would get his tail around the limb and there he'd swing, and there'd be four or five cartridges discharged. The boys with pea rifles could shoot the tail off and the possum would come down. I was the small boy who was dragged along to carry these stinking possums. I would be floundering along about eight or ten feet behind my father. He would flash the light on to the ground occasionally in the bush so he could see where logs and stumps were, but ten feet behind, I didn't have that advantage and I would flounder along bumping into logs and barking my shins.

Those skins were worth possibly a pound a dozen, which was good money in those days. They were very smelly. When you got them on your back in a sugar bag they would invariably urinate, and that would run all down your clothes, and we would get home and mother would order you to throw your clothes out the door before you came in.

If you were very lucky you got a brushtail possum. The skin of a brushtail was worth ten shillings in those days.

TIM: I guess all animals and birds were viewed as fair game in those days.

DON: Yes, I recall that very sadly. My father, having been a hunter, thought that virtually anything that moved was fair game, and he had a passion for shooting wedge-tailed eagles. They did, I suppose, occasionally take a lamb, but also took rabbits and so on. When one of these magnificent birds came around, my father wasn't satisfied until he shot it. He used to nail them up on the wall of the big old barn which stood alongside the road, and I remember having four or five of these great birds—they had a seven foot wing span—nailed up on the barn.

My father was very proud of this, of course. And I recall when he was a very old man, not long before he died, he said, 'You don't see any wedge-tailed eagles these days.' And I said, 'Yes, I daresay you did your share of getting rid of them.'

I suppose he did some thinking on that, because it was very wicked really. They are quite a harmless bird, and that seemed to be the pattern, 'If it moves shoot it'.

TIM: He wasn't alone was he . . .

DON: No, he wasn't alone.

At the hamlet of Gladstone we turned off towards the Mt William National Park and on the honesty system picked up some bagged firewood conveniently for sale outside a farmhouse. It's always great to have a camp fire if you can, and we thoroughly approve of the practice of taking your own wood into national parks and conservation areas although far too many people still hack into the surrounding bush to barbie their chops.

On the southern end of Mt William National Park is a protected inlet called Ansons Bay where my grandfather, Frank Bowden, used to love going fishing. I recall seeing old sepia photographs of serried rows of bream laid out on a grassy bank beside a beaming, bearded, grandfatherly fisherman. Frank Bowden died before I was born, alas, but I'd always wanted to go to Ansons Bay and had never had the opportunity although I had lived in Tasmania for my first quarter of a century. Now it was time. We thought we'd find a good bush camping spot there, and then explore Mt William National Park and further south to St Helens.

With plenty of time in hand—the distances we planned to cover were quite small—we ran in to the northern end of the park and had a picnic lunch at Stumpys Bay, watched closely by mendicant Forester kangaroos. Limited camping is possible there, but the facilities are fairly basic. Because of the drought the small lagoon, no longer open to the sea, looked and smelt a bit 'fruity'. Some workers constructing a boardwalk to the beach told us that a week before the water got so warm that all the bream, flathead and other fish died and they found them floating belly up. The under-construction boardwalk to the beach revealed fabulous views north to the offshore islands of Clarke and Cape Barren. Mt William National Park was established as recently as

1973, partly to preserve the Forester kangaroos which flourish in open grasslands and were co-existing uneasily with farmers. They are attractive animals, clearly relishing their new sanctuary, and the occasional lunch-time treat from visitors—who of course are officially requested not to feed them!

Stumpys Bay is also the starting point for the renowned Bay of Fires three-day walk, where groups of ten are guided along the region's spectacular white beaches and granite headlands. After one stopover in a fairly basic bush camp, they spend their last two nights in the splendour of the upmarket Bay of Fires Lodge, an environmentally friendly, architect-designed hideaway where the exertions of the past two days can be assuaged with fine Tasmanian wines, upmarket cuisine and soft beds in a remote and beautiful location now attracting visitors from all around the world. (The Bay of Fires was named in 1773 by Captain Tobias Furneaux, after he noted camp fires or perhaps some burning off by Aboriginal people. Furneaux was captain of HMS *Resolution* on James Cook's second voyage. He was separated from Cook's ship HMS *Adventure* for some months, and during that time charted most of the south and east coast of Van Diemen's Land.)

On the bargain basement spectrum of camping, Uncle Dak had recommended Policemans Point on the southern side of Ansons Bay, now a conservation area but where free bush camping was allowed. Happily we found we had the point almost to ourselves and discovered a secluded bush bay to put The Manor up only metres from the water's edge. Such Grade A camping real estate locations are still possible in Tasmania if you search for them. I set up our portable barbecue over the camp fire, ringed by stones in the old fashioned way, and barbecued chicken fillets. Over a glass or three of red, we sat by the camp fire and planned our sight-seeing for the next few days as the firelight flickered and highlighted the gnarled trunks of the gum trees enclosing our private hideaway.

As we were about to go to sleep, we became aware of a curious dull roar, gradually becoming alarmingly loud, and coming from the direction of Ansons Bay. I slipped on some shoes (not thongs after my jack jumper experience at the Arthur River) and took a strong torch to investigate. We were camped near the narrow inlet to Ansons Bay and what we were hearing was the tidal surge as the enclosed water hurled itself dramatically back into the ocean in a flurry of white caps. I decided that local fishermen must have to pick their moment to try their luck in the open sea.

Next morning we could not get any Tasmanian radio, and found the Melbourne and Victorian forecasts unhelpful. We decided to make our way around to the Ansons Bay settlement on the northern side of the inlet and then explore the Mt William National Park, including the historic Eddystone Point Lighthouse near its northern boundary. It took us half an hour to wend our way inland to cross the Ansons River and then double back to the northern side. (As we crossed the river we noticed a trailer designed for kayaks, for the pampered hikers from the Bay of Fires walk, who can elect to paddle downstream for ten kilometres to Policemans Point.) The east coast tends to be in a rain shadow even in good times, and the countryside was in deep drought—bare fields with straggly sheep nibbling forlornly at God knows what in the dirt.

By the time we entered the polyglot collection of shabby fishing shacks at the Ansons Bay settlement—I'm sure my grandfather would have recognised many of them—we were looking forward to finding a public toilet. Surely the town must have one? As we nosed about the higgledy-piggledy tracks, most leading to dead ends, I saw an old bloke (probably my age now I come to think of it) walking his dogs. He confirmed our growing suspicion that no public toilet graced the Ansons Bay settlement. And where was the local shop?

'It went broke two years ago—and the local council is bloody hopeless.'

Apparently you could pick up a waterfront block, with a shack, for $80 000 until fairly recently, but prices were 'going up a lot'. He was able to tell us of a 4WD track which wasn't signposted, but would take us up into the national park without having to retrace our steps to the perimeter road we were planning to use. So, Ansons Bay is not only a town with no beer (or pub), but a town with no shop. Following his directions we drove past the boarded up general store to the 4WD track north, stopping briefly for a wander into the scrub, shovel in hand.

It was fortunate we had met our friend with his dogs, because the sandy track he recommended as a short cut was most picturesque and ran through low scrub and sand hill country with an occasional unconcerned Forester kangaroo looking curiously at us from shady hollows. My father often used to quote the old army adage: 'Time spent in reconnaissance is never wasted'. That is certainly true with our style of travel. Just taking the time to chat with locals invariably brings added insights and information about where you are, and where you might go.

Glimpses of the white granite tower of the Eddystone Point Lighthouse to the north-east confirmed we were heading in the right direction, and we rejoined the 'main' dirt road for the last few kilometres. We were pleased to see no other vehicles in the car park, just below the now unmanned lighthouse keeper's cottages.

The Eddystone Point Lighthouse wasn't built until 1889, despite the fact that northbound ships were continually being wrecked by coming too close to the north-east coast of Tasmania. The discovery of a submerged rock off St Helens, to the south, in 1875, prompted the decision to build a lighthouse, and Eddystone Point was chosen because of its more prominent position and wider coverage of the area. The local granite was tested and found suitable for building a tower, and plans were drawn up by 1879. But nothing was done for another ten years despite further shipwrecks on this wild, rocky coast.

The lighthouse keepers and their families were exceedingly isolated—by sea and land. The jetty was exposed and had to be rebuilt several times after having been destroyed by storms. Even in the early twenty-first century, the approach roads to Eddystone Point remain unsealed. In the late nineteenth century basic services—even visits by doctors or priests—were scarce. In her book *Guiding Lights*, Kathleen Stanley tells of a Catholic priest of French origin, with the androgynous appellation of Father Mary, who did what he could for the remote communities of the north-east.[1]

> Such was his reputation for compassion for his fellow men of all creeds and stations that, when Kendrick's daughter, Lucy, became very ill, there being no doctor in the area, her father had no hesitation

---

1 Kathleen M Stanley, 1991, *Guiding Lights: Tasmania's Lighthouses and Lighthousemen*, St David's Park Publishing, Hobart

in saddling his horse and riding off to seek counsel from Father Mary. His journey both ways along the St Marys-Falmouth 'sheep track' took a whole day and a night. On his return he carried, with Father Mary's blessing, a bottle of medicine for his daughter and a bottle of brandy 'to be useful'! Unfortunately Kendrick fell asleep on his horse and dropped and broke the 'useful' bottle. The medicine arrived intact and whether by reason of its virtue or good luck or simple faith, Miss Lucy was able to tell the story 88 years later.

As we walked up the steep path towards the lighthouse I noticed a white 4WD Toyota parked near the elegant, sweeping stone staircase that led to the tower's entry door. I supposed the driver was doing maintenance of some kind on the light, and as we got closer I said cheerily, 'It's just as well we got here in time for your next tour.'

'Well', he said with laconic Aussie understatement, 'the door is open and if you were to walk up the spiral staircase to have a look at the light I mightn't have seen you.' What a bonus! The staircase itself was a wonderful feature, built of decorated cast iron, painted white. The Eddystone Point Lighthouse is one of the few still operating with its original cage of nineteenth century glass prisms, revolving slowly on a geared pedestal once powered by a clockwork mechanism from a weight hauled up the interior of the tower every day by the ever-present lighthouse keeper. It is powered these days by an electric motor. We were able to climb up a short ladder right into the middle of the light, where a modern halogen globe now provides the light source flashed around by the ornate circular cluster of revolving prisms twice in every fifteen seconds. It was simply wonderful to be able to see (and photograph) the old technology still in use. A rusted but solid steel door led onto the narrow outside gallery, but it would not move. I thought it was locked but found out later from our obliging maintenance man that all it needed was a bit of shoulder. A pity, but we had no complaints. I'd have hesitated to try that anyway. We were lucky enough just to be in there. A few more campers pulled into the car park as we drove away. Our timing had been perfect.

We drove to Deep Creek, which is an alternative camp site for visitors to the national park, beside a pretty lagoon. We had considered camping here before being seduced by the isolated pleasures of Policemans Point. The Deep Creek camping ground had a long-drop dunny and two water sources, a fresh water tank for drinking and rough ground water hand-cranked from an ancient cast-iron pump with a long curved handle.

Because of the short distances involved we still had most of the day left and headed south to St Helens, the biggest town and fishing port on this part of the east coast. St Helens is on the shore of a major protected inlet, Georges Bay. We turned off to run down to Binnalong Bay at the head of the inlet, a popular holiday and resort area. The east coast is red granite country and has a benign climate. We drove past a little beach so beautiful that we just had to stop and photograph it. It was protected by low, smooth granite rocks, attractively highlighted by patches of red lichen. A family with small children were paddling and swimming in the calm, clear, shallow water. It was idyllic.

Camping is allowed at Dora Point so we drove in there to check it out—perhaps for next time! The same smooth granite rocks we admired on the coast formed natural bays for the camp sites, shaded by casuarina trees. It was so pleasant that we decided to have lunch there but when I went to use a low rock for a picnic table, I found an obscene pile of cigarette butts—about a hundred of the ghastly things—dumped by previous campers. We found somewhere else.

It was time to drive in to St Helens, which has an impeccable historical pedigree. St Helens Point, on the southern side of Georges Bay, was seen and named by Captain Tobias Furneaux in 1773 (shortly before he spotted and also named the Bay of Fires) and the excellent harbour in the bay was used by whalers and sealers in the 1830s until the first white settlers arrived in 1850. In the days when such things mattered, the free settlers in the St Helens area took great pride in not having any convicts in their ranks. Things remained rural and peaceful enough until 1874 when a mountain plateau in wild country to the north-west, Blue Tier, was found to be almost entirely composed of rich tin-bearing ore. The town of Weldborough, on the northern side of the mountain, became home to some 3000 people—nearly 1000 of whom were Chinese, brought in from Canton as cheap labour, and for three generations Weldborough was home to one of Australia's biggest expatriate Chinese communities—with its own fan-tan gambling parlour and joss house. (The ornate joss house has been preserved and can be seen today in the Queen Victoria Museum in Launceston.) In 1893 a Chinese opera company gave two performances in the town. But by 1945 the tin had largely been worked out and a combination of lack of work and the pressures of the White Australia policy saw all but a few of the Chinese miners return to China.

The rich history of this area is well represented and displayed in the St Helens History Room in Cecilia Street, where visitors can also get mud maps of local walks and information on how to self-drive to historical sites out in the countryside. The high country around Blue Tier used to be thickly forested before the miners and timber getters got at it but the giant mountain ash and other hardwoods were cut down to make elaborate flumes to channel water from storage dams to great waterwheels, providing power to massive stamp batteries that crushed the ore. The History Room has a working scale model of one of those batteries. The Anchor Mine, the biggest enterprise, opened in 1880. In 1900 the fifty head battery was doubled, so that 75 heads could operate at one time, each capable of crushing three tons of stone every hour.

There are some evocative photographs and other memorabilia including a section on the Chinese at Weldborough. Most of the Chinese miners were bachelor workers, but not all. The patriarch, Maa Mon Chin, labour boss and storekeeper, came from China with his wife and children, as did a few other emigrants. Some married European women, attracting the ire of the correspondent for the Launceston *Examiner*, who wrote in 1880 that such women must be 'The scum of the earth to unite with such degraded human beings'. Other Chinese to marry Australian girls included Chin Mon Tock, Lee Wong and Him Sheen. As Tasmanian writer Cassandra Pybus notes in her essay *Lottie's Little Girl* :[2]

In 1945 as the peasant army of Mao Tse Tung fought the Kuomintang, only Billy Bow was tin scratching on the Blue Tier, Cha Lee Harm Jarm, the joss house caretaker, made a living selling vegetables around the Tier. He was the last of the Chinese in

2  Cassandra Pybus, 1998, *Till Apples Grow on an Orange Tree*, UQP, Brisbane

Weldborough. Except, that is, for the Chintock family, descendants of Chin Mon Tok who had come to Weldborough from Ballarat in the 1880s with his European wife.

Wherein lies a tale that is etched deeply into the heart of Tasmanian folklore and sense of island identity. You see, although for many years Tasmanians felt rather forgotten and neglected on the world's stage, the inhabitants of the heart-shaped island at the bottom of the world took great comfort from the notoriety of two extremely famous international film stars, Errol Flynn and Merle Oberon, *who had been born in Tasmania*!

Errol Flynn certainly was born in Hobart in 1909 in Queen Alexandra Hospital—which also saw my own humble entrance into this world twenty-eight years later. Flynn's Tasmanian pedigree is verifiable and iron-clad. (A friend of my father's, Philip Waterworth, went to school with him at Hobart High School during World War I, before Flynn was expelled for rambunctious behaviour.) So Errol Flynn is indisputably a dinky-di son of Tasmania.

But Merle Oberon? That's an on-going debate that continues to swirl passionately about to this day. I will plunge in fearlessly nevertheless. To the pro-Tasmanian Merle lobby, the exotic, almond-eyed film star was the illegitimate daughter of a Chinese hotel chambermaid, 'Lottie' Chintock, who had been seduced by the owner/manager of the St Helens Hotel, John Wills Thompson—who already had a wife and children on site. The beautiful, disgraced, Eurasian Lottie is said to have gone to Hobart to work as a maid and have her child at a house in Battery Point owned by an Indian silk merchant called O'Brien. (This version of the story has him as Indian, but there aren't many Hindu or

Muslim O'Briens around.) Anyway, according to this account, the kindly O'Briens adopted little Merle—O'Brien/ Oberon, get it?—and took her to India. She had to get to India for reasons I'll make clear in a moment.

Cassandra Pybus, who beavered away at this story in the mid 1980s, spoke to people who swore on stacks of bibles that they knew people who had been to school with Merle. A school was even identified, the Model School in Hobart. Alas Cassandra could find no records of her being there, nor could she find any birth record for Lottie Chintock. This is odd because Tasmania has one of the most comprehensive and efficient births, deaths and marriages registers in the southern hemisphere, dating back to the arrival of the first convicts and their masters in the Derwent estuary in 1803. Cassandra also went to Weldborough in her quest and found a photo of Lottie (Violet) Chintock on the pub wall. But she was unable to see Lottie's half-brother, Mr Chintock, because—she was told—he refused to talk to journalists who always misquoted him and, anyway, references to his half-sister distressed him because she was illegitimate. At the St Helens History Room, clearly a bastion of the 'Merle was Lottie's daughter' school, a retired bank manager told her in a conspiratorial whisper that he was personally doing an oral history project with Mr Chintock, that he had all the evidence, and that it was very hush-hush. And so it has remained.

But the following quote from a short biography of Merle I found on the Internet introduces a very different story:

'Merle Oberon', (born Estelle Merle O'Brien Thompson), 19 February 1911—23 November 1979, was a film actress, known for her sultry looks. Born in India to a British father and a Singhalese

mother, Merle came to England for the first time in 1928. Her first
major film role was as Anne Boleyn in *The Private Life of Henry VIII*
(1933). In 1934 she played the female lead in *The Scarlet Pimpernel*,
opposite Lesley Howard . . .

Born in India? Well yes, as revealed by her biographer,
Charles Higham, in his book *Princess Merle*.[3] In this version
of the Merle Oberon story the Mumbai-born actress, nick-
named 'Queenie' Thompson, acted in amateur theatre in
India as a girl and went to London with her mother in 1929.
There she attracted the eye of the film director Alexander
Korda, who not only persuaded her to change her name to
Merle Oberon, but married her and cast her in his films—
Cathy in *Wuthering Heights*, and George Sand in *A Song to
Remember*, among many others.

Actresses of mixed race were not acceptable in those
days, so either Korda or one of his publicists invented
Merle's Tasmanian origins. After all, Tasmania was solidly
Anglo-Celtic and sounded exotic, even if few people knew
where it was. So the dark eyed Eurasian beauty, Estelle
Thompson, from Bombay, became Merle Oberon, a white
upper-class Hobart girl who moved to India from Tasmania
after her distinguished father died in a hunting accident.
Merle went along with this invented past, but was always
vague when asked about her childhood in Tasmania.

In fact she avoided the place completely until 1978—the
year before she died—when she made her one and only
visit to her 'birthplace', possibly at the instigation of her
fourth husband, a younger actor, Robert Wolders. The trip

3 Charles Higham, 1983, *Princess Merle: The Romantic Life of Merle Oberon*,
  Roy Coward-McCann, New York

turned into high farce. At one stage she pointed out Hobart's imposing, sandstone Government House to Wolders, saying the turreted Gothic-revival seventy-four-room mansion was where she was born and raised. It all went pear-shaped when she attended a lord mayoral civic reception in her honour at the Hobart Town Hall. On her way there her driver said how wonderful it must be to be back in her homeland after so many years. Merle Oberon quipped that it was a pity she hadn't been born there! When the questions about her island upbringing at the reception became more pointed, she became distressed, collapsed and had to be helped from the room.

The whole story fascinated film-maker Marée Delofski, who worked for two years trying to get to the bottom of it all. Like Cassandra Pybus, she could find no birth certificate showing that 'Lottie' Chintock had given birth to a daughter, nor could she nail any authoritative evidence that Merle Oberon had ever been in Tasmania, despite some bizarre testimony featured in her excellent documentary which was broadcast on ABC-TV in 2002. A former journalist turned dog breeder, when interviewed by Delofski, said that Merle's features clearly proved she was of Chinese descent. The breeder said she had done a lot of judging at dog shows and had learned to distinguish features.

Marée Delofski got lucky when she began filming in India. In Mumbai (formerly Bombay) she met a priest, Father Richard Lane Smith, whose mother had been a babysitter for Merle. He had also gone to school with a man named Harry Selby—the man who had claimed in Charles Higham's biography that Merle was Anglo-Indian. Selby was now living in Toronto, so Marée tracked him down. Selby had told Higham that he was Merle's nephew. In fact, Delofski discovered, Selby had located Merle's birth certificate in the labyrinthine Indian government records office, and unearthed a closely guarded family secret. Merle wasn't his aunt, but his sister! Marée Delofski explained:

> It seems Harry's mother, Constance Selby, had given birth to Merle when she was fifteen and her mother had taken the baby and raised Merle as her own preventing Merle's real mother from claiming her. When Harry learned that his mother was Merle's mother and not her sister, it helped him to understand why his mother always fretted for Merle. Merle, however, never directly acknowledged the Selby family, except by sending them small amounts of money from time to time. When Harry tried to visit Merle, now famous and living in Los Angeles, she refused to acknowledge him.[4]

With an Indian birth certificate located and living family memory of her origins captured on film, I'd say it was game, set and match to the Indian lobby, but many diehard Tasmanians are not prepared to give up their famous actor even in the face of convincing evidence. I thought it best not to mention Merle Oberon when Ros and I visited the St Helens History Room.

I did ask, though, whether there was any evidence of the tin mining to be seen and a very helpful woman gave us a printed mud map and instructions on how to find the remains of an old crusher, now overtaken by the rain forest on the southern slopes of Blue Tier in an area known as Goulds Country. The area was named after the geologist Charles Gould, who explored the area in the 1860s. The

4 Marée Delofski, *Director's Notes*, 2002

biggest town, just at the top of the tier, was Lottah. But that was in the late nineteenth century and it is a sleepy hamlet today, although Goulds Country is charming despite the loss of its giant eucalypts in those early years. It is steep country gashed with deep gullies and there are occasional small farms. We drove up to Lottah and followed a narrow winding road down the escarpment. A small crudely lettered sign— we nearly missed it—directed us to a track into the rain forest beside a bubbling rivulet that once helped rotate a water-wheel to power the stamp battery we hoped to find.

The path meandered through towering ferns and fallen, rotting logs. Ros was the first to spot two great cast-iron wheels on a shaft, rust-red in the gloom and tilted at an angle of 45 degrees. Nearby was the line of once rampant stamp batteries, the crusher heads still attached to the cams that rotated them. I could just make out the fading inscription of the manufacturers, IEE SALISBURY, LAUNCESTON, 1883. The battery must have been a fearsome sight in its hey-day, gobbling up tons of ore with ear-splitting efficiency. Now the rain forest had reclaimed its own territory. We were very glad we had persevered to find it, and grateful to the St Helens History Room staff for their advice.

It was now late afternoon, but benefiting from summer daylight saving and a long twilight we returned to the Tasman Highway, went off to Pyengana (famous for its cheddar cheeses) and on to the St Columba Falls, which at ninety metres are among Tasmania's highest. A well graded walking track led down to the base of the falls, which weren't looking their best because of the drought. But the cheeses at the Pyengana Cheese Factory looked exceed-ingly delicious and proved to be so. Cheese-making began in the area a century ago because transport difficulties made it impossible to get other dairy products like milk and cream to market quickly enough. The cheddar cheese is still made in the traditional clothbound 'wheels'.

We took a short cut along a forestry road to rejoin the route north to Policemans Point at Ansons Bay, and to spend the last night in our splendid waterfront bush camp. We drank a libation or two of red wine, were serenaded by wattle birds and grilled some chops over our camp fire under a clear sky peppered with brilliant stars.

Off by 9 am, this time with The Manor in tow, retracing our steps to St Helens where we refuelled and headed down the coast towards Bicheno, another fishing port and rapidly developing tourist area. With less than 100 kilometres to travel, it was not going to be a challenging journey—but a very scenic one. The east coast is one of my favourite Tasmanian haunts. It has the best climate in the state because most of the rain gets dumped by the winds of the Roaring Forties on the mountainous west coast, shielding the east coast which, even in the most extreme westerlies, gets lots of brilliant sunshine between occasional showers of quite welcome rain. I say that because the only downside for farmers in this area is lack of moisture. The road south from St Helens hugs the coast and is remarkably undeveloped. Grazing paddocks run right down to the coastline, where red granite rocks and promontories shelter charming beaches with dazzling white sand. Looking at all this—and at a Mediterranean blue sea—makes you wonder how it could have remained unspoiled for so long. Then you start to notice the occasional architect-designed house in the middle of a five-acre or ten-acre block with an absolute water frontage which some mainland smarty probably picked up for a song before real estate values started to move. They are still absurdly low priced compared with Victoria, New South Wales or Queensland's Sunshine Coast, but the well-kept secret of Tasmania's east coast is now well and truly out.

When I last drove this way ten or more years ago, it was not possible to keep to the coast all the way to Bicheno. At the tiny town of Falmouth, 30 or so kilometres south from St Helens, you had to turn inland and drive 10 kilometres up a steep, winding road through St Marys Pass to the town of St Marys, then turn south-east again and negotiate the hairpin bends of Elephant Pass to return to the coast at Chain of Lagoons. But in recent times the 22 kilometres of 'missing link' coastal road has been constructed, so we cruised along relishing the ocean vistas and noting the increased building activity on recently subdivided blocks between the road and the coast.

We had plenty of time to run in to the Douglas-Apsley National Park for a picnic lunch. Thankfully, this park has preserved a large area of dry eucalypt forest, typical of much of the original east coast cover. It was declared a national park as recently as 1989 due to concerns about woodchipping and the felling of large swathes of old growth forest. There are good gravel roads giving access to the park from the Tasman Highway, and basic camping grounds from which to explore rocky river gorges, waterfalls, birds and wild life and cool off by swimming in the Apsley River.

Bicheno doesn't have much of a harbour, but what it has is very picturesque. Fishing boats shelter in what is known as The Gulch, a protected channel between two small granite islands and the shore. Sealers and whalers used it in the early nineteenth century, and fishing boats in later

Not a bad first campsite—waterfrontage on the shores of Lake Hume, near Albury. This is the life!

The utterly magnificent Julius Creek Forest Reserve composting dunny in north–east Tasmania. It even had a visitors' book.

The sombrely named Suicide Bay, at Cape Grim on the very tip of north–west Tasmania. Murder, not suicide, allegedly took place here in 1828 when four convict shepherds are believed to have murdered 35 Aborigines on the rocky beach of the bay below. Even on a bright sunny day I thought the place looked sinister.

Tasmanian Aboriginal leader Brian Mansell points to where vandals, or art thieves, levered away a slab of priceless, ancient rock etching at Sundown Point on the west coast of Tasmania. I must have asked him to smile for the camera because he certainly wasn't happy about what happened.

When the going gets tough . . . I was glad Brian Mansell was driving *his* Land-cruiser on this fearsomely rocky section of coastline, south of the Arthur River, as we searched for recently located Aboriginal middens.

Over thousands of years, rising sea levels have submerged Aboriginal rock etchings. Remarkably, in 2002, this deeply etched fragment of sandstone was washed up on the beach at Preminghana.

The typically white quartzite rock of the west coast outlines the ribbon of recently constructed road through the eastern side of the Tarkine Wilderness. It was built by my brother Philip!

Fellow tourists on the upper deck of *Lady Jane Franklin* admire the incomparable reflections on the dark waters of the lower Gordon River during a tour of Macquarie Harbour, on the west coast.

*Left*: Now in his eighties, Bob 'Cowboy' Crane is still milling the Huon pine logs he first encountered working as a horse-boy with his father in the 1930s.
*Right*: With fireman, Caroline, in the cabin of Abt No. 3 engine.

The steam locomotive, Abt No. 3, waits at Dubbil Barril Station to begin the 1 in 20 climb up over the King River gorge, locked on to the sprocketed teeth of the unique Abt railway system. To travel on the recently restored West Coast Wilderness Railway is an unforgettable experience.

*Left*: My Uncle 'Dak' Diprose (left) and Les Burr, take a break from axing in the front scarf of a huge mountain ash near Ringarooma circa 1948. The scarf they cut was 8 ft wide, 4 ft deep and over 2 ft high. *Right*: The nineteenth century-crafted glass prisms are still doing their original job in the Eddystone Point Light on the north–east coast of Tasmania, as they have done since 1889.

The rain forest has reclaimed the machinery that once operated the water-powered battery stamps of the Blue Tier mines in north–east Tasmania following the discovery of tin in the 1870s.

The Bowden family's east coast weekender *Askelon* (top), a vertical weatherboard shack with an asbestos roof—and million dollar views—looking east over Spring Beach towards Maria Island (bottom).

On a blissful summer's day, Ros simply couldn't resist photographing this idyllic east coast bay, near Binnalong Bay, just north of St Helens.

The magnificent stone walls of the church at Port Arthur. Much of its stonework was shaped and crafted by convict, boy artisans imprisoned on nearby Point Puer, some as young as ten years of age.

*Left*: A moment's reflection in this underground punishment cell at Saltwater River on the Tasman Peninsula. Convict coal miners would have endured complete darkness in their long periods of solitary confinement. *Right*: Peter Adams' Peace Garden on his property, *Windgrove*, overlooking Roaring Beach on the Tasman Peninsula.

Peter Adams hopes his Peace Fire, fortuitously located over an ancient Aboriginal charcoal midden, will burn for 600 years. The slow combustion fire is contained by the top of a corrugated iron tank.

The dolerite rock formations off the east coast of Bruny Island seemed like weird sculptures.

The skipper of our high-powered excursion catamaran, Robert Pennicot, piloted *The Albatross* around the spectacular rock formations off the south–east coast of Bruny Island as though it were a dolphin.

Penelope and The Manor at a beach-side campsite at Cockle Creek—our farthest point south in Tasmania. Ros is preparing a celebration dinner.

*Left*: Ros—of the aching knees—on the South East Cape track. The boardwalk crosses a button-grass plain bog. *Right*: Forestry Tasmania's spectacular Tahune Airwalk is cantilevered over the Huon River. Visitors can also see the aftermath of clear-felling on the hillside to the south.

Recent clear-felling is usually marked by a 'visual management zone'—Forestry-speak for a screen of trees between any nearby roads and the devastation of the forests. But a private contractor erred and visitors driving in to the Tahune Airwalk can see for themselves what clear-felling actually does to the environment.

They don't make caravans like this any more—home for a family of three. Alas, the 1950s-vintage, curved, ply-board roof failed to keep out a torrential downpour the night this photograph was taken.

Visiting Tasmania's excellent small vineyards is highly recommended—I took to the practice with enthusiasm. At Cooinda Vineyard I tasted a glass or two of Pooley pinot noir with Tasmania's (Australia's?) oldest female vigneron, Margaret Pooley, aged 87.

The Bowdens at the base of the 87-metre tall *Eucalyptus regnans*, dubbed 'The Big Tree', in the Styx Valley, south–east Tasmania. Many of these giants are being clear-felled for woodchips.

These telegraph pole-sized eucalypts have replaced the noble mixed rainforest that was clear-felled in the Styx Valley. The area in front has recently been clear-felled for a similar plantation. Note how the rows of heaped earth run straight down the hill instead of following the contours. Imagine how much of this soil gets washed away as a result.

The high country around Cradle Mountain, in Tasmania's north–west, has Tolkien-style overtones. King Billy pines and tiny tarns are fringed by the ubiquitous cushions of button-grass.

The chalet, *Waldheim*, built by Cradle Mountain's pioneer settler, Gustav Weindorfer, had collapsed by the 1960s. This replica is faithful to the Austrian visionary's original design.

Behind *Waldheim* a short forest walk winds through ancient, gnarled King Billy pines, celery top and myrtles. I tried to find another description, but 'enchanted forest' is the only phrase that comes close to doing it justice.

*Climar*, at Campbell Town, was designed by Marjorie Blackwell (now Bligh) in the 1950s. The music notes that run along the fence denote Marjorie's favourite song, *Melody of Love*.

Now 87, Marjorie Bligh has always been an indefatigable fighter against waste. She developed the technique of crocheting discarded plastic bags into useful objects like handbags and hats.

years. The Gulch used to be known as Waubs Boat Harbour after a feisty Aboriginal woman called Waubedebar, who was enslaved by sealers—regrettably a common practice in those frontier times. Waubedebar, a very strong swimmer, became famous for rescuing two sealers when their boat was wrecked offshore, and the townspeople later constructed a memorial to her over her grave. Since the 1960s the extremely profitable abalone industry has used Bicheno as a base, and the town is seeking now to capture its share of the tourist market, emphasising its wild, rocky coastline, a better-than-average blow hole (where incoming seas contained by a rocky cleft burst up with a cloud of spume and spray), surrounding attractions like private wild life parks and proximity to the Douglas-Apsley National Park. We decided to prop at one of the local caravan parks to do some washing, and eat at a restaurant recommended by friends. After expanding The Manor from trailer to living mode—I often think it is rather like the improbable space that magically appears inside Dr Who's telephone box Tardis—I heard a curious whistling sound emanating from Penelope. As I watched, the left rear tyre subsided slowly to the ground. Oh well, if you have to have a puncture you might as well have it in camp, in the middle of a town with a garage almost next door. That's certainly preferable to struggling with a jack and spanners on the side of the road in some god-forsaken spot in the rain!

With most of the afternoon available and feeling touristy on a nice sunny day, we wandered down to the blow hole and looked at a curious granite boulder nearby that is so finely balanced it rocks gently to the rhythms of the sea. Then (having changed Penelope's tyre) we drove to a wild life park several kilometres to the north of Bicheno that we'd noted on the way in. It had a curious mix of domestic and wilder life, like tiger snakes and Tasmanian devils. An eclectic collection of chooks, ducks, Cape Barren geese, native hens, peacocks and tame wallabies roamed in the public areas, all pooing indiscriminately so that fancy foot-work was essential. We arrived at feeding time because Tasmanian devils are nocturnal animals and have to be bribed to wake up. The devils were small, young and very sluggish. One of the keepers did his best for the shutter-bugs and, rather gamely I thought, picked up a baby devil which promptly bit him. Even though it was a baby it had formidable teeth and the devil's famously wide gape. The keeper had to speak sharply to it, and it let go reluctantly. They are not friendly creatures.

The keeper then moved to a larger enclosure where a couple of wedge-tailed eagles with broken wings rather pathetically hopped around on fallen branches, competing with seagulls for the scraps of meat being thrown to them. I always find these places faintly depressing, but couples with children seemed to be getting their money's worth.

That night we found Mary Harvey's Restaurant excellent—Ros said her fish was the best she had ever eaten. As fish is not at the top of her food chain, this was high praise indeed. It was washed down with a local Tasmanian sauvignon blanc. The east coast, with its benign, dry climate, seems to have a vineyard on every visible hillside, all swathed in white bridal-veil-like nets at this time of the year to keep birds away.

I wondered aloud who Mary Harvey was, and the proprietor, clearly bored to distraction by being asked this question, obligingly produced a fact sheet. Mary was the copper's wife at Bicheno in the 1850s. Like Waubedebar, she was a formidable woman. There were three stories about Mary Harvey. The first described the time when her husband, Constable Harvey, caught a man stealing potatoes and the thief overpowered him. Mary hid her baby in the bush, grabbed a stick and belted the villain (who was still hammering her husband's head with a rock) over *his* head. She failed to knock him out, but he got away while the going was good. Constable Harvey was a fairly tough cookie too, and returned to duty a few days later.

On another occasion Mary heard about some whalers who had absconded from police custody. (I'm not sure whether from Harvey's lockup, or from another area.) Her husband was away, but Mary went out on horseback, located the whalers and enticed them back to her house with offers of food. After she'd fed them, they allowed her to lock them up!

The third Mary Harvey story has echoes of Waubede-bar's sea-going bravery, involving the rescue of two boys from a shipwreck. Again, she was on her own at the police house. She organised two inexperienced men to row a lifeboat out in stormy seas, and encouraged them out to where the boys were hanging on to a small capsized dinghy. One of the boys, it is said, lost his hold and disappeared, but Mary jumped overboard and rescued him. Both boys were saved.

**Travel Diary Thursday 6 March**

We are on our way to Coles Bay and the Freycinet National Park, surely the jewel in the crown of Tasmania's east coast, although there are many other sparkling contenders. I know the area well, because I holidayed at Coles Bay as a child, and have been there many times since. You might say it is a place to die for—and I nearly managed that about twenty-five years ago! There will be no camping tonight as we are staying with friends who have a holiday house there.

The red granite peaks on the Freycinet Peninsula were first seen by Europeans 160 years before the French explorer Nicholas Baudin spotted them in 1802 and named them after the Freycinet brothers on his expedition. Not even St Helens, named by Furneaux during Captain Cook's second voyage in 1773, can outdo this Tasmanian coastal feature in the purebred historical stakes, having been sighted by no less a person than Abel Tasman in 1642. He had already sailed around the south of the island that would later bear his name, and the rocky peaks of Freycinet Peninsula were probably the last piece of Tasmania he saw before setting an easterly course towards New Zealand and Batavia in the Dutch East Indies. The Dutch explorer noted and named Schouten Island, and mistakenly believed the peninsula to the north to be a string of islands.

The first feature you see as you drive in towards the peninsula from the Tasman Highway are the distinctive three-pronged peaks of The Hazards—not named because they are difficult to climb, but after a nineteenth century American sealing captain, Richard Hazard, who worked from this area. The Freycinet Peninsula encloses not only Great Oyster Bay but a large, almost completely enclosed waterway, Moulting Lagoon. As its name suggests it is a wonderful breeding ground for birds, but regrettably not part of the national park. Driving past the lagoon we could see large numbers of duck-shooting hides, for although some Australian states have banned duck shooting Tasmania hasn't, and it is a popular pastime with locals and visitors from the mainland who can't do it at home. (We heard on the radio news the next day that conservationist activists were planning to spoil the coming season by wearing brightly coloured T-shirts and standing next to the shooters in their hides, thus scaring the ducks away. They've done this in past seasons and, so far, no one has been shot. It's probably only a matter of time. The spoilers also try to get to injured ducks and save them. It must be an amazing spectacle. Some smart Tasmanian entrepreneur should try to sell tickets to watch it all.) As usual Moulting Lagoon was populated by graceful long-necked black swans, swimming serenely among the brush-hides. The hunters aren't allowed to shoot them.

Tasmanian Aboriginal members of the Oyster Bay tribe enjoyed the hunting and fishing at Coles Bay for thousands of years before *mynheer* Tasman sailed by. Over the millennia they created enormous shell middens behind the sheltered beaches of the bay, now largely destroyed by the efforts of one Silas Cole. In the 1830s he mined and burnt them to create lime mortar for building, then had this tranquil, lovely place named after him. Most of nearby Swansea's main buildings were constructed with Silas Cole's mortar. Coles Bay during the whaling times must have been unspeakable. A contemporary description of a whaling station gives some idea:

> . . . we approached the station and entered on calm waters, thickly spread with oil. Occasional chunks of fat and entrails swam on the surface and ringed it with greasy ripples . . . On the flensing stage . . .

two carcases lay steaming in dismemberment. From the vast mass of meat a wide stream of blood ran down slowly to the sea.[5]

Schouten Island, to the south, was mined for coal from 1840 to 1880, and also for tin. Both the island and the peninsula were farmed until, fortunately, the area was declared a game reserve in 1906 to stop the slaughter of native animals. In 1916 the island and Mt Field, fifty kilometres north-west of Hobart, had the distinction of being declared Tasmania's first official national parks. Schouten Island joined the park in 1977, followed by the Friendly Beaches coastal region in 1992.

For most of the twentieth century and beyond, Coles Bay has been a popular holiday destination for those who could get there. The road in was a narrow, rutted, sandy track. In 1935 Ron Richardson, a former bank clerk-turned entrepreneur, built what he called The Chateau, a fitness and health resort which he supplied by flamboyantly hurling his Rolls Royce along the goat track of the access road at improbable speeds. Fishing shacks were built but when I first went there you could hardly call it upmarket. Today, however, it is just that, with Ron Richardson's old chateau transformed into a resort, and others being planned for the shores of the bay.

Fishing at Coles Bay was legendary. As a boy I remember my father taking me out in a small dinghy just a few hundred metres (or yards as they were then) from the shore fishing for flathead. In the Tasmanian way, a lead sinker was topped by two hooks on shorter traces and baited with a bit

5 Pamphlet, *Freycinet National Park: The European History of Tasmania's First Coastal National Park*, Parks and Wildlife Service, Tasmania

of meat to start with, and then chunks of cannibalised flat-head. You didn't have to wait long for a bite. Sometimes you would have two fish on *before* your line hit the bottom. The sand seemed to erupt into a brown cloud of flathead. They were so voracious they would even bite bare hooks. I remember putting a line down once just to test that. But, no more. I'm told you can still get a feed but you have to go out a lot further, and work for it.

On the ocean side, you could fish for crayfish off the rocks. My parents used to stay with friends, David and Betty Waterworth, who had a shack at Coles Bay. We used to take a picnic lunch and walk over to the smooth, orange granite rocks that led to the sea. You had to have a reason-ably calm day to do this. David had several cray rings, as we called them: hoops of iron, with shallow nets laced to them. Bait was tied to a rope across the middle of the ring, and three lines led up to a float, attached to a longer rope. All you did was toss this into the water from the rocks, and it floated down out of sight. It was a hit and miss business really, but sometimes, if you were lucky, you could actually look down through the clear water and see a big crayfish crawl over the lip of the ring to get to the bait. Sometimes the big old cunning ones would leave their tails hooked over the edge of the hoop for a quick getaway. The trick was to suddenly pull the cray ring up so that the crayfish was jerked to the bottom of the net. We generally caught four or five large ones like this.

Not long after I was married—I was in my early thirties—I took Ros down to Coles Bay to stay with the Waterworths. David still knew some prize spots and we headed off with the tried and trusty cray rings for some crayfish off the rocks. It was a clear, still, autumn day with little wind. I had become a keen spearfisherman and had a full-length wet suit and neoprene helmet which you needed in order to spend more than about three minutes in Tasmania's super-chilled waters. On this occasion, from my diver's perspective, I was able to tell David when a crayfish entered his cray ring, or suggest that he move it if it was badly placed on a sloping rock. I even dived down and repositioned it for him a couple of times.

Then I took my spear gun and swam out looking for a fish—and this is when I nearly finished myself off. Like many potentially tragic accidents, it happened in an innocuous way. I saw a nice trumpeter, a magnificent eating fish, and dived down to stalk it, the buoyancy of my wet suit equalised by a belt hung with heavy lead weights. The water was beautifully clear, and the underwater scenery was just gorgeous with tumbled boulders, columns of kelp and the occasional abalone shell clinging to an exposed rock. I fired at the fish and missed. To my chagrin my spear wedged itself under a large rock, about three metres down. Leaving the handle floating at the end of the line, I returned to the surface for a few restorative breaths, then dived again to free it.

The wretched thing was stuck fast, and I stayed down a bit too long trying to pull it out before heading up for some now urgently needed oxygen. Just picture the scene. On the rocks were David and Betty and their two daughters with Ros, all sitting placidly in the sun, while I was diving no more than three metres from the edge of the rocks. As I rocketed back to the surface for more air, I was suddenly stopped dead. Jesus! What was going on? I looked down and saw that the line from the spear to the suspended spear gun had twisted around my right thigh. A quick glance upward revealed I was trapped about half a metre below the surface! Sunshine and air were so near, but so far away . . .

They always say that you have more time than you think in a diving emergency before you need to take another breath, or black out. In a split second I remembered that I was diving without my knife, usually carried in a holder on my weight belt. The right thing to do was to work out which way the line was twisted around my leg, and untwist it. But I panicked and just gave a godalmighty heave. Fortunately the line either pulled out of the end of the spear or broke, I'm not sure which. Probably the former, because the spear lines are made of tough braided nylon cord. I surfaced, spluttering and desperate, tearing off my mask and snorkel in an effort to get air more quickly. No one else was aware that anything had been wrong, nor could they have done anything about it. I have often thought that might have been a ridiculous way to die, suspended just below the surface of the water on a lovely calm day, my partner and friends blissfully unaware of my predicament. It would have spoiled the picnic rather . . .

As we drove in to the Coles Bay settlement I saw that it had changed beyond my memories of it, but we located our friends' house, Andrew and Elizabeth Kemp, beautifully situated with a view of The Hazards from the deck and dining room. Tourism has brought more roads to Coles Bay and our friends later drove us up to the lighthouse at Cape Tourville, which has a short but very scenic walking track around it. Because of the elevation we had great views of the coastline and even a glimpse of Wineglass Bay, a magic spot which can only be visited by boat or by climbing over a saddle of The Hazards. But you then have to climb back! (There is a suggestion it was named not because of its wineglass shape, but by being stained claret red by the blood of slaughtered whales in the nineteenth century.) I could even see up the coast to the scene of my spearfishing close call, and experienced a slight shudder at the base of my spine just thinking about it even after more than a quarter of a century.


We could have dallied longer at Coles Bay, walked to Wineglass Bay and explored the Friendly Beaches—but we had experienced these beautiful places at other times. It was the Friday before a long weekend and we had planned to meet up with my sister Lisa and her husband David Roberts at the family weekender at Spring Beach, south of Orford, that evening. The weekender, Askelon—a little vertical weatherboard shack with an asbestos roof—is an integral part of my 'Tasmanian Dreaming'. As much as any thirteen year old could, I helped build Askelon during its construction phase in 1949 and 1950. (My father chose that name because the Spring Beach locality reminded him of the old Roman town of Aschaelon—spellings vary—in Palestine, on the shores of the Mediterranean which he visited during World War II.)

Askelon is still remarkably the same more than half a century on, although it has been expanded out the back into the original car port to create an extra bunk bedroom for the brood of my father's grandchildren that emerged in the latter part of the twentieth century. The term 'shack' still applies, although it is a shack with a million dollar view, looking east towards Maria Island (named by Abel Tasman in 1642 after the daughter of his patron Anthony Van Diemen), over a shimmering, turquoise sea. For the first twenty-five years of my life I had my summer holidays there, and many, many weekends. During the building phase my parents, Peg and John, used to set off from Hobart on a Friday night after Father finished work in a Series 48 Holden, towing a battered wooden trailer filled with timber and tools, kids in the back seat and a small, black (farting) dog, Bill, on the rear floor. I have written about these times in my autobiography *Spooling Through*.[6]

We planned to abandon The Manor and stay at Askelon for the long weekend before heading further south on our coastal journey to the Tasman Peninsula, and Port Arthur. With the whole day ahead of us, and less than 100 kilometres to cover, there was plenty of time to dally and re-engage with my beloved east coast.

Not long after rejoining the Tasman Highway from the Coles Bay road we turned right, following signs to the Freycinet Vineyard. Although it was only 10 am I felt it was not too indecently early to at least taste the crisp east coast riesling we hoped to buy. Tasmanian cold climate whites are exceptionally good and I felt my taste buds begin to salivate as we drove past the lines of vines draped seductively in their white bridal anti-bird veils. Yes, the tasting room was open at that early hour, but no riesling! They were out of last season's joy juice and could not help me. Would I be interested in a pinot noir? Unreasonably I felt quite grumpy about this, having fixated on a riesling. Very sportingly they suggested I try the Coombend Estate (which we had driven past to get to Freycinet Vineyard). Not only did they have some riesling there but the woman plying us with the bottled sunshine seemed vaguely familiar. You know what they say about Tasmania—everyone knows or is probably

6 Tim Bowden, 2003, *Spooling Through: An Irreverent Memoir*, Allen & Unwin, Sydney

related to everyone else. In this case we had known each other in our schooldays and later teenage socialising. It would have seemed churlish not to buy some wine under those circumstances, and we did. Good stuff too.

There is plenty to do and see in Swansea, which is Tasmania's oldest municipality. The Glamorgan Shire was created in the 1820s. Morris's Store is one of the oldest buildings and has been trading continuously from 1838. Its bluestone walls are offset by the white mortar provided by Silas Coles from the Oyster Bay tribe's ancient middens. We noted the Swansea Bark Mill and East Coast Museum, recreated to show how the black-wattle bark was processed to produce tannic acid, a basic ingredient used in tanning heavy leathers. The bark mill was one of the few local industries that survived and kept operating through the Great Depression, doubtless helping keep Swansea alive.

Three kilometres south of Swansea is Kate's Berry Farm. Knowing it was the raspberry season I was keen to get some of my favourite fruit, which can only be enjoyed in season (other than the frozen fruit which never tastes as good). We drove up the hill towards the farm, passing fields of straw-berries with—I later found out—Kate busy picking them. At the restaurant and shop I said I'd have some fresh rasp-berries thanks. 'We don't have any,' said the woman behind the counter, rather gracelessly I thought. I said I found that surprising, as I thought I had arrived at a berry farm. 'Never mind, I'll have some fresh strawberries instead.'

'We don't sell those either.'

'Hold on, I can see someone picking them from here!'

Apparently Kate's Berry Farm never sells fresh berries to the public, but you can buy pots of raspberry or straw-berry jam and eat raspberry ice cream—as well as the ubiquitous Devonshire tea routine with scones, jam and cream in the restaurant. I did buy a take-away raspberry ice cream cone, but we didn't linger.[7]

About a kilometre further south from the preserved berry farm, the Tasman Highway bypassed a most interesting feature known as Spiky Bridge. This is a convict-built bridge (1843) which was cleverly built from local stone, without the use of mortar. Its side walls are studded with vertical stones, hence its name. The highway runs within sight of the sea, with great vistas, until it turns inland just after crossing the Little Swanport Estuary (and river) and then weaves through grazing and orchard country to Triabunna. In my youth, when Tasmania was known as the 'Apple Isle', there were extensive apple orchards here. They were grubbed out years ago and now there are many more hectares of new walnut plantations. This represents a major investment on the east coast by the agricultural companies Webster and Vecon. The plan is to supply fresh, new season walnuts to European markets by August each year. I found out that in the 2000 season, the harvest was 12 tonnes of walnuts worth $60 000, but within five years the production will be 4000 tonnes worth more than $16 million. Or so it is hoped.

Triabunna, which I remembered as a sleepy fishing port, is also on the move. It is the service town for a big wood-chipping operation and shipping terminal across Prosser Bay. It is a twenty-four-hour-a-day operation and its lights can be seen from Spring Beach and Askelon. The woodchips are shipped directly to Japan and, until regulations were

---

7 We had a more friendly, fresh-raspberry experience in northern Tasmania a few weeks later. See Chapter Nine.

brought in to stop it, the transporters used to pump out their water ballast, collected originally from the filthy waters of Tokyo Bay, straight into poor old pristine Prosser Bay, unfortunately pristine no longer. This practice caused all manner of unwanted organisms, like exotic seaweeds and alien starfish, to flourish in plague proportions.

The once undisturbed coastline has been assaulted vigorously by industry over the years. There used to be wonderful kelp beds all along this part of the coast. The great columns of *Macrocystis* grew up from the sea floor and streamed their stems and long leaves along the surface of the sea. When you went fishing you could tie your dinghy painter to them, and try for cod and other kelp-related fish. Skin diving in among those great kelp columns was a surreal, sublime experience. However in the 1950s the Commonwealth Scientific and Industrial Research Organisation did a study to assess the quantity of this type of fast growing kelp on the east coast. The CSIRO estimated, in their wisdom, that commercial harvesting of between 35 000 and 40 000 tons of dried kelp could be sustained, based on three harvests a year.

In 1963, Alginates Australia Ltd began harvesting and processing the kelp from their base at Louisville, between Triabunna and Orford. (They produced a kelp setting compound that was used in toothpaste, ice cream and other products.) I remember, when this started, the locals predicted that the kelp beds would be ruined, and there would not be enough to keep the factory running. They were right. Special kelp-cutting barges were brought in to cut the kelp down to a depth of a metre below the water level. Of course they got greedy and pulled out five times the recommended harvest. This despite discovering that the kelp beds could only be harvested once a year, not three times as forecast by the CSIRO. As the local kelp beds declined, Alginates Australia brought in a bigger harvesting vessel in 1967 to range even further up and down the coast. And when—as the locals had predicted—the kelp failed to grow back, the company applied for and got a licence from the government to take bull kelp (a different species that attaches itself to rocks with thick stems) as well. By 1973 it was all over, and the company closed its factory at Louisville. The kelp beds I remembered as a boy never came back.

Since our visit I have learned that the future for the few remaining kelp forests in Tasmanian waters is dire. A recent study by a marine biologist from the University of Tasmania, Dr Karen Edyvane, showed that the kelp forests off Tasmania's east and south coasts declined on average by nearly fifty per cent between 1944 and 2000. Global warming may also be a factor, but the kelp is also suffering from over-fishing of the species that usually keep sea-urchins and other predators of the under-sea forests under control. Dr Edyvane says:

Kelp loss in Tasmania is as important as coral bleaching in the Great Barrier Reef. They [the forests] are ecological canaries of the health of the ocean.[8]

There were other consequences from the ill-thought out Alginates operation on the east coast. The Prosser River above Orford was dammed to provide a water supply for

---

8 Leigh Dayton, 10–11 July 2001, 'Out of the blue, a desperate cry for kelp', *The Weekend Australian*

the processing plant. The Prosser estuary silted up, large fishing boats could no longer use it, the sand bar to the ocean shifted and even the fishing was stuffed. A pretty good effort, environmentally, wouldn't you say? At least it gave Orford a town water supply. Another minor benefit is that the company's old wharf at Louisville is now used by the ferries that take tourists to Maria Island.

I recalled this as we drove across the Prosser River bridge into Orford. The Tasman Highway turns right here and follows the Prosser up and out of the valley towards Hobart. We kept straight ahead for the five kilometres to Spring Beach, further down the coast. (My grandfather's full name was Frank Prosser Bowden, but we never knew of any family connection with the river.)

My heart leapt as we came over the hill that leads down to Spring Beach—there is a sudden revelation of cobalt blue sea, wide white sandy beach, and the familiar profile of Maria Island, not seen in combination until that moment. Seconds later we turned up the driveway to Askelon and ran up beside the house to a level spot where we could unfold The Manor. (We weren't going to sleep in it over the long weekend, but we needed to keep the fridge going and have access to our belongings.)

Walking into the front room of Askelon took me back to my childhood. The house could be described as small, but my parents were ahead of their day with its design. The convention, in the late 1940s, was to have the kitchen, where 'the little woman' busied herself over the stove, decently tucked away from the living area. 'Not so,' said my mother, who had endured a similar arrangement in the family home. 'Not on holidays. I want the kitchen where the action is.'

So the living area of Askelon still looks quite modern. The main room faces east, with a double glass door opening out onto a floor-level terrace and deck. There are two single beds in the north-east and north-west corners of the room, for afternoon naps or overflow guests. The open fireplace is on the western wall, with a circle of easy chairs around it.

Near the southern wall of the living area is a 6 feet by 4 feet Huon pine table, and off to one side is the kitchen alcove, with a small stove, and a huge Huon pine dresser with a sink cut into the middle of its bench. There is no room for the fridge, which is just outside the back door, but the dresser contains all the saucepans, cutlery and cooking impedimenta in its lower cupboards and central drawers, while the open shelves house the plates, mugs, cups, glasses and essentials like flour, sugar, salt and spices. All close by the sink, so that during the washing up (there is nor never will be a washing up machine) putting away is all within an arm's reach. At times of family celebration, like Christmas, twelve people can sit around the Huon pine table.

These days the outhouse dunny has been moved indoors next to the bathroom, and the two original bedrooms have been augmented by the bunkhouse where the car port used to be. It all works extremely well—mostly because of the Huon pine table and dresser. And therein lies some family folklore. My father could do rough house-building style carpentry, but not furniture. What to do about the kitchen alcove? One day he went to a second-hand auction house in Hobart, Burns Mart, now long gone. In one corner he spied a huge Huon pine dresser. He whipped out his tape measure and calculated it would fit exactly into the kitchen alcove, solving *all* his problems. When the auction day arrived, he went in early and stood beside the dresser. Hobart being

Hobart he knew most of the people who wandered past and took an interest in it. One was an acquaintance, Gordon Colebach. My father said, 'What do you want this for?'

'I'm building a dinghy. I plan to use the bench top for the transom and the shelves will be handy in my workshop.'

Father said, 'Well, I want it for the kitchen in my shack and I'm prepared to go to twelve pounds for it.'

'Oh my goodness,' exclaimed Gordon, and headed away quickly.

And so it went through the day until the auction began. When the dresser came up, Father just put his hand up and left it there. Hardly anyone else bid. They knew Father was remorseless. I don't recall what he paid for it, but it wasn't much for such a unique piece. The Huon pine table also came from Burns Mart. It is absolutely plain so that the exquisite grain in this most rare of timbers can be admired. One of the two planks making up the table top is nearly a metre wide. Huon pines are very slow growing, so the tree it was milled from could have been 1000 years old, perhaps even older.

(Many years ago my parents lent Askelon to a family member who shall remain nameless. It rained for a week, so he decided to do something useful and painted the Huon pine table *green*. It took a long time to get it back to its rich honey-yellow glory.)

My sister and her husband, who weren't due until after 6 pm, said they would bring the dinner so Ros and I made a cuppa and sat on the deck in front of Askelon gazing over towards Maria Island. Now a national park, the island was once exploited in every possible way and its history is littered with failed enterprises. In the early nineteenth century, whalers and sealers operated from its northern end (later named Darlington) and from Whalers Cove on the eastern side, in Reidle Bay. In the days before the national park was established I used to camp there with some mates. You could still see great chunks of whalebone half buried in the sand at the head of the cove.

The first inhabitants, of course, were the Tasmanian Aborigines, who called the island Toarra Marra Monah. The Oyster Bay tribe used to travel to the Tasmanian mainland in bark canoes, using tiny Lachlan Island as a convenient resting place. It was nevertheless a risky five kilometre journey in open waters.

I've written earlier about the problems colonial administrators had finding a safe and secure place to send hardened convicts who were repeat offenders—that is why Sarah Island in far-off Macquarie Harbour was selected on the west coast. Things couldn't have been all that flash either for the convicts who had to build the Darlington settlement from scratch, but Thomas Lempriere, who arrived at Darlington in 1926 as the commissariat clerk (essentially the second in command to the commandant), later described Maria Island as 'one of the sweetest spots in Van Diemen's Land'. In her book *Maria Island: A Tasmanian Eden* Margaret Weidenhofer quotes from Lempriere's unpublished diaries, which indicate a stark juxtaposition between the life of the jailers and the jailed.[9]

*Wednesday 8 November*—Mutmare, the overseer of the carpenters, got some Spirits from the Sergeant, & got drunk. 50 lashes always makes him sober.

---

9 Margaret Weidenhofer, 1977, *Maria Island: A Tasmanian Eden*, Darlington Press, Melbourne

*Saturday 9 December*—I had an inspection of bedding today & was regaled with a fine display of fleas.

*Monday 25 December*—Christmas. We dined at Major Lord's . . . We had for dinner a Roast Goose, leg of Mutton boiled, & caper sauce, boiled fowls, Roast Duck, Pigeon & Giblet Pies, gooseberry tarts etc.

One suspects the convicts did not do nearly so well.

Most of the major buildings at Darlington, the commissariat store and the penitentiary were constructed during the first period of convict occupation from 1825 to 1832, until the colonial administration in Hobart decided it was all too far away and too expensive. But this decision was reversed ten years later in 1842 when Darlington was re-opened, this time as a probation station. A second settlement was established at Long Point, about halfway down the island near the isthmus at Chinamans Bay, and by 1850 the two sites were connected by a road that still exists today. At one stage there were 600 convicts at Darlington but by 1851 both stations were closed and the convict era was over.

Enter one of my favourite historical characters, the ebullient Italian businessman and entrepreneur Diego Bernacchi, whose various enterprises ranging from silk worms and viticulture to cement-making dominated Maria Island's history from 1884 until well into the 1920s.

There seems no rational explanation for Bernacchi's continuing obsession with this beautiful island off the east coast of Tasmania—it is as though the highly intelligent, well educated and initially wealthy businessman was bewitched by the place. Maria Island became a grand passion and took over his life.

The love affair began the first time Bernacchi laid eyes on the island, in February 1884. The businessman, his wife and two young sons had arrived in Hobart a few weeks earlier to take up eighty acres of land, but never did so. Instead he convinced the Minister for Lands of the day that the benign climate of Maria Island was ideal for silk making and viticulture and applied for a lease of the island for a modest sum.

Two months later the Bernacchi family moved to Darlington with a huge pile of luggage as well as dogs, horses, sheep, pigs, cows, poultry and bullocks. As he waited for confirmation of his lease from the government, Bernacchi told a special correspondent from the *Tasmanian Mail*, who was his guest for several weeks, of his plans for the island:

> ... the island would be utilised in every possible way: dairy produce, fruit, hops, cereals, manufacture of conserves ... and, of course, wine and silk. His host had already expended about 1000 pounds on Darlington and had sent cocoons of silk ... obtained from a property in the Derwent Valley ... to be examined in Europe.[10]

Bernacchi spared no expense, even importing Italian and Swiss vignerons who had been working in Victoria. By 1886 he had 60 000 vines planted and growing in and around Darlington, so he was serious about his plans for a Maria Island-based wine industry. In April 1886, a parliamentary party went to the island to inspect operations, and Bernacchi invited the Tasmanian treasurer to inspect his books.

---

10  Margaret Weidenhofer, *Maria Island: A Tasmanian Eden*

There is a great story told about this visit. As I heard it many years ago, the delegation arrived only to be entertained lavishly by the Bernacchis. So well were they wined and dined, it seems, that it was almost dark before they got around to inspecting any of the vineyards. The plan was to cut the first bunch of grapes for that year's vintage. Mrs Barbe Bernacchi, so the story goes, cut the nominated bunch with a pair of silver scissors, but one of the less-lubricated members of the party noticed the silk thread tying a fat bunch of Victorian-imported grapes to the vine. Why would the Bernacchis bother to do that? They had scads of grape bearing vines, as contemporary accounts confirm. The story is apocryphal but refuses to die.

By 1888 Bernacchi had managed to get Darlington renamed 'San Diego' and was quickly dubbed 'King Diego' by the general Tasmanian populace. The Maria Island Company Ltd was floated in 1887 and 'King Diego' announced plans to expand into fishing, agriculture and the working of cement, limestone and marble deposits on Maria. These were the glory years for the Bernacchis, with Darlington now a small town with a hotel and even a coffee palace. European trees were planted—some can still be seen today—and houses constructed for the workers, many of whom were of European origin and who had their own clubhouse with imported foreign language newspapers By 1887 Maria Island wines—riesling, hock, claret and cabernet sauvignon—were exported to Melbourne.

However in 1889 the Bernacchis and their four children (two had been born on the island) moved from Maria Island to a grand house at Louisville, from where today's tourists voyage to Darlington from the failed Alginates industry wharf. Failed enterprises, alas, are synonymous with the

history of Maria Island. 'King Diego' was a man of enormous
enthusiasms and he had a charismatic ability to attract
funding for his schemes. His interests in a Maria Island wine
industry declined in proportion to his soaring ambitions
for a cement industry based on large limestone and fossil
cliffs near Darlington, mined and transported to the cement
works by a steam railway. But the sums didn't work out, so
by January 1892 the Maria Island Company went into
liquidation. 'King Diego' wasn't fazed by that, however, and
immediately registered the Bernacchi Patent Natural Portland Cement Co. Ltd in Victoria, in the same year!

However by 1897, the Bernacchis had returned to
Europe. Although now a man of reduced means Bernacchi's
infatuation with Maria Island continued and he remained in
contact with friends in Tasmania. His wife died in 1914
and some time later he sailed to Melbourne, arriving just
before the end of World War I. In 1919 'King Diego' was
once more in residence at Darlington and the cement works
got going again. In 1920 National Portland Cement came
into being, a convict-built dam behind Darlington was
enlarged for a water supply, new plant and machinery were
ordered in from overseas and Darlington's population grew
to 500 people. The revived cement works project was officially opened in 1924, and Diego Bernacchi was present.
But it was King Diego's last hurrah. Shortly afterwards he
fell ill, left his beloved island for the last time, and died in
Melbourne in 1925. He did not live to see the demise of the
cement works yet again, killed off three years later primarily by the 'tyranny of distance', of shipping to distant
markets from an exposed wharf that was often unavailable
to shipping for weeks at a time. The cement works closed,
finally, in 1929.

The huge chimney and cement storage silos at Darlington were clearly visible from the front of Askelon until the early 1970s when they were demolished as they were thought to be unsafe, at the time the island became a national park. Today Maria has many convict-built buildings at Darlington, many of them preserved because of Bernacchi's use, and the island has reverted to the beautiful, peaceful place it must have been when he first fell in love with it. It is well worth a visit.

As Ros and I gazed reflectively at the island, recalling the times we had been there together, exploring Whalers Cove, Chinamans Bay and Darlington, one of Tasmania's abrupt weather changes blew in from the south-east, slowly obliterating the island in a grey mist. We moved inside as light rain began to fall, and lit the fire. I turned on the radio to hear that this south-easter was going to clag in on the east coast for the next three days—the first spell of rainy weather we had experienced since arriving in Tasmania three weeks before.

It was perfect timing to arrive at Askelon to rest up while it rained, meet up with family, and prepare ourselves for the next phase of our journey to Port Arthur, Hobart, and as far south on the island as we could get by road.

'Things could be worse,' I said to Ros as we clinked our glasses of Coombend Tasmanian riesling while the cheerful crackle of the kindling taking hold in the open fireplace promised a warm and cosy evening.

# six

## The Convict Stain

**Travel Diary Monday 10 March**

It rained fairly consistently during our long weekend at Spring Beach, but with a roof over our heads and a log fire, this was no hardship. We even managed to do some planning for our travels over the next few weeks. By the time we had packed up and disentangled our lives from the accommodating Askelon, the weather looked as if it was starting to lift. There were patches of blue sky and shafts of sunlight illuminating the forested flanks of Mt Maria as we continued south along the coast towards the Tasman Peninsula and the convict ruins at Port Arthur. Ros said rather wistfully that she had enjoyed the comforts of living in a house for three days, particularly when she got up in the night to go to the loo. I knew in my heart she was not really straying from the true camping path, but told her to pull herself together nevertheless.

Not so many years ago the coastal route we planned to take would not have been possible. The only way east and south would have been to retrace our steps to Orford and then take the Tasman Highway towards Hobart. But forestry roads have been upgraded—possibly with tourists in mind—and it is now possible to continue past the hamlet of Rheban (scene of many a flathead-fishing excursion from Askelon) and head into the thickly forested hills of Wielangta (less thickly forested since Forestry Tasmania has been at them) through Kellevie to join the Arthur Highway again at Copping for the run down to the Tasman Peninsula. The rain had made the unsealed roads greasy, so careful driving was called for.

Most of the original forest of the east coast has been lost to farming, logging and now more recently woodchipping, but Forestry Tasmania has graciously spared a few areas of what are called 'relict' rain forest, where gullies and deep valleys have retained pockets of pristine rain forest which have never been burned because they are always moist. One twenty-hectare relict forest can be experienced in the Wielangta area, where Forestry Tasmania has constructed a circular track and board walk along a rivulet creating an enjoyable twenty-minute walk. We stopped to do this walk which—given the added bonus of recent rain—gave a fresh interpretation to the term 'rain forest'. The mottled-green mosses and lichens coating banks of the creek and the ancient trunks of the myrtles were tipped with crystal clear droplets, some jewel-like when caught by the weak sunlight that filtered through the upper canopy. There were also fine blackwoods, sassafras, silver wattles and lush ferns. Before we climbed back up to the road we could see that the bridge over the creek was constructed as many such bridges are in Tasmania by using huge logs felled during the building of the original road.

We joined the Arthur Highway at Copping, and

continued for ten kilometres through farm land to Dunalley. There a swinging bridge crosses the canal, which allows fishing boats and smaller vessels to avoid going right around the Tasman Peninsula by connecting Frederick Henry Bay with Marion Bay. In convict times there were a few guards stationed at the narrow spit (then called East Bay Neck) as an insurance that escaping prisoners would not make it off the peninsula. The primary line of containment was at Eaglehawk Neck, another twenty-three kilometres south, where the Tasman Peninsula was again reduced to a narrow isthmus. There, as early as 1831 (the Port Arthur convict settlement dates from 1830), savage dogs were chained in a line across the neck of land, the chains designed so that the dogs could just touch but not fight each other. A story was put out for the benefit of would-be escaping convicts that the waters were shark infested—they weren't—and platforms were built out into the sea on either side of the line with a dog on each to give warning if an escaper tried to swim around the barrier.

The line was lit at night with lanterns, and a garrison of some thirty troops was permanently on hand. It was remarkably effective and only a few resourceful individuals ever made it past the line. One was the celebrated bushranger Martin Cash who, with two companions, swam past the dog line on Boxing Day 1842—perhaps the guards had Christmas hangovers—and stayed out for twenty months before being captured in Hobart Town. (Although Cash shot and killed a policeman while being recaptured and was sentenced to death, he managed to avoid the gallows and eventually died in his bed, a free man, at the ripe old age of sixty-nine, shortly after writing his memoirs!)

Another ingenious, but failed, bid to cross the dog line was made by one William Hunt, a strolling player by profession before he was transported. Hunt acquired the skin of a large kangaroo, put it on and hopped artistically towards the Neck, but he had to shed his skin and reveal himself quickly when one of the guards decided to shoot the surprisingly large marsupial.

Just before Eaglehawk Neck we turned off the main road to see a natural feature on the coast called the Tessellated Pavement, where a slab of sedimentary rock is fractured in astonishingly straight lines, looking remarkably like paving stones. The view down the coast towards the looming bulk of Cape Huay was awesome with sinister-looking black clouds rolling in from the sea, disgorging raggedy edges of heavy rain onto the cliffs. Some friends had described a good camping spot near the Lufra Hotel which overlooks the 'pavement', but it had been turned into a car park.

Crossing the Neck where the dogs used to be (they lived 'on the job' with wooden barrels as their kennels), the Arthur Highway turns back towards the west coast of the peninsula. At Taranna we turned off to the right, leaving the main road which went on to Port Arthur. We had time to explore what I think is the best tourist value on the peninsula, the coal mines at Saltwater River. As we would discover, what remained of the main convict settlement at Port Arthur is now completely enclosed, and you have to buy a ticket to get in. At Saltwater River you can wander around freely through the sandstone facades of former administration buildings and barracks, see underground cells and make your own way—guided by excellent interpretive signs—to what can be seen of the shafts and workings. Because of the lemming-like rush of tourists to

Port Arthur, you can often have this superb site completely to yourself.

Like Port Arthur the buildings at Saltwater River have wonderful water views, but it is unlikely the convict coal miners appreciated them or even had much time to look, because Saltwater River was a place of punishment from Port Arthur—where punishment had been refined to a high art—for repeat offenders 'of the worst sort'. Four underground cells were constructed deep in the coal mine workings to punish those who offended further!

There was great excitement at Government House in Hobart when coal was discovered by surveyors at Plunkett Point in 1833. At that stage what little coal the colony had was being imported from New South Wales. Lieutenant Governor Arthur—who had initiated the building of the Port Arthur penitentiary three years before—immediately ordered the coal seams to be mined, and why not by the most recalcitrant convicts? Not only were the coal seams hard to get at, and to mine, but it was lousy coal anyway, exploding in fireplaces and scattering 'small pieces in great quantities, to the detriment of carpets, furniture, ladies' gowns etc.'[1]

At their peak in the 1840s the coal mines were staffed by 579 prisoners, not all of them down the mines, but many employed on building projects. Some of the narrow shafts began to fill with water and constant pumping—by convicts of course—had to be maintained. Because of the punishment aspect, the authorities were not concerned how hard it was to mine underground. Men worked bent double in the cramped, wet shafts. Lady Franklin, wife of Sir John

---

1 Thomas Lempriere, 1839

Franklin (who succeeded Governor Arthur), went there in 1837 and described how little carts were 'pushed before a man who, leaning against it which he must do when stooping, pushed it on. Whilst going uphill an additional man is saddled on before.'

The crowding and chaotic working conditions at the coal mines were in contrast to the tight controls and solitary confinement at Port Arthur. There was official concern that the convicts would 'learn from others' vices'. Homosexuality was rampant and uncontrollable in the dark recesses of the underground workings, described as 'sinkholes of vice and infamy'.

In an effort to curb such acts additional lighting was placed in the tunnels, auger holes were made in the doors and shutters of sleeping wards and visits by constables were made at irregular times. Over one hundred separate sleeping cells were built in 1846 to keep prisoners segregated at night.[2]

Homosexuality was considered a serious crime in the nineteenth century and carried the death penalty. In 1845 two prisoners at the coal mines, Job Harris and William Collier, were arrested and charged with raping another prisoner. They were hanged for this offence in January the next year.[3] But it was impossible to keep the convict workers apart at the mines, and venereal disease was rife among the unfortunate miners. Additional punishment cells were built below ground, the remains of which can still

2 2003, *Coal Mines Historic Site: Tasmania's First Operational Mine*, Parks and Wildlife Service Tasmania
3 Ian Brand (undated), *The Port Arthur Coal Mines, 1833–1887*, Regal Publications, Launceston

be seen today. The coal mines were closed by the government in 1848 on both 'moral and financial grounds'.

We found it a fascinating area to visit on a nice sunny March day early in the twenty-first century—even though it was undeniably a bugger of a place in its day. The remains of the sandstone administration buildings are on a smaller scale than the Port Arthur ruins, but extremely atmospheric in the bright autumn afternoon light and I could not stop myself indulging in an orgy of photography.

We retraced our steps to Taranna on the Arthur Highway from Saltwater River, driving past extensive sand flats, reflecting cameos of the headlands and timbered bays in wide, shallow pools left by the falling tide, and continued south towards Port Arthur. About four kilometres out we turned left and followed signage to a very well situated caravan park on Garden Point overlooking a bay where circular salmon farm pens floated on naturally protected waters. The park was quite new and even had some en suite camping sites. The camping bays were well laid out in natural bushland and there was a walking track around the foreshore leading to the historic Port Arthur site. We even had a water glimpse, as real estate agents are wont to say. A nuisance shower of rain enveloped us just as we began to set up camp and expand The Manor's canvas walls, but if you have to have rain it is preferable to have it when you set up camp rather than when you're packing up, because then you have to fold wet canvas in over your beds—about the only drawback of our style of camper.

A larger version of The Manor was parked next to us. It needed to be larger because a family with four children were living in it—and its annexe—with pushbikes and boogie surf boards scattered about on the grass. We heard lessons under way after three high-spirited little boys and their elder sister (all under ten years of age) had been corralled inside. The schooling was necessary because, we learned later, the family planned to be on the road for ten months. At least they had an in-house professional: their father was a school principal from Victoria. They seemed very pleasant people except I thought they blotted their copybook the next evening when they all ranged into the surrounding bush and broke off branches and sticks for their evening barbecue—despite the fact that the park had wood for sale for just that purpose. Not a good lesson in conservation.

The rain had cleared away overnight to produce a bright, sunny morning for our visit to Port Arthur. When Lieutenant Governor George Arthur arrived in Hobart Town in 1824, he presided over a society where convicts vastly outnumbered free settlers. As I mentioned earlier, security was a grave concern for colonial administrators in Tasmania as the possibility of a convict uprising could not be disregarded. Most of the constables in the police force were recruited from former convict ticket-of-leave men. When Arthur arrived, convicts were divided into seven classes. Class 1 convicts were the ticket-of-leave men, who could work for wages but could lose their status if they behaved badly. Class 2 were the assigned servants, given to settlers as free labourers, really. Their masters had to feed and clothe them, and in return the convicts had to do whatever work they were instructed to do. About fifty per cent of the transported convicts were in this category. Class 3 convicts were employed on public works projects by the government, Class 4 worked on the road gangs, and Class 5 did the same work as 'hard labour' in chains. Class 6 convicts were repeat offenders who had been convicted of offences in Van Diemen's Land (Maria Island was first settled to accommodate the Class 6 convicts), and Class 7, the worst of the worst, had to serve their sentences in chains. These Class 7 men were originally sent to Sarah Island in Macquarie Harbour to get them safely out of the way—and get some useful work out of them cutting timber and boat building.

The Port Arthur site was selected by Lieutenant Governor Arthur as a secure prison, reasonably close to Hobart Town, and as soon as he was able to do so he closed down Sarah and Maria islands. By 1833 he had brought all the Class 7 and 6 men to the new prison on the Tasman Peninsula. A military man with a brave war record, Arthur saw himself primarily as the chief executive officer of an extensive penal settlement. By all accounts he was an efficient administrator, forceful and determined but untroubled by self-doubt. He wanted everyone to know where they stood and enforced his will by strict discipline. Although what he did seems repressive by modern standards, he was remarkably liberal for his time. He was determined to implement the sentences of hard labour meted out to the transported convicts but he also believed in their reformation by encouraging good conduct, and rewarded such behaviour with the highly sought-after tickets-of-leave. Conversely, he punished transgressions fiercely and let it be known back in Britain that Van Diemen's Land was no home away from home. It's interesting to note that only about 12 000 of the 70 000 convicts transported to Van Diemen's Land between 1803 and 1854 ever saw the inside of a cell at Port Arthur. Most convicts clearly took advantage of the available opportunities to start new lives.

The early years of Port Arthur, while it was being built, were the 'flogging' period, where corporal punishment was the preferred option. But in 1838 a report by a British parliamentary committee—the Molesworth Committee—reassessed the whole system. It found that the assignment system, where convicts were sent out to work for individual settlers, wasn't working. Many of them were having too easy a time of it, in the committee's opinion, and were becoming corrupted by a system that also 'encouraged their vicious propensities'.[4]

While there was little doubt in Governor Arthur's mind that if Port Arthur was to work it had to be a deterrent, at the same time he said that 'coercive measures must be bounded by humanity; if they are not, the criminals are driven into a state of mind bordering upon desperation'. In other words, hard labour had to be within the bounds of human endurance—if the chain gangs and soul-destroying dawn-till-dusk pounding away on treadmills could be so described. Anyway the Molesworth Committee recommended that Port Arthur be run in a similar style to a new American theory that the penitentiary system should 'inspire terror . . . to improve the moral character of an offender'.[5]

It's difficult to judge, of course, through the mists of history, but I wonder if a re-offending nineteenth century convict might not have chosen a short sharp flogging or two, rather than the punishment regime of solitary confinement and sensory deprivation brought in with the building of the 'model' or 'separate' prison. This 'prison within a prison' opened in the early 1850s—just as a mirror-image

---

4  Ian Brand, 1975, *Port Arthur 1830–1887*, Jason Publications, Hobart
5  Ian Brand, *Port Arthur 1830–1887*

prison in Pentonville, England, was closed on the grounds that it 'created more mental problems for the victim than it ever cured'.[6]

In the separate prison, inmates were locked in tiny cells opening into galleries where warders patrolled constantly in slippers, their footsteps further muffled by matting. Snooping and spying ensured that prisoners had absolutely no contact with each other. The prisoner slept in a hammock. The only articles in the cell were a set of corner shelves, a small table and stool and a bucket for the other kinds of stool. Strict silence was the order of the day and night, and even the warders did not speak to the prisoners but communicated by gesture. This lack of contact was maintained in the exercise yard, where prisoners walked alone for an hour, facing the wall if another prisoner was escorted past them. As if that wasn't bad enough, any misdemeanour was punished by a spell in the 'dumb' or 'dark' cell, where they experienced total sensory deprivation— complete blackness and utter silence.

The hope was that the prisoner in solitary confinement would contemplate his soul and misdeeds and, by inner contemplation, attain salvation—based on a concept evolved by the Quakers. Few, if any, managed this. Instead most became mentally ill—a known consequence of the failed English Pentonville experiment which 'unnecessarily spawned a tragic harvest of prison lunatics'.[7]

Even though religion was supposed to be vital to their salvation, the unfortunate 'model' prisoners were not permitted to attend services in Port Arthur's imposing

6 Alex Graeme-Evans, 2001, *A Short History Guide to Port Arthur 1830–77*, Regal Publications

7 Alex Graeme-Evans, *A Short History Guide to Port Arthur 1830–77*

church—the walls of which still stand and are one of the site's most recognised and photographed features. Instead, a special chapel was built beside the separate prison, constructed with fifty upright stalls so the prisoners could not even glimpse each other, just the preacher:

> Each man was locked in his stall by an iron rod which passed through every stall door. Facing the stalls were the preacher's pulpit and two boxes which were occupied by the guards. This was the only place in the Separate Prison where prisoners were allowed to use their voices. The convicts, therefore, eagerly joined in the hymn singing.[8]

It is a wonder there is much of Port Arthur left for tourists to see. It was closed down as a convict prison in 1877 and its name changed to Carnarvon, by those who bought some of the buildings, to try to erase the convict stain. The site was ravaged by bushfires (the interior of the church was gutted in 1884), and dressed stone from the other buildings as well as timber and fittings were plundered at the end of the nineteenth century and into the twentieth. Many of the substantial buildings were built on poor foundations by people with limited construction skills, and no sense of heritage developed, because Tasmanians were deeply uneasy about their convict past.

(It has only recently become chic to have a convict ancestor. I recall in the 1950s when my father's eldest sister, Dorothy Bowden, discovered that we had not only one but two First Fleet convict ancestors, she wrote to tell my Uncle Eric in Adelaide of what she thought was most interesting

---

8 Ian Brand, *Port Arthur 1830–1887*

news. Adelaide prided itself on its lack of a convict past. It probably still does. Eric wrote back saying: 'On no account must any word of this reach Adelaide.')

Fortunately in 1916 the Tasmanian government decided to buy the most significant parts of the site as a reserve, to preserve what remained. Today Port Arthur is Tasmania's most visited tourist attraction. The ninety-eight hectare site is contained, and you can either just wander around the remains of the penitentiary, separate prison, the church and other buildings, or take a guided tour. Except in August, the admission price includes a harbour cruise.

Ros and I decided to wander around and also pay a bit extra for a boat trip and tour of the Island of the Dead, Port Arthur's cemetery. Only the non-convicts scored headstones and there are seventy-six of them. The convicts were buried in mass, unmarked graves. In order to better preserve this much-visited site you aren't allowed to explore by yourself so our wise-cracking Pommy guide was compulsory, but he knew his stuff even if his jokes were well worn and delivered for the 1365th time.

Port Arthur, with its crumbling stone memories of Tasmania's convict past, used to be the island state's second biggest tourist drawcard after Hobart and the line of nineteenth century sandstone buildings on the waterfront at Salamanca Place. That was so until Sunday 28 April 1996 when a disturbed young local man, Martin Bryant, inexplicably took a collection of guns to Port Arthur and went on a murderous rampage, shooting people he knew, like the elderly couple who ran the Seascape Guest House, as well as indiscriminately firing at tourists innocently visiting the popular historic site.

Bryant, a loner with blue eyes and startlingly blond shoulder-length hair, calmly ate a substantial meal on the deck of Port Arthur's popular Broad Arrow Café before producing his military-style rifle and carefully and accurately firing at other diners. In just fifteen seconds he killed fifteen people and by the time he left, a minute later, twenty people were dead and another eleven wounded. As he strode from the scene he fired through the windows of tour buses parked outside the café, killing four people and wounding more. Getting into his yellow Volvo he drove back towards the toll gates, stopping only to murder a young mother, Nanette Mikac, and her two young children, Madeline and Alannah, who were playing in the parkland. During this most chilling episode, Alannah instinctively tried to hide behind a tree. Bryant stalked and shot her.

The killing continued at the toll gates where he forced four people from their car and shot them before abandoning his own car and hijacking their BMW. At a nearby service station Bryant stopped a Toyota Corolla driven by Zoe Hall, commanded her companion, Glenn Pears, to climb into the boot of the BMW and took him hostage. He then shot and fatally wounded Zoe Hall.

Bryant returned to the Seascape Guest House, where he had already left the bodies of David Martin and his wife. It was Martin's seventy-second birthday. Bryant, who knew the Martins well, had shot both of them earlier. With Pears as his hostage—he too was shot and killed—Bryant kept police at bay through a long night, chatting to them on his mobile phone until his batteries failed, all the time firing occasional shots out into the darkness. At 8 am on Monday Bryant set the guest house alight, probably intending to die in the flames with his victims. But faced with the excruciatingly painful reality of incineration, he tore off his burning clothes and rushed out, naked, into the police cordon, to be captured and taken to the Royal Hobart Hospital for treatment to the burns on his buttocks and back. He had killed thirty-five people, injured twenty-two, and achieved the frightful distinction of being the worst mass murderer in Australian history. Those who compile statistics on such events have reported that more than 2000 people, including 690 emergency staff, underwent critical accident stress counselling as a result of the incident. The on-going legacy of grief for the families and friends of the victims of Bryant's rampage was profound and will never end.

Bryant's crime was so ghastly that—coupled with its past grim history—tourists simply could not bear to go to Port Arthur. Visitor numbers dropped drastically for the next three years, causing a devastating impact on the local economy of the Tasman Peninsula which is inextricably linked with the Port Arthur site.

An immediate problem in 1996 was what to do about the tainted Broad Arrow Café site. A carved Huon pine cross was erected on the waterfront at Masons Cove and inscribed with the names of the victims as a focus of grief where wreaths and floral tributes could be placed. As time passed the debate about a permanent memorial was vigorously argued. Some favoured obliterating all traces of the Broad Arrow Café from the face of the earth. Others said that elements of it should be incorporated into a permanent memorial to those who had died.

Five designers were asked to submit their ideas to a newly created Port Arthur Memorial Committee. Apparently all the original plans submitted by the five designers were rejected by the committee, which had no members who were artists, architects or historians. The chair of the committee wanted to have the Broad Arrow Café as the focus of the memorial, and some months after all the initial plans had been rejected Hobart architect Torquil Canning was approached to see if he would reconsider his early objections to the incorporation of the café. He did what he could given the brief and the limited funds available. When Ros and I visited Port Arthur in the summer of 2003 we saw the finished result, an open memorial garden with one bluestone wall of the original café, its brick chimney retained, seen across a memorial pool. On a corner of the pool, just below the surface, lie thirty-five golden leaves, to commemorate the lives of Bryant's victims. Carved into the basalt paving of a path leading to the pool are lines by local resident and poet Margaret Scott:

> *Death has taken its toll,*
> *Some pain knows no release*
> *But the knowledge of brave compassion shines*
> *like a pool of peace.*

We found the memorial stark and sombre, as memorials must be to some extent, but rather bleak. I was aware that one of the designers who was asked to submit a concept for the memorial, Peter Adams, believed that the committee's approach had prevented what might have been an internationally significant memorial which would not only have commemorated the thirty-five victims of the Port Arthur massacre, but might have drawn on the history of the site and incorporated an element of hope for the future. Adams, a sculptor, has a property overlooking Roaring Beach on the western side of the Tasman Peninsula and I had been told he decided to incorporate his ideas for a memorial on his own land. Ros and I planned to visit his property the next day to meet him and see his concept first hand.

As the name suggests, Port Arthur was built on a superb harbour. In its heyday it supported a flourishing ship-building industry which constructed some of Tasmania's biggest ships in the 1830s. The whole Port Arthur site evolved into a big industrial complex, the labour of the convicts being extremely important to the growing colony. Today no traces remain of the many trades-related shops—shoemakers, blacksmiths, nail makers—that once flourished on the waterfront. Port Arthur also grew its own fruit and vegetables to combat the scurvy that was a problem in the early days, banished eventually by the fresh food produced in Government Garden—mostly potatoes, cabbages and turnips. Draft animals were not kept on site because of fears the convicts might use them as transport for escaping, although later on some dairy cows were kept to provide milk and cream for the hospital and from 1854 a farm was established with cattle, a piggery and a slaughter house.

There is an aura about Port Arthur: its history of human oppression and punishment seems engraved in the stones and, without wishing to seem overly dramatic, it seems to seep into your soul after a while.

Your entry ticket enables you to come and go within a set time, so we decided to take a break from reminders of past infamy and drive further down the coast to a feature called Remarkable Cave, which has been shaped into a series of arches by sea erosion over the millennia. As we drove away from the enclosed Port Arthur site I noticed a rather faded sign to Point Puer and, on an impulse, turned along a rutted track until we reached a locked gate. I knew that Point Puer was the infamous boys' prison. The Isle of the Dead is only a few hundred metres from the tip of Point Puer, and we had seen the promontory from the catamaran that had taken us to that island. There wasn't much evidence of habitation. We could make out a few low stone terraces and the remains of a stone jetty.

In fact the site is in the process of being surveyed and 'interpreted' for visitors, but there were no 'keep out' signs. We found it was possible to walk about a kilometre and a half from the locked gate to where some restoration work was being done to some of the low rock walls and what looked like the opening to a large oven. It was likely the stone had been shaped by the junior convicts themselves, as stone masonry was one of the crafts that they were taught. Indeed many of Port Arthur's major buildings, including the church, were constructed from stone chipped by the toiling boy felons.

Extraordinary as it may seem today, boys as young as ten years of age were sentenced to transportation by the British judicial system, generally for stealing and petty theft. Young they may have been, but some twelve year olds were experienced villains. Thomas Lempriere, who ran the Commissariat at Port Arthur, reported that one twelve year old, sentenced to seven years for stealing, admitted to thirty prison sentences before that—all for stealing. In his first thirteen months at Point Puer he was tried for twenty-four offences, *none* of which was for stealing.[9]

Governor Arthur soon found that assigning these juveniles to free settlers was a recipe for disaster as the boys

9  Ian Brand, *Port Arthur 1830–1887*

were 'entirely useless and generally so mischievous are these corrupt little rogues that they are the dread of every family'.[10]

The solution was to send all the juvenile offenders to Port Arthur and Point Puer, which could be seen across the bay from the main settlement but which separated the boys, aged from ten to eighteen, from the adult convict prisoners. The Juvenile Establishment at Point Puer was occupied by 1834. After that the prison system just kept shovelling the lads into it. There was even a designated 'young offenders' convict ship, *Frances Charlotte*, the first of eight ships carrying juveniles between Portsmouth and Van Diemen's Land. From 1838 to 1841 some 1200 boy convicts were transported and most of them finished up at Point Puer. There they were subject to strict discipline and were taught various trades. Punishment for misdemeanours included solitary confinement in a cell with a diet of bread and water and, as a last resort, being 'breeched'—a euphemism for flogging, although we are told this was rarely done. Their treatment was regarded as humane by the standards of the day, and many of them were certainly tough little cookies. But the bashing and near death of an unpopular overseer by some of the boys is a matter of record.

Walking along the point we also saw the remains of some tunnels. What they were used for is unclear and currently a matter for debate by historians and archaeologists. By this stage we were 'convicted out' and after having admired the natural sculpture of Remarkable Cave, we headed back to camp for dinner and what we thought was a well-earned sleep.

---

10  Alex Graeme-Evans, *A Short History Guide to Port Arthur 1830–77*

If there is a piece of paradise on this earth, the sculptor and environmental philosopher, Peter Adams, has come close to finding it with his coastal property Windgrove, overlooking Roaring Beach and Storm Bay on the western side of the Tasman Peninsula. To get there we drove to Nubeena, which is the largest town on the peninsula, but you wouldn't know because it is scattered along the waterfront of Wedge Bay among the trees and is where the locals have their week-enders. The name Nubeena means 'crayfish' in the language of the Tasmanian Aboriginal tribe who once fished there.

We turned left at Nubeena and ran along a narrow dirt road for about six kilometres until we came to the turnoff to Windgrove. Peter's property is on sloping land running down to a rocky coastline, with Roaring Beach audible away to the south. It is a popular surf beach and the swells roll in from Storm Bay channelled through a narrow gap between two prominent rocky headlands. Good for surfing, we learned, but a dangerous place to try to swim. The property overlooks a dramatic seascape with no other dwelling in sight. Peter's elegant wooden house is hidden away in a grove of trees so that it does not impinge on the skyline. (The house is a recent refinement. He lived in a bus for seven years developing his eight-hectare Peace Garden before he got around to building it.) He specialises in wooden sculptures, sometimes incorporating natural stone, and is engaged in a host of other projects, some of which we hoped to see. He emerged from his studio to greet us as we drove up.

'How long have you got?' he asked. I thought at least two hours, which became three. But a month would not have been long enough to explore the subtleties of this sublime place. In fact some lucky souls can spend a month or longer. Since Peter built his house, incorporating art studio and multi-purpose hall, he offers his converted bus (and the freedom of his home) to 'artistic refugees' who need time and space to work on their projects. The bus now has a corrugated iron roof and an upper storey—a platform with sea views and ceramic pots as seats!

We began our all-too-brief tour of his two-kilometre coastal walk at the Peace Garden, which incorporates a seven-metre spiral-carved, blue-gum log sculpture that is reflected in the adjacent pool.[11] Although it seems to emerge from the pool itself, it rises from a circular womb-like base crafted in Tasmanian slate and entered into a little further down the slope. On the upper side of the pool is a huge—six-tonne—split dolerite boulder, its revealed inner faces polished to mirror smoothness. To one side is an ancestral midden site devoted to significant stones donated by visitors. (Later I was able to send Peter stones from Central Australia and Antarctica.) The Peace Garden, with its associated sculptures, marks the beginning of a two-kilometre coastal walk, along which Peter has selected certain vistas with carefully positioned sculptural benches where people can stop and contemplate the surrounding bush and the coastal seascape. Some of the seats are sculpted from single pieces of wood, mostly Huon pine and myrtle, with the Adams trademark of water-rounded stones cleverly inset into the wood in perfectly fitting, nest like indentations.

At the entrance to the Peace Garden is an inscription: *Peace within the individual, peace between people, peace between humanity and the rest of the living world.* Peter explained

---

11 Peter Adams welcomes visitors to Windgrove by prior arrangement.

the symbolism around the Peace Garden in relation to the inscription.

> PETER: I set this up as a visual representation of how we might walk the path towards peace. It begins with the past, represented by the ancestral midden, moves around the pond to the present which is the split stone, and continues on to the womb of the earth, representing the future—where hope and enlightenment are the hallmarks, not fear and terror.
>
> TIM: So what is the symbolism of the split rock?
>
> PETER: The notion that if we embrace life fully, we will definitely be broken open. Out of our hearts breaking open, out of our suffering, we can gain compassion which, in turn, leads us towards tolerance. Here the reconciliation process can begin. Beyond that, the polished beauty of the split rock shows that the beauty within each individual is not revealed until we are opened up. We shouldn't live in such a protected way that we don't feel pain. People try to protect themselves too much. So whether it's drugs, or alcohol, or hiding behind closed walls or gated communities, they shut themselves off from life and in so doing remain victims of fear, mistrust and cowardliness.

I asked Peter to tell me about how the decision to create a memorial in and around the Broad Arrow Café to commemorate the thirty-five victims of the Bryant massacre had been reached:

> PETER: Five of us were selected to design a memorial at Port Arthur. It seemed to me important to consider the history of Port Arthur as well as the more recent history of the massacre. I wanted to create a memorial there to honour everything that had come through Port Arthur—to tease out all the negativity. It was as

though all the convict history had been swept under the carpet in a kind of utter denial. I thought we should create a memorial that would acknowledge the past—whatever that past was, good or bad— in honour of all the people who had come through. Of course the thirty-five victims would be honoured in a very prominent manner, but we should also leave room to honour past and future events. The Memorial Committee, though, saw this as too grand an idea and outside the scope of the massacre. As one person said, they didn't want to belittle the grieving process for those families of the thirty-five victims.

I said that in fifty to a hundred years' time people would come to Port Arthur, as they do now to the World War I memorial, and walk right past it. We should have a memorial that is 'experienced', and kept up to date, something that will stay alive and be meaningful for all visitors. One of the things I incorporated in the memorial was an on-going 'raking-of-sand' at the base of the standing ancestral stones, similar to what is done at a Japanese temple. People would sign up in advance. They and their family would come for that day, possibly every year. Every day of the year somebody would have the honour of the raking. However there were a lot of politics involved and the committee had their own vision of what the memorial should be. I also fought against the preservation of the Broad Arrow Café as a memorial. I could see the reason for keeping it as a historic aspect, if they thought that was necessary, but to incorporate that into the memorial lessened its potential power. The analogy was that if Martin Bryant had shot his first victims in one of the buses, would that bus have been used as the memorial?

So I wanted to focus on those long term issues. And make it big enough so that the memorial had a positive impact on the site. It is now a big memorial for thirty-five people, but I find it a little sterile. It lacks power. A memorial has to hit you. It has to take you and uplift you. It should take you into and through the pain of the past, and exit you through hope and a better world.

As we strolled back towards the Peace Garden, I noticed a wisp of smoke coming from underneath what looked like the top of a corrugated iron water tank. Peter Adams told me that it was an eternal flame, a cleansing fire dedicated to honouring the path of peace and reconciliation. He mentioned, in passing, that he planned to keep it burning for the next 600 years!

It has been burning continuously since 6 April 2002 and it works a bit like a slow combustion stove. Peter tends it daily and obliging neighbours look after it if he goes away. The concept of the fire came from an Aboriginal woman originally in Cape York, who heard about Windgrove from friends.

'She said, so I was told, "That's nice—for a white man!" Several days later she got a letter from her Cape York elders asking her to go and see them. They presented her with a stone, saying that there was some place of significance being created in Tasmania, and that she needed to come and put that stone there. So she did eventually do this, at Windgrove, but while here she also wanted to create a peace fire—for peace between blacks and whites, men and women and humans on the earth. She said, "I want to bring father god back to mother earth and make us understand the importance of that." So I was made custodian of the fire, and it is my job to look after it.

'We dug down to where we were going to put the fire, and about a metre deep we hit a charcoal midden, with stone tools. So it seemed that Aboriginal people had had a camp there and I thought, well, they would want fresh water. So I searched around and right over there in those trees is a seep—and when this land was more forested, the soil retention would have lasted longer, and there might have been a year-round seep right there. You can see naturally why they would have chosen this place to camp. Overlooking the beach, with access to it, and water.

'I decided on the 600 years time span only because it seems impossible. For Aborigines, or Eskimos or other indigenous people it's not . . . I wanted to demonstrate to us westerners that this notion of "long time" is important. People come here and can't comprehend the ancient age of some of the trees we are cutting down. The peace fire and its seemingly impossible commitment to 600 years gives them an experiential sense of what it means to cut down a 600-year-old tree. It is definitely a teaching and learning process. How will it be looked after in fifty years time? Who knows? But that shouldn't stop us from beginning the commitment.'

I wondered how Peter, as a conservationist, could justify burning a log fire for 600 years?

'I believe,' he explained, 'that the benefits of burning this wood are clearly evident in a spiritual sense. For those scientific rationalists out there, how about this for a justi-fication: I've calculated that the tonnage this fire would burn over 600 years equals what Forestry Tasmania and the timber company Gunns cut down in the first three hours of a working day. Just think about that—*the first three hours of one day*! So if we were to stop the cutting of the forests for just three hours over 600 years, that in a sense equals what we are going to do with this fire. I don't see that as an issue.'

I thought he had a point.

Peter invited us to his house for a cup of tea. In the early days, when he set up house in the bus, he had to bring his drinking water from Hobart. Now he has tank water and electricity from solar panels which, I noticed, managed to power a spanking new iMac computer with a liquid crystal screen. Being a Macintosh man myself, I commented on this. Peter said the iMac was a big advance on his ancient Powerbook 170, which got so cranky—particularly in the winter—it had to be warmed in his wood-fired oven in the morning before it would boot up! (Those interested in the daily life at Windgrove and Peter's projects can access his website at www.windgrove.com.au, or access his on-line journal 'Life at the Edge' at www.cobbers.com/pa.)

The ingenious high-backed stools—wooden of course— that we sat on were made of very thin, obviously very tough wood, with the bark still visible. (The everlasting bark is a characteristic of Tasmania's unique horizontal scrub, only found in virgin rain forest.) They were made by craftsman Craig Dorrington. The rare timber is incredibly strong, but Peter told us that much Tasmanian native rain forest timber which could be used for furniture and other crafted products was not being salvaged adequately from clear-felling forestry operations in old growth forests. As I was to find out later, even professional saw-millers were outraged that they were not permitted to remove precious timbers like celery-top pine, myrtle or even horizontal, because of the wasteful practice of taking out the eucalypts for saw logs and woodchipping, and simply burning all the rain forest trees before replanting with a sterile mono-culture of eucalypts.

Another of Peter's long term projects—presumably in fewer than 600 years in this case—was to regenerate the natural timber on his own property, devastated by years of clearing and burning by pastoralists.

After only a few hours at Windgrove I was keen to set up house in the vacant bus and begin writing the great Australian novel. I would need to work alone, so I explained to Ros that she could take Penelope and The Manor back to Sydney by herself, after dropping off a few clothes and my computer. I'd keep in touch by email from time to time. She seemed resistant to this sudden change of plan and even Peter looked nervous.

It is more than a year now since we visited Windgrove, and writing about our visit has rekindled this fantasy for me. On a whim I checked out Peter's website and found that, apart from finding and photographing a baby possum in his donation box at the Windgrove entrance gate, he had been experimenting with growing tomatoes nourished by sea water! There were even photographs of his tomato plants—with tomatoes on them—as evidence. The diary entry, however, was for 1 April.

In his Great Tomato Hoax, Peter had both the Greens and the Tasmanian Conservation Trust allegedly up in arms that he had put a white plastic pipe across the sands of Roaring Beach to pump up salt water to his tomatoes on the hill. (He'd curved the pipe artistically for his website photograph so it looked like a beach sculpture.)

His project to cultivate 'Roaring Reds' to supply pre-salted tomatoes to McDonald's hamburger joints throughout the entire world is now stalled, and his business slogan 'Better Red than Green' is dead in the unobtainable salted water. (This April Fool's Day spoof, with photos, can be viewed on his online journal in the archives section for 1 April 2004.)

**Travel Diary Wednesday 12 March**

Drove away from Port Arthur on the kind of sparkling, still, sunny morning which always lifts the spirits. It is amazing how the drought-stricken paddocks have reacted to the rain of a week ago and are already green. Such a contrast to the dry, white grass we saw on our way in. To continue our coastal journey we have to retrace our route from the Tasman Peninsula to Dunalley, and then to Hobart via the old towns of Richmond and Campania, on the eastern side of the Derwent estuary. This relatively flat, arable land was originally settled in order to become the granary and vegetable-growing area for Hobart Town. Richmond, a miraculously preserved Georgian village, has some of the oldest buildings in Australia, and boasts the nation's most venerable stone bridge, built in 1823 to facilitate traffic between Hobart Town and Port Arthur.

We have 'the tyranny of distance' to thank for the historical time capsule of Richmond. As early as 1874 a causeway was constructed across Pittwater to the town of Sorell to shorten the distance not only to Port Arthur, but the east coast. The main highway bypassed Richmond, until then a strategic military post and convict station. Happily for today's visitors, the town became a sleepy rural backwater for the next century and is now a magnet for tourists. It is bursting with antique shops, craft outlets and tea rooms. Should you have a craving for a Huon pine honey-twirler you will find one in seconds, as well as Huon pine-made anything you can think of—bowls, cheese boards, chess sets, mixing spoons, mirror holders, desk sets and paper knives. That aromatic, yellow timber has such a fine grain that it can actually be turned in a lathe into Huon pine wine goblets with sides as thin as glass. Ros spotted some Huon pine perfume for men, but I said I didn't want to smell like a log—immediately inviting the obvious rejoinder. Some husbands never learn.

The most visited sites in Richmond are the gaol (which pre-dates Port Arthur) and the magnificent stone-arched bridge. We were on a mission to find a toast rack. Now this may seem quaint, but toast racks are very hard to come by these days. Ros wanted one for when we had guests staying overnight: a touch of graciousness on the breakfast table instead of having to rush from the toaster juggling slices of hot toast with bare hands and clunking them onto a guest's plate. Yes, there were toast racks to be had in most antique shops—in silver for well over a hundred bucks. Ros wasn't *that* keen, nor did she want to have to clean and polish something all the time. Happily an obliging antique shop proprietor—without marked enthusiasm I have to say, but he did do it—was able to produce a silver-plated, slightly battered toast rack for $20. His shop specialised in Huon pine furniture, old and new. As he wrapped up our bargain toast rack (we found out it had once graced the tables of the Windsor Hotel in Melbourne) I asked him whether business had picked up since the new roll-on-roll off ferries, *Spirits I* and *II*, had begun operating.

'The answer to your question is yes,' he said. 'Two years ago, Premier Jim Bacon warned us to gear up for a massive increase in tourism when the ferries came on stream. I bought in at least $200 000 of extra stock, and recently I've been shipping it off in truckloads to the mainland.'

I asked him who was buying the Huon pine dressers, tables and sideboards.

'Mostly young couples who are spending a week or ten days touring Tasmania by car. They call in, make a buying decision, and ask me to ship it to them later. In past years you had to think six months ahead, or even a year in peak holiday time, to get your car on the ferry. Now young business people can find they have a week's holiday available so they just drive down to the Williamtown terminal in Melbourne and off they go.'

I couldn't help thinking that it was a pity the B & B and caravan park industry hadn't taken their premier's excellent advice with similar alacrity. With twice the population of Tasmania streaming through the island each year as tourists, it was prudent to book accommodation well in advance.

We had in fact booked ahead for our accommodation that night at Campania House, surely one of the most stylish B & Bs in Australia. We would be sleeping in the oldest private home in Australia to open its doors to guests, and not only that, our hostess would be a personal friend, Paddy Pearl, widow of the celebrated Sydney author, journalist and bon viveur Cyril Pearl. Paddy had left her Paddington terrace in Sydney seven years before to take on single-handedly the restoration of Campania House, and then run it as a B & B. Because of the way we were travelling and camping, B & Bs weren't on our agenda—even if we could have got into them. But it was difficult to pass by this opportunity, and we had been meaning to look Paddy up ever since she moved to Tasmania.

Campania is only a few kilometres north of Richmond, near the Coal River which is now a premier wine growing area. Not wishing to burden Paddy too early in the afternoon with our presence we turned off on a whim to the Cooinda Vineyard nearby. It was typical of the small boutique vineyards we love to visit: a relatively small holding with a modest tasting room, and hopefully personal contact with the people who grow the grapes.

Like many similar holdings—and some bigger ones—Cooinda's wine is made by Andrew Hood, a microbiologist turned winemaker who began making wine for friends with small vineyards in 1990. In those days he rented space in existing wineries, but in 1994 built his own, Hood Wines, between Richmond and Cambridge. Today Hood's winery makes him one of the 'big five' winemakers in Tasmania, and has his own Wellington label. His wines, and those he makes for other vineyards, regularly win prizes. His Wellington 2000 pinot noir—a grape that grows particularly well in Tasmania's cool climate—was selected for Qantas first class international flights. Andrew Hood now produces wine for thirty vineyards, with nearby Meadowbank his biggest client, but including Frogmore Creek, Coombend (where we bought some riesling on the east coast), Elsewhere, Providence (also visited by the Bowdens in the east Tamar region), Laurel Bank, Pembroke and many more.

We wondered whether Cooinda Vineyard was open, as it seemed deserted. We wandered around and peered in the window of the tasting room, and were just about to return to Penelope when the tiny figure of an elderly woman appeared around the side of the house and introduced herself as Margaret Pooley. Would we like to taste some wines? We certainly would.

She unlocked the tasting room, and showed us the range of wines on offer. Many of them had the Pooley label, and still the penny did not drop. Finally Margaret looked at me searchingly and said, 'I think I know you. Have you ever lived locally?' Thinking that this might be the legacy of many years fronting the *Backchat* viewer reaction program on ABC-TV, I said that I came from Hobart originally but hadn't lived there since the 1960s.

'Of course!' she said. 'You're Tim Bowden. You would have known my daughters Diana and Pat.' I had indeed known them. They were both very attractive, dark-haired girls, and we had attended many parties and dances together in the late 1950s and early 1960s. In fact Margaret said one of her three daughters had a crush on me at one stage. And I never knew! I hadn't met Margaret before but I did remember her late husband, Denis, an Englishman who worked in the car industry and was passionately fond of rally driving, wining and dining—although even in those pre-breathalyser days, not at the same time. In the Hobart of the 1950s dining out was not a sophisticated experience; roast lamb and two veg was about it. Drinking wine was usually associated with derelicts swigging port and sweet sherry out of brown paper-covered bottles. The only dry table wines around, I recalled, seemed to be Cawarra Claret (undated) and Quelltaler Hock. Denis started a wine and dine club and, in later years when the Tasmanian wine industry began to establish itself, founded Cooinda. Margaret reminded me that Denis had been one of six founding members of the Beefsteak and Burgundy Club, in Hobart, which was still going strong.

Denis died in 1995, and his son John inherited his father's twin passions of quality cars and wine. Cooinda was currently being managed by his son (Margaret's grandson) Matthew, with some help from his grandmother—who admitted to being eighty-seven, although wearing her years lightly. Having selected our wines—some sublime pinot noirs and riesling—Margaret took us into the house to look at family photographs and sample some of her legendary shortbread. As we left she pressed a gift pack of shortbread into my hand for Paddy Pearl (who I thought would be lucky to get it) and also a bundle of long, thin fire-lighting spills she had rolled from old newspapers. Most Tasmanians still have log fires, and I remember my father speaking of fire-lighting spills when he was recording his childhood memories on tape for a book on his life.[12]

I remarked to Ros as we drove away that this was vintage Tasmania. Call into a vineyard on impulse and find that it's like a rerun of 'This is Your Life'.

We arrived at Campania House at about 6 pm. Paddy Pearl, full of vitality as ever, met us at the door. It is a wonderfully elegant house in the Georgian style so it has generous windows and wood panelling. When Paddy bought it she found all the panelling had been painted over by previous owners and had to be taken down, section by section (by Paddy herself). She then trucked the panels to Launceston in batches to be stripped, sanded and oiled. (It takes about five coats to bring cedar back to its original condition.) When the panels arrived back in Campania, Paddy employed local unskilled and unemployed lads to complete the work. She was delighted that, later, they managed to get jobs with the skills they had acquired working for her.

I asked Paddy about the history of the house and she said its sandstone and cedar construction, in classical Georgian style, was begun by George Weston Gunning, of the 73rd Regiment, shortly after he arrived in Van Diemen's Land in 1810. The house has one of Tasmania's few sandstone

12 Tim Bowden, 1989, *The Way My Father Tells It: The Story of an Australian Life*, ABC Books, Sydney

cantilevered staircases, a drawing room, large library and a distinctive and intimate dining room. We asked Paddy to show us around the house before dinner. It has three levels, the formal bedrooms with open fires being on the first floor. There are more attic bedrooms on the upper level, with great views over the valley.

The house has been lovingly restored, and Paddy and Cyril's antique furniture from their Paddington house suits it perfectly. They lived in France for many years, and Paddy is a gifted and innovative cook as we were about to rediscover.

The only other guests were Sandy and Keith Wellington, who were celebrating their fifth wedding anniversary. Both had been married before but when they decided to wed had eloped to Tasmania from the mainland. They rang Paddy and asked if she did weddings. She did, but how many people would be there? Two! Paddy had to get a neighbour, Betty Ireson, in as a witness, and Betty joined us for dinner too, five years on. The Wellingtons had not been to Tasmania before their wedding, but were so enchanted with the place that they had moved from the central New South Wales coast to Burnie where they now live.

We felt honoured to share such a special occasion! After dry sherry and champagne in the drawing room, we moved to the dining room for a gourmet feast: thick borsch with smoked eel and beetroot savouries, followed by a whole salmon lightly baked (earlier in the afternoon and left to set), served on a slurry of home-made mayonnaise and topped with horse radish sauce. This was accompanied by a sensational cous cous and mixed vegetable compilation, and a local Meadowbank riesling so delicious that Ros and I immediately made plans to go to the vineyard the following day to buy some more. Then came a range of gourmet Tasmanian cheeses—cheddar, goat, brie and blue—topped off with fresh plums stewed in wine. When the Wellingtons produced a bottle of vintage 1989 French champagne to celebrate their wedding anniversary, it seemed churlish not to help drink it.

It rained heavily all night, but the walls of Campania House were so thick that we heard nothing. It is also possible we may have been anaesthetised, to some extent, by the excellent repast.

Somehow we found ourselves hungry enough the next morning to do justice to breakfast served by Paddy in her modern kitchen, choosing porridge and mouth-watering scrambled eggs with fresh herbs. I remarked to Ros that we could get used to this kind of life quite quickly. She said it was high time we got back on the road.

Having been born and bred in Hobart, it is very difficult for me to see the city with the eye of an outsider. But it always gives me an enormous surge of pleasure to drive over the foothills of the Meehan Range, heading west from Cambridge, and suddenly see the vista of the great, blue, sprawling bulk of Mt Wellington towering over the Derwent estuary with Hobart squeezed between its lower flanks and the harbour. Never mind about the north-south debate, it is a spectacular location for a capital city dominated, of course, by the mountain which at 1270 metres (over 4000 feet sounds higher to me) can be snow-capped at any time during nine months of every year and even occasionally on Christmas Day!

Mt Wellington not only dominates the city, but also its weather. It is like a monstrous weather-cock. No wonder weather is a perennial topic of conversation for Tasmanians. When the prevailing westerlies blow, the mountain can suddenly disappear. Hobartians know that the rain will hit the city ten minutes later and that they have time only to dash for shelter, or put up their umbrellas. Then, not long after, the sun will break through, often with a spectacular rainbow arcing from mountain to sea.

It was the harbour that prompted Captain David Collins to move the initial settlement at Risdon (chosen by Lieutenant John Bowen in 1803) to Hobart Town a year later. Hobart is one of the world's great natural harbours, although its mercantile significance has declined since the roll-on-roll-off ferries have favoured the shorter sea-link with Melbourne. As you drive over the high curve of the Hobart Bridge you can glance south down the Derwent estuary towards Storm Bay, knowing there is nothing beyond that but Antarctica.

I don't normally have to think about accommodation in Hobart, because I have a brother and sister living here. But this time we had Penelope and The Manor in tow and were planning to spend only a short time in Hobart before continuing our coastal journey to Cockle Creek—the furthest south it is possible to go by vehicle in Tasmania— so we needed a caravan park.

There are very few caravan parks available in Hobart. None at all in the city, and only one in the southern suburbs. We had booked well ahead to that caravan park in Sandy Bay, on the lower slopes of Mt Nelson, but no sooner had we booked in and made The Manor habitable than I read in the Hobart *Mercury* that this park would be closed later in the year by the Hobart City Council (which owned it) to be turned into a retirement village. The next available park to the south was at the town of Snug, thirty-six kilometres away! It seemed crazy, with tourist numbers picking up as they were, and I fired off a letter of protest to the *Mercury* about it. The letter was published—but my pathetic gesture was the equivalent of farting against thunder and I heard later that the park did close as planned.

Somehow Hobart has managed to preserve a great deal of its nineteenth century heritage, particularly at Salamanca Place on the waterfront where sandstone warehouses (now converted to art galleries, bookshops and restaurants) and historic hotels lie cheek by jowl in a straight line for several hundred metres. This area of Hobart, including Victoria and Constitution docks (where the Sydney Hobart yacht race finishes), has colourful wooden fishing boats moored within metres of floating fish and chip barges as well as upmarket fish eateries. Ros and I decided to meet up with my brother Nick Bowden, his wife Fran and youngest daughter Amelia, and my sister Lisa and husband Dave Roberts at Salamanca Place for an evening meal. Lisa and Fran chose a restaurant they said was reasonably priced, with good tucker. For some curious reason it was decked out in an African theme, bestrewn with Zulu shields and masks and large photographs of tigers and hippos. The menu featured some African dishes, but not to the exclusion of more conventional fare.

I was aware that Tasmania's tourism industry had roared into high gear, bringing with it welcome new jobs for Tasmanians and mainlanders alike. This was good news for the state's economy, but was putting strains on the service industry. The young woman who came to open our first bottle of wine seemed unsure of how to do it. As she fiddled with the folding corkscrew she said, shyly, that this was the first time she had ever opened a bottle of wine. The TAFE institutions and colleges of hospitality are clearly finding it difficult keeping up with the demand for trained staff.

'I'll show you how to do it,' I said gallantly.

After we had reprovisioned ourselves for the next leg of our travels, I suggested to Ros that we did something suitably touristy, not something I normally do in my home town: 'Let's drive up the mountain.'

I was born in 1937, only three years after the road to the top of Mt Wellington had been built as a Depression project initiated by the newly elected Labor premier AG Ogilvie. It became known as 'Ogilvie's Scar' and as a young boy I remember the finished road slashing across the forward slope of the mountain like an ugly wound, with great rock falls tumbling down from the blasting and construction.

The line of the road can only just be seen today from afar, as the vegetation has returned to mask Ogilvie's Scar. Its surface is now sealed, and the summit can be reached in less than an hour. On a good clear day the views to the north, east and south are incomparable—providing you can stay upright. I have never been to the summit of Mt Wellington without bracing myself against a howling gale. When I was about fifteen, a friend and I walked up the mountain in the late afternoon to camp in a public hut near the summit, in the hope of seeing the sunrise over Hobart. I don't think I have ever been so cold—even in Antarctica. There was a light covering of snow when we woke, shivering, in our sleeping bags on the raw, wooden floor of the hut. Outside a thick mist swirled miserably. We could hardly see twenty metres in front of us to find the track and retreat down the mountain.

Ros and I struck it lucky. It was clear and sunny, with some streaky, high cloud and even the wind wasn't too bad. From this vantage point you can see all the way to the east coast, including the unmistakable profile of Maria Island. Looking south, down towards the D'Entrecasteaux Channel, I was able to point out to Ros the northern tip of Bruny Island, where we planned to be the following night.

# seven

## Farthest South

We were bound for Adventure Bay, on the eastern side of Bruny Island. How could we resist such a name? The bay had enticed just about every early European adventurer you can think of, beginning with Abel Tasman in 1642, then a who's who of explorers, including Captain Tobias Furneaux (captain of *Adventure* on James Cook's second voyage), who named the bay after his ship in 1773. Matthew Flinders's first Australian landing was in the bay and the French explorer Bruni D'Entrecasteaux—twice in 1792, and in 1793—finished up having the island named after him, even if the Anglo-Celts of early twentieth century Tasmania couldn't cope with the French spelling and changed it to 'Bruny'. And let me not forget the other French explorer of south and south-east Australia, Nicolas Baudin, who called in to Adventure Bay for wood and water in 1802. The great Captain Cook himself popped in just before heading off to Hawaii and his death. Captain Bligh was practically addicted to the place, having arrived there first on James Cook's *Resolution* in 1777, then again in the ill-fated *Bounty* before the mutiny, and finally in 1810 after he had been deposed as governor of New South Wales by the rampaging Rum Corps. Let's face it, Bruny Island has an unbeatable pedigree in early explorers and, strangely (as noted in the *Lonely Planet*), tourism, although important to the island's economy, is still low key. Maybe we were going just in time.

Like Maria Island further up the east coast, Bruny is divided by a narrow, sandy isthmus. The northern half of the island, once thickly timbered, is now cleared for mixed farming. The bigger, southern half is more mountainous and forested and has a national park on its southern extremity although there are some farms as well, mostly on its western coast.

In my youth, the only way south from Hobart to Kingston was a narrow winding road following the coast, over Bonnet Hill (past the historic nineteenth century sandstone Shot Tower where hot lead was dropped down the interior of the tower into cold water at the base to make shotgun cartridges) and then on to the D'Entrecasteaux Channel towns of Snug, Kettering and Woodbridge. Now there is a fast road that climbs away from Hobart from upper Sandy Bay, over the hump of Mt Nelson, by-passes Kingston and feeds you straight on to the Channel Highway in about ten to fifteen minutes without indecent haste. The old way used to take at least half an hour to Kingston, longer if you got stuck behind a labouring truck on Bonnet Hill.

The vehicular and passenger ferry to Bruny Island leaves from Kettering, about forty-five kilometres from Hobart. Snug, Kettering and Woodbridge are fishing towns and used to be apple producing centres when Tasmania was known as the Apple Isle, before the Common Market in Europe stopped all that imperial mercantile favouritism. Penelope and The Manor joined the heavier trucks on the lower deck before sedans were driven up a ramp onto the top deck. The journey takes about fifteen to twenty minutes to the northern end of Bruny Island, leaving only a modest thirty-five kilometre drive south, across the isthmus, to Adventure Bay on the eastern, ocean side of the island—which is why all those early explorers chanced upon it.

Our journey had some poignant memories for Ros. Always an independent gel, at the age of fifteen Ros informed her mother that she and two girlfriends proposed to ride their bikes from Taroona, a southern suburb of Hobart, to Adventure Bay during a long weekend. They found the journey rather longer than they expected. Ros thinks now that they had no real idea of how far it was or how long it would take. So they hitched rides with trucks and with a tattooed bloke in a panel van (Ros said one of the tats was a heart next to the word 'mother' on his arm so they thought he must be harmless). In 1955, Tasmania—and perhaps Australia—seemed more innocent.

There were odd things about that journey. Somehow all the cooking utensils got left behind so they sustained themselves on dates and boiled tins of condensed milk over a fire to make caramel, which they ate straight from the can with a teaspoon. At Adventure Bay they found someone who let them sleep in a shed on their property. Some of the local lads began to hassle them but the three girls told them to bugger off and they did! Ros thinks now that the lads weren't used to a group of young girls telling them forcefully to go away. She can't remember the details of the trip home, but they didn't ride their bikes very much so probably they hitched again with an obliging truck driver. Ros's mother did insist that she ring her on the Sunday to say they were OK.

Adventure Bay has two caravan and camping grounds, and on a whim we chose the one right in the southern corner of the bay. We were glad we did. We hadn't booked ahead because we don't need a powered site, and that makes camping a more flexible option. To our great joy we were allotted a beach front location.

After getting The Manor up and sorted out, we wandered along to the Adventure Bay Caravan Park office to check out some walks or other activities. They recommended an excursion in a fast catamaran around Fluted Cape and down the south-east coast of Bruny Island but we would have had to book straight away for the next day. We passed on that and asked about walks. As it happened we were camped almost on the beginning of a coastal track around the southern shore of the bay to Grassy Point, near Penguin Island, named by Furneaux who had captured a curious yellow-crested penguin there. It was only a two-hour walk, which we could fit in before dinner, and what better way to spend the latter part of a sunny afternoon.

Penguin Island marks the southernmost point of Adventure Bay, and a dramatic change in the geology of the island. Just out of sight, to our right, were the sheer dolerite cliffs of Fluted Cape, best viewed from the sea. Adventure Bay was the birthplace of the whaling industry in southern Tasmania, and its pioneer was our old friend Jorgen Jorgenson, former Van Diemen's Land Company surveyor on the north-east coast and later (briefly) King of Iceland. The doughty Dane acted as mate and guide in the whaling vessel *Alexander* in 1804, and showed the captain where whales could be flensed on Grassy Point, at the end of our walk.

We had been told that we could see traces of some whaling cottages at Grassy Point built by another colourful master mariner and entrepreneur, James Kelly, in 1818. Three years before that, Kelly had circumnavigated the whole of Tasmania in a small five-oared whaleboat, discovering in the process major west coast features like Port Davey, Port Macquarie and the Gordon River (named after the man who lent him the lifeboat). Ros and I could clearly make out the oblong foundations where Kelly's stone cottages had been, sited among the tussocks and sea-worn stones on the point. Seeing them made our walk even more rewarding. I discovered later that this site had been examined recently by archaeologists, which is why the foundations were so evident.

By the way, the toilet block at the caravan park was festooned with huge whale bones, recovered locally. The whalers hunted the so called 'right' whales and took mothers, calves and bulls indiscriminately. It is estimated that the population of some 100 000 or more right whales was so decimated that today there are only 3000—but the population is slowly recovering.

On the way back along the coastal track I was walking in front and telling Ros a fascinating story that she told me later she had heard many times before, when I heard a sudden gasp and a sickening *thump*. I looked around to see that Ros had inexplicably thrown herself full length on the track behind me. She had tripped on a root—probably bored into carelessness by my interminable anecdote—and bitten the dust. It could have been much worse. Her face just missed a jagged rock although she grazed her cheek and nose on its side. I helped her to her feet and found that she also had a bleeding hand, skinned knee and a raft of yet-to-emerge bruises. Ros made light of all this—she is more stoic than her partner—and managed to walk back to camp unaided. (We are but a hair's breadth from unexpected disaster in this life.)

Back at camp we saw the couple who run the caravan park walking their dog at 4.30 pm, at a time when you would expect them to be run off their feet with customers seeking sanctuary. Apart from having their priorities right, we realised that they must time their walk according to the ferry timetable. No one can book in until they drive from the ferry point to Adventure Bay and the couple know the timetable by heart!

With Tasmania's long twilight, the sun didn't set until nearly 8 pm and we could see how the caravan park is ideally situated, with magnificent views of the bay. But I never cease to be amazed at certain breeds of caravan travellers who seem unimpressed by their natural surroundings. I could not imagine, on a night like we had in such a magic place, why anyone would sit inside a van watching their favourite soapie on the telly—but that is what many of our fellow campers were doing.

**Travel Diary Saturday 15 March**

An unexpectedly mild night—perhaps because we are so close to the water—and a fine sunny morning. We decided to drive to a remote eatery, the Hothouse Café, which commanded sweeping views of the isthmus, and was famous for excellent coffee, then return to Adventure Bay to see the eclectic collection displayed in the privately owned Bligh Museum which was only open between 10 am and 3 pm daily. The plan was then to drive to the Cape Bruny Light Station on the southern tip of the island, which first operated in 1838.

Plans are made to be changed and our first glitch was to find the Hothouse Café shut. We were in such desperate need of a coffee that we drove in to find out why. Cheeky really, but the proprietor was accommodating, even though she was supervising preparations for a big wedding later in the day—the reason for the closed sign at the bottom of their drive. We promised to have our caffeine injection quickly and then go. She asked us what we were doing and whether we were going on Robert Pennicott's catamaran tour of Fluted Cape and the southern coastline.

She said Robert took his boat into amazing places. Although she had been running the Hothouse Café for twenty years she had not seen around the corner from Penguin Island—where we had been the day before—until one of her kids insisted she take the trip. As *The Albatross* had surged around the point, revealing Fluted Cape from the vantage point of the sea, she said, 'Fuck! This is amazing'. Inspired by her candour we decided to change our plans. It was 10.15 am and the boat left at 11 am. We dashed back to the caravan park and managed to get seats literally at the eleventh hour.

Robert Pennicott, the owner/skipper, was an engaging young bloke, an ex-fisherman who knew every rock on the southern Bruny coast because he used to try to set his pots in gulches closer to shore than any other fishermen would dare. We paused briefly in the bay beside our caravan park, where Robert pointed out the blue gums near the shore. They did not flower every year but had done so the previous year and after a few days, according to our skipper, the flowers produced a nectar that was alcoholic. The trees were besieged by about eighty yellow-tailed black cockatoos which supped heavily from the nectar and then proceeded to disgrace themselves by behaving in a larrikin and abandoned manner, giving new meaning, said Robert, to the expression 'pissed as a parrot'.

Before we left the shelter of the bay Robert addressed the anticipated passenger paranoia about seasickness, and distributed some herbal pills based on ginger. With lashings of open air and calm seas, I would have thought seasickness unlikely. Yet at least seventy-five per cent of those on board took the pills. The placebo effect certainly worked because only two young Japanese girls felt queasy, but not enough to be sick.

The dolerite cliffs of Fluted Cape are 276 metres high and drop vertically into the sea. They were almost impossible to photograph because Robert took *The Albatross* so close to their base that not even a wide angle lens would have helped. Our skipper handled the catamaran as though it was an extension of his arm, steering principally with his port and starboard engines and suddenly dashing through an opening so narrow between a rocky pinnacle and the sheer rock cliffs that you would think it impossible to negotiate. He also pointed out a tunnel into the rock face (mercifully too narrow for us) which turned sharply and came out again about 200 metres further along the cliff. One of his party tricks, when he was a fisherman, was to get an unsuspecting passenger and gun his dinghy straight into the tunnel, and then swing around the hidden corner. He said one particularly voluble foreign student didn't talk for some hours after that experience.

We saw sea eagles, shearwaters, gannets, Antarctic gulls and shags. Robert would head into a spectacular gulch and then slowly swing *The Albatross* around so that both port and starboard passengers could photograph the scenery. He didn't need a PA system as his voice cut through engine and sea noise. How he keeps it up six days a week for three hours a day (sometimes twice a day) can only be imagined. He was an excellent guide, funny, knowledgeable —obviously a conservationist (rare for a fisherman)—and the whole trip was a class act.

The farthest south you can go on this part of the coast is Friar Rocks, one of which has a hole right through its middle. The area is home to thousands of fur seals, which are a different species from the Antarctic variety, which can be unfriendly and stroppy to tourists particularly in the breeding season. Robert said that abalone divers dived among the fur seals quite happily. The only problem was the possibility of being mistaken for a seal and eaten by giant white pointer sharks, which regularly snack on these graceful mammals. A bonus for us visitors was soft sunlight on the basking fur seals and rocky gulches in the dolerite rock, splashed with orange lichen above the high tide level.

On the way back to Adventure Bay we surfed with bottle-nosed dolphins, swimming right beside our boat. Robert said they normally put on a special show when he stopped *The Albatross*, but seemed preoccupied that day. He thought there might be killer whales about, which would explain why they were on the move. He told us of one occasion when pods of killer whales formed a barrier and baled up a whole lot of dolphins in Adventure Bay, then took turns to dash in and feed on them.

(A tourist who obviously hadn't had a great deal to do with boats told Ros of a significant revelation: 'I've discovered that if you put your feet apart it's easier to balance.')

On the return trip I asked Robert a bit about his background. He was a professional fisherman by the age of twelve. He lived at Tinderbox, near the D'Entrecasteaux Channel, and his father was a fisherman. At the age of eleven he used to 'borrow' his father's dinghy and nets and catch fish to sell from door to door. His father got sick of the damage to both boat and nets and told him he would have to pay his way—and he would charge him $5000 dollars for use of the equipment for a year.

Robert made $12 000 by catching crayfish and fish and selling them, door to door, in Kingston and Margate—quite illegally of course. He left the fishing business for a while to work in a credit union, went back to fishing, and then ran a fast food business. He said fishing was fun for three months of the year but fairly boring for the rest, so he decided to go into tourism with his own purpose-built boat for eight months of the year. Good luck to him, and his stamina. He had an offsider to help with the passengers, but the virtuoso performance by the skipper made for one of the best value tourist trips I have ever experienced. And we nearly didn't go! We paid $14 deposit to the caravan park to book but still owed him the balance of $70 per head. As we docked at the Adventure Bay jetty he asked would we mind going along to the local store where there was also a booking office, and pay there. When we did so about two hours later Robert happened to be there and I asked him if he'd ever been let down. It turned out he'd only ever been dudded by two couples the whole time he had been doing his trips. Perhaps only in Tasmania would you find a tourist operator who put his trust in the honour system.

Our plans changed again after Ros went to the obliging caravan park owners and asked if we could leave The Manor in the car park while we drove to Cape Bruny to see the lighthouse. The woman there said, 'Why do that? You've seen it all on Robert's trip anyway.' We decided to get away early the next day to leave time to have a quick tour around North Bruny before heading for the ferry and our foray to the farthest south you can drive in Australia—Cockle Creek.

Away by 8.15 am, which was a smart pack up for us. The routine is so familiar that we don't even have to speak to each other, an added bonus in the early morning. This time, on reaching the isthmus, we parked and I climbed up to the Truganini Memorial and lookout, high on the ridge of the connecting sand bank between the north and south of the island. (Ros was still feeling a bit stiff and sore and decided not to tackle several hundred steps to the vantage point.) Truganini—believed to be the last full-blooded Tasmanian Aboriginal—came from Bruny Island and was a daughter of Mangana, chief of the Bruny Island tribe. She died in 1876 aged about sixty-four, after a remarkable life that saw her entire race decimated by disease and murder perpetrated by European settlers. She had a rough start in life. While still a child her mother was stabbed to death by a white man, her uncle shot by a soldier, and her sister abducted by sealers. As a young woman, returning to Bruny Island from the mainland of Tasmania, she saw her two companions, including her intended husband, attacked and drowned by two white men.

She was quite small in stature and described as vivacious and intelligent. When the 'Great Conciliator', George Augustus Robinson, began his state-wide quest to contact all surviving Aboriginal people in 1835, she joined his party as an interpreter. Robinson's aim was to remove all remaining Tasmanian Aborigines to Flinders Island to save them from European guns. There were then only about 100 left. Truganini went to Flinders Island as well, and eventually returned to Oyster Cove—in sight of her birthplace, Bruny Island—with the last sixteen surviving Aborigines in 1856.

Truganini was aware that Aboriginal bodies had been stolen and dismembered as scientific curiosities (including that of her husband William Lanne) and was haunted by the fear that her body would be similarly mutilated after death in the 'interests' of science. Despite her known wishes, her skeleton was displayed in a glass case in the Tasmanian Museum and Art Gallery from 1904 to 1947. I remembered seeing it there when I was a young boy, and that it gave me nightmares. But in 1976 her remains were cremated and the ashes spread on the waters of the D'Entrecasteaux Channel.

The climb to her memorial and lookout was well worth the effort, with panoramic views over the isthmus on the eastern and western sides. I could see right down to Adventure Bay and Fluted Cape, and even up the eastern coast of North Bruny. We had time before meeting the ferry to run up to the northernmost tip of the island, Dennes Point. This is where Bruny Island is closest to the Tasmanian mainland, across a short strait to Tinderbox (where the eleven-year-old Robert Pennicott used to pinch his father's dinghy and nets). When Ros and her two friends took their bicycles down to Adventure Bay in the mid 1950s, the ferry used to operate from Tinderbox to Dennes Point.

Unfortunately this service had ceased by the time I became motoring editor of the *Saturday Evening Mercury* in Hobart at the ripe age of nineteen. Back in the 1950s, going for a drive on Sunday afternoon was all the rage and I thought it would be a great idea to write a series of articles about where the good burghers of Hobart might go in their Holdens and Morris Oxfords. In one article I sent them down to Bruny Island, and across to Dennes Point on the by then nonexistent ferry. A few readers—more than a few actually—wrote to tell me of my error and I imagined a queue of indignant Sunday travellers waiting for the ferry that never came. In reality I doubt if I had that much influence!

We found it had been raining on the north of the island and the narrow dirt roads were greasy and tricky. After gazing across the strait to Tinderbox, we headed down the west coast towards the ferry departure point. On the way we passed a turnoff to Barnes Bay, which again triggered old memories. Tucked away in a northern inlet, Barnes Bay has perhaps the most sheltered anchorage for yachts in southern Tasmania. As it is within a day's sailing, or motoring, from Hobart, it was and doubtless still is a popular overnight stopover for yachties. It was so in my father's era, and indeed before that. One of Father's contemporaries was Guy Webster, whose own father was a retired admiral— and an impatient, testy one at that, particularly when skippering his own yacht. On one occasion Admiral Webster (Ret.) was manoeuvring into Barnes Bay to spend the night. He didn't have an engine, so things were a bit tense. His son Guy was waiting at the bow ready to drop the anchor.

As my father tells the story the moment was judged and the Admiral shouted, 'Let her go!' Nothing happened, so the old boy shouted again, more urgently, 'Guy, drop the bloody anchor.' Still nothing. By this stage the yacht was in danger of running aground, and he was relieved to hear the splash and rattle of chain and then silence. But the yacht still had forward motion. The Admiral boomed out yet again, 'Guy, is the anchor overboard?'

The immortal reply came back from the foredeck: 'Yes Father—over, but unattached!'

I made an occasional voyage to Barnes Bay myself on a small yacht, *Pirate*, owned by a former school friend, Brian Hull. It has to be admitted that a fair amount of serious drinking took place in Barnes Bay. It was an era before throwing beer bottles over the side became a no-no, and it's a wonder the entire bay wasn't filled up with them. It was the fashion of the day to have your own pewter beer mug—conveniently slung around your neck with a lanyard, considered convenient for barbecues. One night on *Pirate* I was about to sup an ale from my pewter mug when a very alarming thing happened. As I lifted it to my lips my arm was frozen, with the longed-for Cascade beer twenty centimetres from my lips. I could not lift it any further. I furtively strained at it, not wishing to attract attention to my dilemma. Could this be the onset of a previously unknown condition, drinker's paralysis? As I fought to get at my beer, the others in the cabin of *Pirate* hurled themselves about in helpless mirth. I thought this was unkind in view of my predicament until I looked down and saw the lanyard on the handle of my beer mug had looped itself around the handle of a drawer under the bunk bed I was sitting on.

Only recently a friend of my brother Philip, Tim Payne, wrote to me to check out a memory he had of me in Barnes Bay. His account (reproduced here by his gracious permission) conveys the essential elements of a night in Barnes Bay in 1958.[1] He was but a lad of fourteen at the time and sober.

The Barnes Bay picnic race was indeed a very festive occasion. At night, after the 'race', a bonfire was lit on the shore, and much drinking and singing of disgusting songs took place late into the night, much to my fascination and amusement. I was intrigued that although many of the singers were so pissed they could hardly stand, their renditions of the verses were perfect.

Deep into the night a sailor struggled to get his dinghy into the water and I helped him. Others staggered down to the shore and asked for a lift. The dinghy was impossibly full by the time the outboard was started, and the noise of that attracted others who waded out and hopped in. That wasn't hard because the gunwale was only millimetres above the water.

The drunken sailor gunned the outboard. Normally this sat the stern of a dinghy further in the water and set the bow up on a bit of a bow wave. In this case, the surge of power made absolutely no difference to the dinghy's position in the water, and not a lot to its speed. As the dinghy hit the first wavelet the men forward swore and stood up as their arses got wet. This reduced whatever stability she had and the dinghy took several tiny waves aboard. I could see it subside into the depths from the light of the bonfire. The outboard motor rendered a peculiarly hollow note as it sank; it didn't die easily. Fortunately no one was at

1  Tim Payne, 2004, *Hello Myrtle: The Meandering Maunderings of a Premature Baby Boomer*, Artemis Publishing Consultants, Hobart

risk of drowning, they could stand up with heads just out of the water at the point the boat sank, although, despite being buoyed by the water, some were so pissed they had to be helped to land, where they lay and swore.

The next morning I rowed our dinghy around the assembled fleet, eerily quiet, and came adjacent to a vessel to find Tim Bowden imperiously peeing over the stern, resplendent in a top hat—nothing else. I said, 'Hello, Tim, good morning' in a sonorous tone. He made a valiant effort to focus on who it was, to no avail. He piddled for an age, turned around, let go of the back stay and stumbled out of sight into the cockpit, shattering his aura of aristocratic composure. He must have found it comfortable there. I paused in my rowing, but he made no move to regain his feet.

Tim Payne claims that I denied all knowledge of this when he mentioned it to me some years ago. I have no memory of that denial, nor of the events he described! Let me simply say that it accorded with the general goings on at Barnes Bay in those days.

Back on the mainland (I mean Tasmania) we turned right from the Channel Highway and climbed over a modest mountain range to link up with the main highway again just below the town of Cygnet. The intrusion of the Huon River estuary meant we had to drive in a big loop via Huonville to cross the Huon River at the first available bridge, then head south again. We were deeply into apple orchard country and stopped at one of the many roadside stalls to buy some new season's fruit. The apples were disappointing, small and sour because of the drought. The trees were bearing fruit more the size of plums or apricots than standard apples.

The weather was overcast and cold—perhaps because we were heading towards Antarctica. We turned down to the beach at Southport for a picnic lunch, but it was a hurried affair. We noted that the public toilets were closed because of a lack of water to flush them. (Tasmanians aren't used to being short of water.) Beyond Southport the roads are unsealed and of indifferent quality, but that did not seem to deter the more intrepid of the caravan brigade who were also heading for Cockle Creek. Walkers who have survived the Southwest Track (some from as far away as Strathgordon near Lake Pedder, or from the beach at Cox's Bight, flown there by light aircraft from Hobart) also finish up at Cockle Creek and can take Tassie Link buses, which call in three times a week, back to Hobart for $50.

At first we found the camping sites to the north of Cockle Bay disappointing, as they were littered with rusting caravans (used as fishing shacks) and a sprinkling of temporary visitors. But as soon as we drove over the creaking wooden bridge across Cockle Creek into the Southwest National Park the camping sites were much more attractive. In fact we scored some waterfront real estate that eclipsed our beachside site at Adventure Bay. We quickly established camp and wandered along the beach as the setting sun broke through the clouds and sent golden light onto the beach and the dark wooded promontories we could see on the other side of Recherche Bay.

After a cold but fine night we decided to walk to South Cape Bay, said to be a four-hour return journey. Ros had some misgivings, still being a bit stiff and sore after her crash onto the track at Adventure Bay. (She made some curried egg sandwiches, cleverly undercooking the eggs slightly to make them moist.) When we saw the Parks and Wildlife noticeboard at the beginning of the walk, it revealed that our walk was a fifteen kilometre round trip. Despite that Ros decided to give it a go, although we both agreed that if we turned back early it would not be a personal disgrace. The track, rather stony at first, wound through an open forest with an understorey of banksias, tea trees of various varieties and heath plants of the Epacridacie family (according to Ros). We couldn't resist photographing the bright purple berries on some *Dianella* bushes.

The country changed dramatically when it moved from dolerite to sandstone, with poorer scrub due to lack of nutrients, again according to Ros. After an hour we reached the Blowhole Plain. This lived up to its name with a stiff breeze which blew us along the parallel boards on the track thoughtfully constructed over the marshy button-grass bogs, which would have been very heavy going without them. The sky began to cloud over, the wind increased and it was getting cooler by the minute. We made an executive decision to turn back. As we did so a couple of *real* hikers hove into view with large backpacks. They were a German couple who had not only walked all of the Southwest Track but had started from Scotts Peak, at Lake Pedder, adding about sixty kilometres to the journey. I was curious about how much weight they were carrying—certainly less at the end of their trip than at the beginning. In my early bush-walking days, a fifty pound pack was considered fairly heavy, so I asked the German bloke if he had started out with eighty kilos! He burst out laughing and I realised I had done my sums on the conversion from imperial to metric the wrong way around. He's probably still dining out on the story.

Ros's knees were sore. God knows what damage she had done to them at Adventure Bay. Had it been my knees I would have probably called for an ambulance but she is made of sterner stuff. We had our sandwiches and fruit sitting on a large log accompanied by more flying nasties than I remembered from when I bushwalked in Tasmania forty years ago. Bumble bees recently imported to assist the pollination of certain fruit and vegetable crops have adapted happily to the bush and can now be found all over the island. European wasps arrived by accident somehow, as if we didn't have enough stinging insects already with our home-grown March flies and our own wasps—not to mention the ferocious and free ranging jack jumper and inchman ants. I saw an inchman wandering towards Ros on our lunch log, and despatched it in case it bit her.

We began to amble back the way we had come. Just as we reached the noticeboard at the beginning of the track a young man, I guess about nineteen, with a surfboard under his arm and dressed in shorts, T-shirt and—so help me God—thongs, was running towards us at a half trot. He didn't even have a day pack or a water bottle. Where was he going? To a famous break at South Cape, he told us, as he was heading down for a quick surf. At the rate he was travelling he'd probably do the round trip in just under three hours, plus a couple for surfing. I think this curious behaviour is something to do with being young! It made us feel like a couple of geriatric old crocks.

Our truncated walk gave us extra time in the afternoon to drive Penelope up the coast to where we had seen a sign indicating the spot where the formidably named Admiral Antoine Raymond de Bruni D'Entrecasteaux had watered his ships during his second visit in 1793. He first discovered and named Recherche Bay (after one of his ships) the year before when he landed on the north-east peninsula of the bay and established and planted a garden of vegetables and fruit trees which he hoped would provide fresh produce for later visits. The causes of scurvy were unknown in the eighteenth century, but fresh food was known to help. (D'Entrecasteaux himself died of scurvy only months after leaving the shores of Australia in 1793.)

The admiral had been sent to the antipodes to search for another French explorer, Jean-Françoise de Galaup La Perouse, who disappeared after leaving Botany Bay in March 1788. Battered by the Roaring Forties, D'Entrecasteaux's expedition made their landfall at Recherche Bay where the exhausted sailors found excellent fresh water, plenty of fish and game. It must have seemed like paradise for the five weeks they rested there, and the scientists on board rejoiced in collecting unknown animals and birds and 100 new botanical species. They didn't have any contact with Tasmanian Aborigines on that first visit, although they knew there were people about.

Historians and heritage enthusiasts were excited in January 2003 when bush walkers Bob Graham and Helen Gee went searching for traces of D'Entrecasteaux's garden amongst the thick cutting grass and scrub on the north-east peninsula of Recherche Bay, and found parts of the line of stones that the original gardener, M de la Haie, had used to mark out his plot, dimensions of which were recorded in the expedition's journal. The find was later authenticated by Anne Bickford, a Sydney specialist in colonial archaeology, and Emeritus Professor John Mulvaney. The *Sydney Morning Herald* of 25 March 2003 carried the following description:

It was laid out with precision in a very straight line, as you might expect of naval fellows. The dimensions are right within a few centimetres. It has two plinth stones in the centre, where water barrels may have been. It is a carefully man-made feature, with soil shovelled in to give depth. It coincides with the mark on the map. One couldn't say more without some excavation.[2]

Remains of a forge and a charcoal pit may be nearby, and the French also set up an astronomical and terrestrial observatory in the area to conduct geophysical experiments.

While the Tasmanian Heritage Act has been invoked by interested parties, including the Recherche Bay Protection Group, at the time of writing, the outlook for the area is uncertain. The Heritage Council of Tasmania recommended to Ken Bacon, Minister for Tourism, Parks and Heritage (no relation to the former Premier Jim Bacon), in November 2003 that he declare a two year moratorium on activities which might diminish the heritage significance of the north-east peninsula of Recherche Bay. Consultation, as they say, was still continuing and no decision had been made on a moratorium by mid 2004. Greg Hogg, of the Recherche Bay Protection Group, noted gloomily in a report in June 2004 that even if the minister adopted the two year moratorium suggestion to prevent activities which might 'diminish heritage significance', this might still permit some clear-felling of forests in the area by private landholders.

The Tasmanian Labor government plays hardball on its logging and woodchipping policies and did so even under

---

2  Andrew Darby, 25 March 2003, 'A French Connection', *Sydney Morning Herald*

the premiership of the late Jim Bacon. His deputy premier (and hard man on forestry) was Paul Lennon and in February 2004, when Jim Bacon unexpectedly resigned as premier after having been diagnosed with lung cancer, Lennon took over as premier. Heritage issues are unlikely to carry much weight in the current political climate, despite some outspoken advocacy by powerful conservationists like the Greens' Senator Bob Brown, and Emeritus Professor Mulvaney, who said unequivocally: 'This is a complex cultural landscape. Its destruction in the interests of short-term wood-chipping would represent vandalism of significant Australian cultural heritage.'

I had heard talk about clear-felling, but after making some inquiries it seemed that the owners did not intend to clear-fell timber on the north-east peninsula, but take out trees selectively. The area has been logged before, several times, as far back as the 1870s. Now thickly timbered and covered in dense scrub, the landscape is not as D'Entrecasteaux's expedition saw it. Then it was open savannah grassland, with occasional eucalypts dotted around, kept so by an Aboriginal firing regime. Today the land owners, according to my informant in the Heritage Council of Tasmania, are prepared to allow a 'curtilage zone'—heritage-speak for appropriate screening around a significant site—for 100 metres all around the waterfront and around any sites discovered in the course of logging.

On the face of it, this does not seem unreasonable. But the problem is getting agreement on an access road that has to cross both Parks and Wildlife territory and Crown land. Local property holders—mostly owners of weekenders—are objecting to any access road at all. At the time of writing no compromises had been reached.

Ros and I drove north from Cockle Creek to where a Parks and Wildlife sign indicated a small bay where D'Entrecasteaux's party are said to have watered their ships on their return to Recherche Bay in the summer of 1793. The French were curious about the indigenous people but failed to meet any on their first visit, and only made a brief contact in the last hours of their second visit. Reading a translation of D'Entrecasteaux's diary, I was struck by the contrast between their gentle initial contact with the Tasmanian Aborigines and the later conflict first with sealers and whalers and then the British settlers in Tasmania from 1803. The first Aborigines seen were encountered by the botanist, M La Ballardière, and the gardener, M de la Haie:

> Their first interview with them established such confidence that it was followed by several others, all equally friendly and of the kind to give the most favourable idea of the inhabitants of this country. We regretted not having made their acquaintance until shortly before the end of our stay. Had we been able to prolong our stay in part, it would probably have been possible for us to gain very interesting information on the way of living of these people that are so close to nature and whose candour and kindness contrasts so strongly with the vices of civilisation.[3]

Dare one wonder how things might have been for the first Tasmanians if the colonisers had been French?

For our last night at Cockle Creek, and our farthest south, we took the last of the firewood we had bought for

---

3 LA Triebel and JC Batt, undated (circa 1950), *French Explorers of Australia*, LG Shea, Government Printer

$5 on the north-east coast for a camp fire and a celebration dinner of grilled scotch fillet, Tasmanian pink-eye potatoes, carrots and snow peas. It seemed appropriate to break out a bottle of halfway decent red from Penelope's dwindling cellar to toast the occasion. It was strangely warm—which in Tasmania can mean rain is coming—and we sat out in the open watching a subtle sunset reflect a pink sky on the calm waters of the bay.

We brought our Coleman pressure lamp with us for outside camping but we didn't need it because of Tasmania's daylight saving, and the extra long twilight so far south. Ros reminded me of the contrast in the Kimberley, where it can be dark at 4.30 pm in the afternoon in the dry season, particularly near the Northern Territory border. In Tasmania it doesn't really get dark until after 9 pm in high summer.

**Travel Diary Tuesday 18 March**

The weather forecast is not all that flash. A westerly change, then showers for the next three days and even snow showers on Mt Wellington! We packed up early in case the rain came, but it didn't. We are heading for Hastings, where there is a thermal pool and limestone caves that I remember visiting as a boy. We travelled first on a dirt road, occasionally coming upon great swathes of raw earth where the woodchippers have clear-felled every standing stick. We stopped so that Ros could take a photograph of this unlovely devastation, which was unfortunate. We heard a roar in the distance, and a timber jinker (without a load), travelling far too fast for the conditions, skidded round the bend in front of us and nearly took us out. It was a close run thing. Could he have known we were photographing the utter desolation that he and his ilk combine to produce?

The gravel road north from Cockle Creek passes through the hamlets of Ida Bay and Lune River before taking a ninety degree turn to the east towards the former timber and logging port of Hastings. It rejoins the main highway a few kilometres north of Southport. We turned left and headed to the Hastings Caves and thermal pool. A smart new visitors' centre has been built near the pool, which was only a few kilometres from the turnoff, and we arrived shortly before it opened at 10 am. The morning was crisp and faintly autumnal, but I was determined to have a swim in the waters warmed by unseen geothermic forces deep beneath our feet.

When I was last here more than half a century ago, the swimming was fairly rudimentary, with startlingly blue water bubbling up from smooth stones on the floor of the thermal pool. Now there were showers and changing rooms, proper toilets, and polite requests to shower before entering the pool. Our genial pool attendant (and later cave guide), Roger, told me that things had to change because of the hordes of tourists using the pool. Some people began to get ear and eye infections from the supposedly healing mineral springs! For some strange reason the management had painted the side walls of the pool a rather dingy brown, which detracted from the brilliant blue of the remembered old pool. The showers were welcome after two days of bush camping at Cockle Creek, but the tepid waters, steady at 28°C, didn't seem to be all *that* warm on a brisk morning.

We drove further west to the entrance of the main limestone cave, actually called the Newdegate Cave, but the complex stubbornly retains the popular sobriquet of 'the Hastings Caves'. The ubiquitous Roger appeared to shepherd the gaggle of early morning visitors along a board walk through the forest, strewn with the giant rotting stumps of trees logged early last century, and up to the locked gate to the Newdegate cave. (Sir Francis Newdegate was once a governor of Tasmania.) The caves were discovered by timber workers in 1917 and were about to be mined for limestone until the distinguished Hobart photographer, JW Beattie, stopped that by mounting a personal campaign to save them through his beautifully composed sepia images. The caves were first opened to the public in 1939.

Ros isn't particularly entranced with limestone caves, but admitted that the Newdegate Cave had its moments. The Hastings Cave complex is formed from dolerite with limestone intrusions. The harsh, in-your-face lighting that I remembered as a boy has been replaced by more subtle illumination to reveal the stalactites, stalagmites and great naturally sculptured features which are no longer trivialised by names like 'the bridal gown' or the 'enchanted castle'. Roger was a good, informative host as we traipsed around the wet concrete paths and iron walkways in a chilly 9°C. One commonsense-challenged tourist said no one had told her she needed sneakers, and she slopped around pathetically in high-heeled sandals whining constantly about her cold toes. (I would have liked to await my moment and push her over a precipice into total darkness when no one was looking so we never saw, nor heard, her again.) How is it that guides like Roger maintain such a level of enthusiasm for something they do three and sometimes four times a day for years?

Returning to the main highway we continued north through Dover to Geeveston, and turned inland again heading west towards the Hartz Mountains and a new tourist attraction, Forestry Tasmania's Tahune Airwalk, where visitors can walk on elevated steel walkways over the forest canopy beside the Huon River. The complex is only twenty-two kilometres from Geeveston on recently up-graded forestry roads. In fact we were in forestry territory, with the usual signs telling us that the thick bush on either side of the road had been regenerated from clear-felling twenty or more years before. Normally the ravages of new clear-felling are shielded from the eyes of visitors, but, due to a misjudgment by a private contractor, the ghastly scars and raw red earth of a recent environmental assault were visible beside the road which brings thousands of tourists each year to Forestry Tasmania's very own showpiece. It looked like the aftermath of a B52 pattern bombing raid in Vietnam. Ros, unsportingly, took a photograph of it. The normal practice is to leave a screen of trees between clear-felling and any nearby roads or vantage points to mask the extent of the awfulness from the travelling public. In this case it hadn't been done.

We lunched at a picnic ground near the Arve River, where orange-striped European wasps took a close interest in our food. There was a danger these cheeky beggars might ride a forkful of cold meat and salad into our mouths if we weren't careful.

Although we had made inquiries at the Forest and Heritage Centre at Geeveston we weren't sure whether we would be able to camp at the Tahune Forest Airwalk site. There were some motor homes in the rather cramped car park, but it didn't seem an attractive option. I went to the visitors' centre and happened to meet an obliging young temporary staffer, Alex, who directed us to an excellent camping spot right beside the Huon River, within reason-able walking distance of the all-important toilet block. He also offered to give us a conducted tour of the Airwalk and its surrounds.

The manager at the visitors' centre didn't seem too keen about this, particularly when he found out I was a journalist and travel writer. Instead he nominated another member of his staff, Rhiannon, a young woman whom Alex had told us was the best qualified person on site: she had a Bachelor of Science degree with a Masters in botany.

The Airwalk itself is absolutely stunning with some 600 metres of horizontal steel catwalks suspended twenty metres above the forest floor. You walk, perhaps disconcertingly for those prone to vertigo, on see-through metal mesh. I saw some visitors staring fixedly ahead as they gingerly negotiated the slightly swaying walkways. Kids didn't seem to mind and dashed happily along the suspended catwalks, whooping with joy. You can gaze down at the forest canopy below, identifying the crowns of rain forest trees like myrtle and sassafras. Its crowning (as it were) glory is a twenty-four metre cantilevered section thrusting out to the south, towards Mt Picton. The viewing platform on the end bounces up and down as walkers (and fearless junior persons) move along the braced walkway to it. There you have an unobstructed view of the Huon River, its dark tea-coloured waters bisecting the forest below. On a clear day (which we had) you can't quite see forever, but you can pick up swathes of recently clear-felled coupes on the flanks of the distant hills. At least the showpiece Tahune Forest immediately around the Airwalk is spared that indignity.

I asked Rhiannon about forestry practices that so many people found abhorrent. She said that Forestry Tasmania liked to have plantations of softwoods and eucalypts 'farmed' close to developed areas. In the bush, the problem was with the composition of Tasmania's mixed forests. Apparently it is quite unusual to have eucalypts as part of a rain forest. She described them as 'wet' eucalypts with a rain forest understorey.

I wondered why you could not just take the eucalypts out, and leave the rain forest. The problem with that, said Rhiannon, was that if the loggers cut the big stringy barks and swamp gums, they broke the canopy of rain forest below as they fell, not only damaging the eucalypts being harvested but allowing sunlight into the rain forest.

The forestry line was that by clear-felling they got their saw logs and pulp logs in one operation, and then either allowed the forest to regenerate itself or encouraged the regrowth of the commercial timber they really want—the eucalypts—by burning and seeding (from the air or on the ground) with seed collected from the surrounding forest.

I thought it unfair to push her too hard on some questions that sprang to mind about this—and in any case she had an appointment that could not be avoided, and left us to continue the enjoyment of the Airwalk by ourselves.

Ros and I had seen a similarly constructed forest air-walk near Walpole, in the south-west of Western Australia, among the tingle trees in the 'Valley of the Giants'. These old trees were fifty metres tall, with very thick trunks, and before 1988 were being loved to death. Twenty years ago no trip to the south-west was complete without a photograph of your car parked inside the burnt-out interior of a par-ticularly massive tingle tree. The rubbing of thousands of human hands had actually polished the bark of some trees, and vital layers of humus around their roots had been trampled away by visitors' feet. The answer was a suspended treetop walk, completed in 1997, which won a prize for design in the Royal Institute of Architects national awards for design excellence in that year.

The obvious question to be asked about the siting of Forestry Tasmania's equally impressive airwalk was why not have it in Tasmania's own 'Valley of the Giants' in the Styx Valley, even closer to Hobart, and near the Mt Field National Park where the world's tallest flowering hardwoods are to be found. There the magnificent *Eucalyptus regnans*, many of them more than 400 years old, rise over ninety metres above the forest floor. Like all tall trees they are difficult to see from ground level. How magnificent it would have been had Forestry Tasmania built their airwalk there! The myrtle and sassafras under the Tahune Airwalk are piddling by comparison, and even the tallest eucalypts are pygmies compared with the colossi of the Styx. Organisations like the Wilderness Society argue that the long term tourist benefits of having such a facility in the Styx Valley would have a far greater economic benefit into the future.

The answer to the question lies in the determination of Forestry Tasmania to allow its favoured forest industry development company, Gunns, to clear-fell and cable-log most of the remaining thirteen per cent of old growth forest in the Styx (less than ten square kilometres has been set aside in reserves) during the next few years, primarily for wood-chipping. Paradoxically, these majestic forest giants are too old—and too big—to make commercially viable saw logs. How this short-sighted historical folly could and can be allowed to happen beggars comprehension. Ros and I planned to visit the Styx Valley as soon as possible to see for ourselves.

Meanwhile Forestry Tasmania—courtesy of Alex—had graciously accorded us one of the most spectacular camp sites of our trip, beside the Huon. We were even permitted to light a camp fire to cook on and sit around as darkness enveloped us. Before dinner Ros noticed some colourful little birds hopping in and out of a bunch of sword grass beside The Manor. Then she thought she caught a glimpse of the head of a big tiger snake seeking a close encounter with one of the dainty little blue-tailed wrens they were both admiring! I hoped she had imagined the snake, but didn't feel like poking the sword grass with a stick to find out. The sound of the vigorous passage of the Huon River beside our camp was no concern of mine as I take out my hearing aids at night. But we were so close to the rushing waters that Ros found it hard to get to sleep and put in ear plugs. I'm sure my snoring had nothing to do with that.

Although rain was forecast, it held off and we managed to pack up dry next morning. But before we had come down from the mountains it started to rain steadily and continued to do so as we drove up beside the Huon estuary towards Huonville and eventually Snug where we had booked ahead at the caravan park. Realising that we were starting to move out of winery country, and needing to replenish out depleted stocks of Tasmanian pinot noir, we called in at the Home Hill winery near Ranelagh.

It was a bit embarrassing, really, arriving before opening time at 10 am, but we thought we could force ourselves to do a little tasting at that early hour. The winery and tasting room—and a smart restaurant set up for a chamber music concert—were all housed in a rammed earth building. We fronted up to the tasting bar and asked the young woman there if we could try some pinot noir. She gave me a tasting glass but did not endear herself to Ros by saying: 'Would you like to try some too, sweetheart?'

'Sweetheart!' yelped Ros, but the young woman kept burbling on oblivious to her distress. We bought a prize winning 2001 pinot noir and couple of 'cleanskins' which were very light in colour and a bit sharpish, in Ros's opinion. It was difficult to form proper judgments at 10 am, but the cleanskins at $12 a bottle seemed worth a gamble. We wanted to take the prize winning bottle to our friends Rod and Jeannie Ledingham at Oyster Cove that night. Rod was one of winemaker Andrew Hood's first customers, and started his vineyard because of Andrew's winemaking plans.

As we got closer to the southern flanks of Mt Wellington, I could make out the familiar silhouette against the grey sky of a feature known locally as the Sleeping Beauty. From our perspective it also seemed that the recumbent damsel was not only well endowed in the breasts department, but also heavily pregnant. We turned off the Huon Highway at Sandfly to cut across to the Channel Highway for Margate and Snug. (I recall an ABC colleague new to Tasmania being amused at a headline in the Hobart *Mercury*: SANDFLY SPORTS ON SUNDAY. He knew that Australians would bet on two flies walking up a wall, but a whole sports day for these minuscule stinging insects seemed excessive.) Just after we turned right my eye caught a sign pointing to Aliens River. Could this be where the expression 'Pointy-headed Tasmanians' originated? On reflection it seemed more likely that some local wit had changed an 'l' to an 'i'.

It was just as well I had booked ahead for the Snug caravan park because the place was completely full.

They only have twenty-two spaces for casual travellers (most residents are permanents) and the manager in the office said she was dreading the day the Sandy Bay park closed in Hobart. Having to say no to people all the time, she said, was both stressful and time-wasting.

**Travel Diary Wednesday 19 March**

Steady rain set in, conveniently after we had made camp. Things could be worse. We are snug (as it were) in The Manor. I am working on my laptop, and Mozart piano sonatas are playing on our portable sound system. Ros is reading the paper and we are drinking a companionable cup of tea. If the rain sets in—and the forecast isn't all that good—we may abandon our plans to camp at Mt Field National Park, near the 'Valley of the Giants' in the Styx Valley, and go into the mountains for a day trip only, from New Norfolk.

We had a great night at the Ledinghams. Oyster Cove is only about twenty minutes' drive from Hobart, and several members of the Tasmanian Symphony Orchestra have taken up residence there. Stephanie (pianist) and Duncan (oboist) were among the guests. One of the happier local pastimes is to set nets for the Tasmanian-bred Atlantic salmon which have escaped (how sad) from their holding pens. Rod also knows a local who can cure and smoke them, and great platters of freshly smoked salmon—if that isn't too much of a contradiction in terms—went exceedingly well with Rod's brilliantly constructed gins and tonics.

I first met Rod in 1989 in Antarctica where he had been leading a summer party in the remote Prince Charles Mountains, south-east of Australia's Mawson Station. No

sooner had his party of famished scientists landed by helicopter on the supply ship *Icebird* when the bastards drank
the entire ship's stocks of gin and tonic in two days! We
forgave them—eventually. The avuncular Scot has clocked
up a great deal of Antarctic experience, going back to the
days when he worked for the British Antarctic Survey
(BAS). In 1968 he was on a field trip high up on the Graham
Land Plateau, on the Antarctic Peninsula, when the aircraft
that came to pick them up crashed. He and his companion,
plus the stranded pilot, made their way back to the coast by
skis and husky-powered dog sleds just like the Antarctic
explorers of the so called 'heroic' age, and had to winter at
Fossil Bluff, on Alexander Island, with five men crowded
into a small hut designed for four with barely enough fuel
and supplies to see them through. They didn't have to eat
their dogs, but it was a difficult time. Their clothing wore
out and had to be sewn and re-sewn. Rod has a wonderful
photograph of his patched up attire, with the arse literally
out of his duds. He's not a small man either.

The Ledinghams have a modest place in Australia's
Antarctic history. In 1977 they were the first married couple
to winter on an ANARE (Antarctic National Antarctic
Research Expeditions) station. The Antarctic Division was
extremely worried about having women winter in Antarctica
because of the fear of sexual tensions in a predominately
male culture. (The first woman did not winter on a conti-
nental station—Davis—until as late as 1981, and then only
because she was a doctor and the only medico available.)
Jeannie Ledingham is also a doctor, and Rod was the officer
in charge of the sub-Antarctic Macquarie Island station.

He has now retired from ANARE, but continues to
voyage regularly to both the Arctic and the Antarctic in

their respective summer seasons as a guide on Russian icebreakers chartered by various companies to take tourists to the polar regions. His vineyard, planted out on the lower north-facing slopes of the Ledingham Oyster Cove property, is a major continuing interest. In 1994 I overnighted with Rod and Jeannie while in Tasmania for reasons which now escape me. It must have been late March because his grapes were almost ready for harvesting and were swathed in the bridal-style white netting designed to keep the blackbirds and other flying marauders away from the ripening fruit. I asked Rod if he'd give me a conducted tour of the vineyard before we got down to the serious business of sampling and demolishing a few bottles of last year's vintage.

As we reached the end of the first row I was astonished to see the ground littered with the carcases of dead black-birds—there must have been at least a score of them. What on earth had been going on?

Rod explained that blackbirds (a pest and not a native Tasmanian species) were particularly ingenious about attacking grapes. They had learned to dive-bomb the nets, pushing them back against the fruit. They then pushed their beaks through the mesh and helped themselves and they also became adept at wriggling in under the nets for an inside job.

At that time Rod had two elderly husky dogs on his property which had been removed from Mawson Station (where their forebears had been since 1954) because of strict new international environmental guidelines about intro-duced species in Antarctica. Incensed at the blackbirds' attacks on his beloved grapes, Rod devised a unique strategy to deal with them. He put the huskies in one end of the row under the nets and drove the blackbirds down to the other end. I didn't ask for details, but the blackbirds obviously became deceased.

Later I could not resist sending him the following ode.

REFLECTIONS ON BLACKBIRD PIE

Sing a song of pinot,
Or why not chardonnay?
Four and twenty blackbirds
Have come to join the fray.
Enter Roderick Ledingham
His huskies at the ready,
Thumping nets and hounding birds
To save his ripening neddy.

# eight

## Chips with Everything

**Travel Diary Friday 21 March**

Returned to Snug caravan park after our dinner with the Ledinghams in time for the mother of all thunder storms. We had just gone to bed when it started—lightning, thunder, the works. It rained two-and-a-half-inches (on the old scale that most people still use) during the night. We shouldn't begrudge Tasmanians the rain because they badly need it. But the forecast wasn't all that flash for the camping fraternity and the weather persons were inconveniently promising rain for a week. We hadn't taken any special precautions for rain when we camped at Snug, but The Manor held up splendidly. It's a bit like being in a tent—everything is fine as long as you don't touch the canvas walls. A corner of my pillow got a bit damp, but other than that we were snug as the proverbial bug in a rug. It even eased off while we packed up, but collapsing a wet camper is not its best feature as the side walls have to be pushed in on top of the beds (admittedly covered with plastic) and when the roof is lowered, it seals in the damp until the next camp.

We were a lot better off than the poor family next to us—
and I suspect they were poor—semi-permanently camped
in one of those 1950s-style plyboard caravans, where one
sheet is bent over in a curve to form the roof. It was quite
small too, and inside was a young couple, their pre-teen
daughter and their white bull terrier dog. The family hound
was usually tethered to the tow bar, but taken inside after
the poor thing howled and freaked out with the thunder as
dogs do. I heard some thumping noises in the night during
the worst of the rain, and peered out to see the bloke fran-
tically trying to pull a plastic sheet over the roof and hold it
down with bricks. It must have been a dreadful night for
them, bedding and clothing soaked and crammed in with a
wet smelly dog as well. They had not emerged by the time
we pulled out of the caravan park through deep pools of
water at the front entrance.

I had arranged a meeting with the Tasmanian writer,
Cassandra Pybus, who lived nearby at Conningham, overlooking the waters of the D'Entrecasteaux Channel and
Bruny Island where her ancestor, Richard Pybus, had been
the first white settler. Cassandra is a former editor of the
Tasmanian literary journal *Island*, and the author of many
books about Tasmania and Tasmanians—although she has
also inscribed her elegant prose on the larger world canvas.
I had read, and particularly admired, two of her books, *Gross
Moral Turpitude—The Orr Case Reconsidered*, and a challenging biography of the controversial poet and right-wing
intellectual James McAuley, *The Devil and James McAuley*.
She has also written about what it means to be Tasmanian
and shares my opinion that, for better or worse, island
people consider themselves a race apart—not only because
of their obvious geographical isolation, but because they

believe their island existence has imbued them with special values.

Cassandra had not long returned from the United States, where she lives for part of each year, when Ros and I joined her for morning coffee. Her sense of being a Tasmanian must have been well rusted on because, although born on the island, she left it when she was nine years old and did not return until she was thirty-seven!

TIM: What brought you back?

CASSANDRA: I had come back about five years earlier on a kind of rather clandestine holiday—and it wasn't actually until the plane came in to land that I remembered that I had grown up here: the process of eliminating the discourse on Tasmania, by my family, from our memory was complete—you never told people you came from Tasmania.

TIM: Was that the 'two-headed inbred syndrome'?

CASSANDRA: Yes, that would stigmatise you. So I completely eliminated this memory until the plane came in to land, and the minute I got into the hire car and was driving around, I was bursting into tears and having all kinds of epiphanies. It got particularly bad when I got down to Snug and turned down that road you would have driven along. You wouldn't have seen today how spectacular it is but on a clear day it is just the most beautiful thing. And I had been dreaming about that road all my life.

TIM: Where had you been living?

CASSANDRA: In Sydney and Melbourne—mostly in Sydney which is a fabulous city as you know, but a different kind of beauty and spectacle. And I suddenly realised that I was in the landscape that I had been dreaming. I mean, I had thought it was just a road in my imagination, and suddenly I found I was really on that road—and the road ended up at this house where my uncle was living at the time.

Then I realised where the road in my dream came from and how it kept calling me back. Years later I met my first boyfriend, who turned up in Melbourne in 1985 and said to me, 'I've been looking for you, your father told me you never got married.' This was twenty years after I had last seen him! We sort of started dating, as they would say way back in the fifties, and he indicated to me that he had been looking for me all his life, and those other three women that he'd married before didn't count (laughs)! I was so unhappy in my circumstances and I was then desperate to get back to Tasmania. I had this idea I really wanted to come back—my mother had moved back down here and I had started to visit her, and I said to him, 'Well if you want to marry me, you'll have to come and live in Tasmania.' And he said, 'Done. I love Tasmania.' So we moved down here, and he has become so intensely involved in Tasmania and Tasmanians that even if I wanted to leave he would never go.

The fact is I couldn't live anywhere but in this landscape. And part of what allows me to live here and be content is the capacity to go and live in other places—to get out of it, to get out of the kind of insularity that begins to make Tasmanians think that there isn't any other world but this little island.

TIM: Your ancestors settled here, did they not?

CASSANDRA: This whole region is crammed full of Pybuses. Just opposite the street where you camped last night, there is a Pybus Street.

TIM: So how much were you aware of this as a small girl?

CASSANDRA: I was completely aware of it. We lived up on the slopes of Mt Wellington at Fern Tree and we used to come down here for Christmas and holidays in this house which was half the size it is now. And there were lots of Pybuses around, there were cousins and second cousins, and there was a sense that this was a landscape that was infused with Pybuses. Now I'm the only one here, which is really interesting. There are Pybuses in Hobart, but none down the Channel any more. I'm the only one, so I like to think I'm continuing the Pybus tradition. My original ancestor, Richard Pybus, was the first white settler on Bruny Island. He was rapidly followed by others, but he was the first, and there is a sense that this is a landscape that we set deep roots down into, even though I'm now the only one here.

This very road, where I am now, the Old Station Road, is the original road of an old Aboriginal station. I used to go there for walks, and I remember playing there as a child and finding broken clay pipes and things like that. So I immediately had to find out more. Richard Pybus's son, Henry Harrison Pybus, had the land immediately adjacent to that, and had at one stage offered to look after the remaining Aborigines for a certain amount of money. The historian Lyndall Ryan told me this, and so I had that sense of my family and these Aboriginal survivors intertwined in some way. Which is why I then started reading Robinson's journals and found out about my ancestor Richard Pybus, and so very early on I started engaging with the question, do I really belong here?

My answer very firmly was that I *did* belong here. But as part of my belonging I had certain knowledge and responsibilities for what had gone on, because my family has been here all that time and I was a beneficiary of the policy that had taken the Aborigines' land. At an emotional level I have no problem about my deep identification with this land and I don't feel that I have to make apologies for that. I belong here and I think that Europeans have established a relationship with the land. I think that a lot of Australians would like to be able to express their common sense of belonging and they should be able to do so without feeling they are offending their own indigenous fellow Australians.

The D'Entrecasteaux Channel towns are commuter distance from Hobart these days with a four lane highway from Kingston to Hobart. So half an hour after leaving Cassandra Pybus in Conningham we were descending the lower slopes of Mt Nelson towards Sandy Bay, where we dropped off The Manor at my sister's house and headed to the supermarket for the last serious resupply before heading north. Ros is much better at this kind of thing than I am, so I excused myself so I could visit an old friend—who can certainly be qualified as old, as he was just about to turn ninety. But Don Cunningham was one of those people whose mind refused to age, and I had promised to see him while in Tasmania. I knew Ros would understand.

We had last met in Devonport in 1989 when I recorded his reminiscences of growing up in the farming hamlet of Kamona, near Scottsdale, on the north-east coast early last century (some of which I included earlier in Chapter Five). His retirement village was near the old Cadbury estate where, apart from establishing a chocolate factory in 1922, the Cadbury management set up a whole residential complex (and sporting facilities) for its workers. The Cadbury chocolate factory still exists nearby. It is a spectacular site for a factory (and a retirement complex), close to the Derwent estuary with fine views west to Mt Wellington and north-east overlooking the river and distant hills.

Don was waiting for me in one of the communal lounge areas. We had a great talk and, on impulse, I took a photograph of him—perhaps sensing that we might not see each other again. That impression was heightened when he told me that he had recently had a curious experience. He said his heart had stopped. He knew it had, and had started to drift into unconsciousness when it kick-started itself again.

'I thought at the time that it was a nice way to go!' Don said, and believed it would probably happen again soon.

He walked with me to my taxi, to say farewell. It was an emotional moment, since I think we both knew another meeting would be unlikely. Then as he walked off I asked the driver to blip the horn, and waved again as I drove away. He did not turn around.

(Almost exactly a year later to the day that I visited Don at Derwent Park I had an email from his daughter, Julie Macdonald, to say that her father had been diagnosed with bowel cancer and was slipping away. I sent a message to him, which he did receive before he died, and emailed Julie the photograph I had taken of him. The family particularly liked the photo and used it on the cover of the Order of Service for 'A celebration of the life of Don Cunningham'.)

I returned to Sandy Bay to find that Ros had not only finished at the supermarket but had packed away all the produce so that we were ready to leave Hobart after the picnic lunch she had also arranged. I was foolish enough to say, 'I think this is the only way to travel' . . .

The weather forecasts were still fairly dire so we thought it unwise to camp at Mt Field National Park, high in the mountains to the north-west of Hobart. Instead we would drive to New Norfolk, on the lower reaches of the Derwent River, spend the night there and leave The Manor in the caravan park for the day while we drove to Westerway, near Maydena—a departure point for the Styx Valley, home of the giant gum trees where, according to conservationists, Forestry Tasmania should have constructed their airwalk in the old growth forest—most of which was still scheduled to be clear-felled. We wanted to see the area for ourselves, and had arranged with Tony Coleman—then proprietor of the Possum Shed Café at Westerway—to have a conducted tour of the Styx Valley.

The road to New Norfolk follows the Derwent River to this historic town, named in 1808 because it was where many of the original settlers—mostly ticket-of-leave convicts—came after the first settlement on Norfolk Island closed down. The area, with its rich river-side soil, was suitable for growing hops—a practice that endures to this day. Lines of poplar trees were planted as wind breaks, so the town and environs have a distinctly European look, particularly in autumn. This impression is reinforced by distinctively shaped oast houses on some of the farms, where the hops were dried on the upper storey.

The river-front caravan park had no record of my booking but obligingly fitted us in anyway. As anyone who has ever stayed in a caravan park will know, judgment on its qualities generally homes in on the toilet block. We found the New Norfolk arrangements quaint, to say the least. For both men and women, the shower blocks were in separate buildings from the toilet blocks—inconvenient for obvious reasons. You also had to have twenty-cent coins to get hot showers, a cost which really ought to be built into the camping fee.

Although the weather forecast had been iffy, we woke to broken cloud and sunshine and made good time to Westerway, on the turnoff on the Gordon River Road, which ended at Hydro Tasmania's Gordon Dam. This dam, completed by the late 1980s, had drowned the original Lake Pedder—which still makes me cross and sad a quarter of a century on from that stupid decision. (Lake Pedder could have been saved by building an earth dam to separate it from Lake Gordon. The Gordon hydro-electricity project could still have gone ahead, but the premier of the day, 'Electric Eric' Reece, instantly knocked back an offer from the Whitlam Labor government to pay for this barrier and the lake was lost.) This disaster did, however, galvanise the conservation movement to ensure that the next dam on the Lower Gordon River was not built, so Tasmania's last major wild river, the Franklin, still runs free.

The clear-felling of old growth forests for timber and woodchips—mostly woodchips—is the current *bête noir* of the conservation movement, and the Styx Valley is at the heart of that debate. Not that the Styx Valley is pristine wilderness by any measure. Parts of it have been logged and relogged for more than sixty years. But it is still home to stands of the tallest flowering eucalypts in the world, the rather prosaically named swamp gum. *Eucalyptus regnans* is its botanical name, which better reflects its regal stature, some specimens in the Styx rising majestically as high as ninety-two metres from the rain forest floor.

We found Tony Coleman at the Possum Shed Café, which is perched beside the fast-flowing Tyenna River, and he introduced us to Richard Davis, who was a saw miller and farmer (and boat builder!) from Ellendale—a nearby farming district. Richard was one of a number of timber industry professionals who were simply appalled not only by the clear-felling of old growth forests but by the shocking waste of rain forest timbers that could be salvaged, but were usually burnt to clear the site for seeding monoculture eucalypts for the next harvest of woodchips. Tony used to run tours into the Styx Valley to take tourists to see the giant swamp gums, but was no longer doing so. He had amiably agreed, however, to take Ros and me into the 'Valley of the Giants' in his little bus, and Richard Davis said he'd come too.

Sixty odd years of forestry have made their mark on the Styx Valley, with great swathes of raw, cleared ground cheek by jowl with coupes of regrowth eucalypt plantations thickly clustered together like telegraph poles. Tony explained, as we drove along, that this kind of monoculture produced a virtual biological desert, with little other flora or indeed bird or animal life of any description. Apparently many Australian animals and birds need a diverse forest with some trees in it more than 100 years old in order to get the kinds of habitat, knot-holes and crevices they need to live and breed.

We were heading for a small area of old growth forest which housed what was called the 'Big Tree Reserve'. You need a structure like the Tahune Airwalk in the south to see these great trees properly. You can stand underneath them and look up, but it is difficult to judge distance. The Big Tree is 87 metres high, and other trees in the Styx get up to 92 metres. These would tower above the twenty-storey Hobart Casino if they were side by side. Mercifully they are not. These great trees are thought to be at least 450 years old, and are the world's biggest hardwoods and tallest flowering trees. The Californian redwoods, which are pines, are the biggest trees in the world as most people know. We walked from the gravel road along a short board walk and marked track to the base of the big tree, and Ros and I linked hands and still couldn't straddle the girth at the base. These trees just take your breath away. They are utterly magnificent.

The walkway and some signage had only recently been put in by Forestry Tasmania, who one presumes would really rather people did not go near these old forests at all, preferring to have them out of sight and mind until they get 'harvested'. However, several years ago the Tasmanian Wilderness Society published some maps and information telling people how to drive to the Styx Valley and find the Valley of the Giants. For a while they organised eco-tours to bring tourists in, but Tony said, for reasons he wasn't quite sure about, that had stopped. He said they were very popular. When people first started to drive in the trees were quite hard to find, with just a couple of mossy, drooping signs by the side of the road to show where the un-maintained track to them began. Following the Wilderness Society's initiative Forestry Tasmania came in and made some board walks and signage, not only giving statistics on the trees but saying how well Tasmania's forests were being 'managed'.

Under pressure, some stands of *E. regnans* have been reprieved from clear-felling and a buffer zone left around them. This does not necessarily mean they are safe. Only a month after our visit in March 2003, a giant mountain ash believed to be Australia's biggest tree, known as El Grande, was 'cooked' and killed in a Forestry Tasmania burning operation that went wrong. (El Grande had only been discovered a year before, but didn't live long after that. It wasn't the tallest of the trees, at 79 metres, but it had a 19-metre girth and a volume of 439 cubic metres: 35 cubic metres ahead of its closest rival in Tasmania.) El Grande only had a 100 metre exclusion zone around it; it was not enough. In what I can only charitably describe as a demonstration of stunning incompetence, the Forestry Tasmania workers charged with 'managing' the state's forests, destroyed it when a nearby regeneration burn got out of control.

When the Tasmanian Greens senator Bob Brown tried to get a senate inquiry into El Grande's demise, he was defeated by a counter proposal from the Tasmanian Labor senator Kerry O'Brien that the Tasmanian government inquire 'whether the tree could be saved'. It couldn't, of course, and Bob Brown was furious, saying: 'It defies belief. This place [the Senate] is sometimes devoid of spirit and heart.'

El Grande's destruction caused a massive mid-winter protest in the Styx Valley, with some 3000 people flocking to attend it. The Wilderness Society and Greenpeace began a tree sit-in sixty-five metres up a threatened mountain ash known as 'Gandolph's Staff' and maintained it for some months.

Curiously enough these 400-year-plus trees are a bit of a nuisance in timber harvesting terms. They are too big and old for saw logs, and are generally split into segments and sent off to be woodchipped. The conservationists say that their preservation would bring tourists (and income and jobs) to the area for the foreseeable future, arguing that the highly mechanised clear-felling practices of the twenty-first century are not only causing timber industry jobs to be lost in any case, but what jobs are left are only short term with the clear-felling of old growth forests due to end in 2010. By then the big trees will be gone anyway, and demonstrated tourism opportunities will be lost forever.

The Styx Valley has been harvested away from public gaze for so long that Forestry Tasmania doesn't bother about 'visual management zones'—forestry-speak for putting a screen of trees between access roads and the devastation of clear-felling and burning. Tony called it 'lawn-mowing and napalming' the forest. He said, 'The best argument against the clear-felling of old growth forests is simply to come to the Styx Valley and see what Forestry Tasmania is doing here'.

As we drove back through the valley, I noticed clear-felled areas that had obviously been hand-planted with lines of eucalypt seedlings. In some cases the furrows were running straight down the hill, rather than being contoured, meaning that again precious top soil would be washed away with the first heavy rain. These fresh young seedlings naturally attract wallabies, wombats, possums, bandicoots and other small marsupials, which feed on them. Forestry Tasmania dealt with this problem, as Tony told me, by scattering raw carrots around and the wild life get used to feeding on them. Then on a certain day the carrots are put out as usual but this time they are coloured blue, laced with 1080 poison. This poison, banned in other countries, is effective but causes the animals who eat it to die a slow agonising death. A few years ago, Tasmania began to hold an annual 'Ten Days on the Island' festival. Tony said the conservationists produced some bumper stickers which said: 1080 DAYS ON THE ISLAND—THE BLUE CARROT STATE.

The whole forestry debate has degenerated into trench warfare, with neither side prepared to give any ground. Richard Davis, a saw miller himself, was against clear-felling but believed valuable rain forest timber—giving employment and income to the boat building, joinery, furniture and craft industries—could and should be salvaged before being burnt on site. Richard showed me a photograph he had taken of a mix of rain forest and eucalypt logs piled in a huge heap, ready for burning, which he could have salvaged had he been permitted. He included the photograph in a personal submission to a Senate inquiry on plantations replacing native forests.

RICHARD DAVIS: Clear-felling is changing the nature of forests forever. Given present forestry management practices, which are directed towards one-fibre production and limited eucalypt saw log production on a rotation of less than sixty years, we will never ever see the special species come back again, such as celery-top, myrtle, blackwood, sassafras, leatherwood—its flowers prized by beekeepers—and the other timbers wanted by furniture makers, craftsmen and joiners. We've probably got another ten or twelve years left of old growth clear-felling at the speed they are doing it now, then it will be gone forever because it just takes too long to grow back. Myrtle, sassafras and quality blackwoods need 150 years to grow back, and celery-top pine needs over 250 years to be suitable for saw logs. And none of these species grow back at all wherever they are using aerial seeding and hot burning after clear-felling.

TIM: What is wasted?

RICHARD: Just about everything, including some of the eucalypts, unbelievably, because they don't cart everything that they could to the chip mills. A lot of the big limb wood is left behind, but most of the minor species get wasted, much of which could be used by the high value-adding craft and furniture industries. I have seen blackwood logs piled up ready for burning which have a 'Category Four'—the best of the special species logs. They will take some out where they have a market for it, but if they haven't they just burn it.

'Styx 19-C' was a coupe that I wanted to salvage for Forestry Tasmania. I offered them firewood prices because the logs in that coupe had been lying in the sun for a long time, and a lot of it was buried and smashed up—but I thought there was well in excess of 500 tonnes in that particular coupe which could have been salvaged. Even so, salvaging is not a good thing to be doing, because we shouldn't be clear-felling in the first place.

TIM: You are in the timber game yourself—how should the forests be managed?

RICHARD: They should be selectively logged, using single stems or small group extraction methods. I'm not averse to seeing major tracks strategically constructed through forests, more for the purpose of being able to control fire than anything. We should only be taking out timber which can be highly value added, and that should be done in Tasmania. The amounts of timber that you would take from each area would vary with the aspect, the type of timber, the soil type and the ages and mixture of the species that are in there. But if I was managing it, I would be trying to maintain forest stability and particularly the hydrology of the land. And even if you only altered it by five per cent, it is important to maintain the biological and ecological integrity of the forests—to live off the interest and not mine the bloody capital all the time!

TIM: Forestry would say it's not economic . . .

RICHARD: That's right, because Forestry is into high resource extraction with a low return, low value adding and a low employment regime. On the other hand I believe we should have a forest industry based on low resource extraction, with high value adding and high employment.

TIM: Instead of sending the chips off to Japan.

RICHARD: For bugger all—about $7 per cubic metre, or translated down, .013 of a super foot. Value added in the furniture industry you'd get at least $20 per super foot return.

TIM: You have a photograph from an area that has been clear-felled. The trees are about the same girth as telegraph poles. How old would that be?

RICHARD: Probably be around twenty-five to thirty years.

TIM: What is the wastage rate from that?

RICHARD: When they flatten it, they'd probably recover eighty per cent because of the small amount of limb wood and small heads which they'd knock off. But it would all go for woodchips. You'd never get saw logs out of that sort of timber because if you thin them out to the stage where single stems could grow you'd probably lose most of them to wind blows. Wood lots like that—you wouldn't call it a forest—have a very small root structure. They just don't expand enough to hold themselves up. If Forestry were to thin them when they were very young, then you'd be back into the economic argument again, of large cost inputs for bugger all initial return. The whole industry is driven by quick dollars.

TIM: Well, how much does Forestry Tasmania make for the state government?

RICHARD: In the financial year 2001/02 it returned less than one per cent to the public purse. Obviously they don't get enough royalties for what they are selling. I guess because the industry is chip wood driven—the vast majority of their income comes from chips—they have to compete against South America and a lot of the Asian countries. That's the royalty only of course. Gunns, the timber company and largest woodchipper in the world, makes millions while the people of Tasmania get cleaned up.

TONY COLEMAN: One thing that Forestry Tasmania and the government constantly harp on is that they have got 'world's best practice' forestry methods. But it is obvious when you come out here that there must be other ways of forest management which would be truly sustainable. The simple answer to them saying, 'Well, look at what other countries are doing to their forests', is that two wrongs certainly don't make a right.

RICHARD: This industry has progressively lost jobs for years and years now. In the calendar year 2002 there were 800 jobs lost in the forestry industry in Tasmania. That is from Australian Bureau of Statistics figures.

They are cutting down the forests twice as fast as they were three or four years ago. Jobs that were lost in 2002 were in the value adding section of the industry—that is, on the processing side. It doesn't have to go on that way.

TONY: Don't blame the Japanese, blame us! They must think we are bloody idiots obliterating our native forests for such a pittance. Their forests are pretty well pristine. I'm not blaming the Japanese for buying ours, because they are just people like you and me. If we could get away with it we probably would too. But we would think the people we were buying the forests from were bloody idiots, selling their national heritage to us for that price. The Japanese must have no respect for us either from a business perspective or an environmental perspective.

Cynics used to say that the Hydro Electric Commission (now Hydro Tasmania) used to run Tasmania. Now that reputation has fallen on Forestry Tasmania. Certainly information on the state's forest industry and practices is extremely hard to come by under Tasmania's tough Freedom of Information legislation. Occasionally a courageous whistle-blower tries to lift the veil of this secrecy. In 2003, a former forests practices inspector, Bill Manning, gave some damning evidence to a Senate committee about the widespread, illegal destruction of public forests. Manning detailed some eighty examples of alleged breaches of fauna protection provisions, including uncontrolled run-off from clear-felled sites into streams and rivers—provisions 'meant to protect the unique creatures of Tasmania's forests, the giant freshwater crayfish, wedge-tailed eagles, [and] the spotted-tail quoll'. Bill Manning said no action was taken on any of these breaches, despite his reports.[1]

Manning confirmed the suspicions of those who believed Forestry Tasmania was a law unto itself by alleging

---

1 Melissa Fyfe & Andrew Darby, 13–14 March 2004, 'There Goes the View', *Sydney Morning Herald*

the industry, through self-regulation, was starving the government of information with a culture of 'bullying, cronyism, secrecy and lies'. The Minister for Forests, Paul Lennon (now premier following the death of Jim Bacon), rejected Manning's claims as 'a farrago of false and inaccurate allegations'.

So far Tasmania's booming tourist industry does not seem to have been affected by the on-going controversy about the continued clear-felling of old growth forests. Perhaps the strategy of 'visual management zones' screening the devastation from travellers' eyes is paying off. Meanwhile Gunns are going great guns, and have plans for a billion dollar chlorine-free pulp mill in Tasmania. Campaigning in the marginal northern Tasmanian federal seat of Bass in July 2004, the prime minister, John Howard, promised the company five million dollars to help create an 'environmentally friendly pulp mill'. Gunns is pressing on with a feasibility study but says 'the mill might not be viable if felling of old-growth forests was ended'.[2]

Green groups and conservationists are gearing up for a stoush to save old growth forests of similar proportions to the campaign which eventually saved the Franklin River. With an eye for the telling, news-making gesture, conservationists have made some sizeable waves. In 2002 they paid $200 000 for a huge billboard near Sydney Airport which showed the Styx Valley juxtaposed with a burnt, clear-felled forest, with the caption 'DISCOVER TASMANIA BEFORE 2003'. Another unforgettable image was the maiden voyage of the third Tasmanian vehicular and passenger ferry, *Spirit*

---

2  Mike Dobbie, August 2004, 'Trees Please', *Shares* magazine, Fairfax Business Media, Melbourne

*of Tasmania III*, in January 2004. As it sailed past the iconic Opera House, four environmental activists abseiled down the side of the vessel unfurling a banner just above its name, creating the message, 'WOODCHIPPING THE SPIRIT OF TASMANIA'.

**Travel Diary Tuesday 25 March**

A very autumnal morning for our departure from New Norfolk, with a classic 'Bridgewater Gerry'—a thick mist that follows the course of the Derwent River right down to Hobart. It was very cold and I was glad of my work gloves, packing up The Manor, coiling up power cords, and hitching up the super-chilled metal coupling to Penelope. As we headed out of New Norfolk heading for Bridgewater, we could see more clearly as the sun began to break through that the fog was faithfully following the river. I stopped to photograph a black swan swimming downstream in the mist against a background of sun on the far shore, and the top of a hill poking up cheekily above a band of white fog.

We crossed the Derwent at Bridgewater—still in the grip of its Gerry—and decided to give the main highway a miss and turn off to the east to Pontville and Campania, then head north on a minor road through Colebrook to join up with the Midland Highway just south of Oatlands. The distances are about the same, but the B31 is much more scenic. By now in full sun, the country just sparkled with a superb combination of colours—dark brown newly ploughed paddocks contrasting with last season's yellow grass set against the bright green shoots coming through after recent rain. It looked like a farming idyll, with sheep grazing companionably in decorative groups.

As we drove through Colebrook, Ros noted that it used to be called Jerusalem. We had bypassed Bagdad on the Midland Highway (without the 'h') and had yet to pass by Jericho.

The Midlands Highway I remembered from thirty years before used to follow a more tortuous route, winding through valleys (it is more mountainous in its southern section) and up Spring Hill to Oatlands, the real gateway to the flatter farmlands that produce much of Tasmania's world-class superfine merino wool. Someone had the bright idea of planting a line of English trees the entire length of the Midland Highway early in the twentieth century, relying on the property owners to look after them. Most of that road has been bypassed now, but the upgraded highway uses the same line of road through St Peter's Pass to the north of Oatlands and poplars and hawthorn hedges can still be seen.

All the towns along the way—Bridgewater, Kempton, Oatlands, Tunbridge, Ross, Campbell Town and Perth—were used as staging posts in the days of horse and coach travel. Most have been bypassed now, but can be visited by tourists and travellers with time to spare. They are colonial time capsules with their Georgian sandstone public buildings and historic inns. The convict-built sandstone bridge over the Macquarie River at Ross is a much-photographed feature, and quite rightly so. Built in 1836, it has 184 panels that decorate the arches, created by two convict stonemasons, Colbeck and Herbert, who earned their freedom by the quality of their work. Each panel is unique, with Celtic symbols, animals and the faces of notable people carved into the sandstone. I haven't seen it at night, but the features are said to stand out superbly when they are illuminated.

Campbell Town, the next town to the north, has a magnificent convict-built brick bridge which, as the town has not been bypassed, still carries traffic on the Midlands Highway. We did have a look at the bridge, but we had two other important reasons for stopping in Campbell Town— to get hot pies for lunch from the best pie shop in northern Tasmania, and to visit The Grange stately home.

Alas, we found that the best pie shop in living memory was no more—it had been taken over by Banjos, the bread and pastry chain, which, given our expectations, induced feelings of deep deprivation and disappointment. The town, however, has been experiencing some unexpected publicity and a dunny-led recovery. I caught up with the story in the *Sunday Tasmanian*, by reporter Phil Beck:

WHERE SPENDING A PENNY REAPS A FORTUNE

The northern Midlands township of Campbell Town is enjoying a mini economic boom—and it is built around toilets. Once virtually ignored by Tasmanian travellers and tourists alike, upmarket public loos have put the town well and truly back on the map.

Motorists now stop, new businesses are springing up and confidence has returned to the town. Until the mid-1990s, motorists who stopped at Campbell Town to relieve themselves took their life in their own hands.

The public conveniences were located behind the court in the main street. Finding them wasn't difficult if you had a sense of smell. They were dark and dingy, damp and dirty. It was in the 1996–97 financial year that a breath of fresh air swept over the town when a new toilet block was built in Valentines Park, a stone's throw north of the court house.

After heated debate the Northern Midlands Council decided that no expense should be spared on the new facilities and allocated $81 261 for the project. As the word got around, motorists who merely remembered Campbell Town for their speeding fines started to stop.

New businesses were, and still are, being established . . .

Ros, who is something of a connoisseur of public toilets, gave the new facility five stars. But I was preoccupied about the sad demise of that good old traditional country town pie shop . . .

The Grange, a huge stately sandstone home, is now an extremely up-market B & B, with five ensuite rooms and a two-bedroom cottage. We turned into its semi-circular drive-way—originally a carriageway of course—between two rather odd-looking gateposts. I knew what they were because my brother Nick had briefed me beforehand. They were metal columns from a photographic telescope pier, used originally to observe and record the transit of Venus in 1874!

Because we experienced another of these rare events on 8 June 2004, most Australians would now be aware that a transit of Venus occurs when the planet Venus crosses the sun's face as seen from earth, appearing as a small black dot in silhouette against the brilliant disc of the sun. Transits are rare, the most recent but one occurring in 1882, so until the 2004 event there was no one alive on earth who had seen one. The transit of Venus has great significance for Australians, because without it we may not have become a nation—or at least an English founded one. The observation of the 1769 transit of Venus was the reason why Captain Cook sailed to Tahiti in *Endeavour*, after which he opened his sealed orders, set off to look for the 'Great South Land' and found the east coast of Australia, later colonised by the British government.

My brother Nick Bowden, a surveyor by profession, is passionately interested in history and in 2000 sent me an article he had written for a surveying journal about how Campbell Town—and The Grange—had played their parts in world-wide observations of the 1874 transit, in this case not by the British, who were also combining with other nations to set up observing teams in various parts of the globe, but by the United States Navy. The US Naval Observatory positioned teams of scientists and astronomers at eight locations, including The Grange at Campbell Town. Before arriving in Tasmania, US Navy captain Ralph Chandler sailed his ship *Swatara* to the Crozet Islands—and Kerguelen Island, deep in the Southern Ocean—but was unable to land on the Crozet Islands party due to bad weather. So that particular group helped out in Tasmania instead.

So why was there so much historical excitement about Venus crossing the face of the sun?

It was all about finding out the correct measurement of the most fundamental distance in astronomy, the astronomical unit (AU)—defined simply as the average distance between the earth and the sun. That is known accurately today, but in the seventeenth and eighteenth centuries there was considerable doubt about the AU. By using observation of the planet Mars from different places on earth and a triangulation method called trigonometric parallax (that's as technical as I'm going to get), the seventeenth century French astronomer, Jean-Dominique Cassini, deduced the AU was equal to about 138 million kilometres. According to my brother Nick that wasn't a bad effort, and within eight per cent of the currently accepted value of 149.6 million kilometres. Anyway, getting the AU right had enormous implications for astronomy and the study of the universe, particularly the improved calculation of distances between the planets and the sun—hence all the excitement about the 1874 and 1882 transits of Venus. Here endeth the lesson.

We had previously contacted the owner of The Grange, Gary Price, and asked him to show us what remained of the 1874 transit observations, having already seen the gateposts. He took us to the rear of the house, where there is a little conical summerhouse—its roof was added later—once called the 'equatorial house'. This was where the then owner of The Grange, and host to the Americans, Dr William Valentine, installed his own astronomical telescope after the transit observations were completed. Some fifty metres away the brick foundations for the transit telescope itself were still visible, as well as a stone platform that would have supported buildings and other equipment.

Unfortunately, according to Nick's research, the morning of 9 December 1874 was cloudy—and it was raining! But at 12.15 pm the rain stopped, the sun started to break through, and the transit, which had already begun, was observed as visibility gradually improved. The observation team managed to expose 200 photographic plates, and the occasion was deemed to be a success—which was just as well after the long voyage and all that preparation.

(On 8 June 2004 a crowd of over 100 people, including many amateur astronomers and twenty-two members of the Royal Society of Victoria and brother Nick, gathered at the Agricultural Society's sheep pavilion to view the transit of Venus on a big screen, with a commentary by the Queen Victoria Museum's Curator of Physical Sciences, Martin George. Like the transit of 130 years before, morning cloud at first disappointed those who had come to watch the rare phenomenon, but at 3 pm the clouds blew away and Martin George, dashing from telescope to telescope, declared himself also 'blown away' by what was observed during the rest of the afternoon.)

There was one other assignation with Campbell Town before we continued our journey north. I drove Ros past a house in the main street that I first noticed in 1963 when I drove to Launceston in my second-hand FJ Holden to join the staff of the ABC as a talks officer (the quaint public service terminology of the day). It was difficult not to notice this unusual house. Its rounded brick rooms (a fashion popular in the 1950s) fronted on to a lush garden which featured a circular fish pond, over which was a hooped bridge. The semi-circular porch led to floor to ceiling glass panels and front door ornamented with a riot of sand-blasted glass animals, trees and geometric designs. The gates, meant to resemble a piano accordion, were bordered on two sides (it was a corner block) with a fence of five metal rungs representing a musical stave, complete with musical notation depicting the song 'Melody of Love'.

The house was designed by Marjorie Blackwell and called Climar—a mélange of the names of her husband Cliff and Marjorie. Before I knew this, my then girlfriend in Launceston, Fiona, and I used to fantasise every time we drove past about who might live there. In 1965 (just before we broke up) Fiona presented me with a book, *Marjorie Blackwell at Home*, which the author had self-published. It was an extraordinary compendium of recipes plus household, craft and gardening hints, all garnished with lashings of Marjorie's favourite sayings and poems.

The house looked rather stark nearly forty years on, its crowded and lush garden replaced by bare lawn and the ornamental pond dry and forlorn. Melody of Love still adorned the fence, but Marjorie had been forced to leave her dream home after the breakdown of her marriage, which occurred the same year I'd received her book. This unhappy reality was a contrast to the domestic bliss that Marjorie portrayed in her first book. In her Recipe for Happiness she wrote:

> Combine one husband, one wife, and a number of children, assorted sizes. (These are optional, but add a delightful flavour.) Using a strong unity, blend well together. Add a pinch of helpfulness, a sprig of loyalty and a dash of patience. Mix a generous portion of smiles, and a few drops of tears . . .

There were plenty of those. In her remarkably frank autobiography, *Life is for Living: The Heartaches and Happiness of Marjorie Bligh*, published in 1986 (Marjorie has had three husbands in her long life), she revealed that life with Cliff, whom she married in 1938, was hazardous to say the least. Early in their married life she was helping him get a load of firewood in the bush when he said: 'Petty (that is what he called me), if I was to kill you and bury you up here with the bulldozer, no one would know who did it, or ever find out. I could say you cleared out and left me.' Marjorie said she took that as a joke!

Later, as her relationship with Cliff deteriorated irretrievably in 1965, he made his feelings towards her known by cutting down her favourite roses, pulling out plants in her garden and smashing her flower pots. The last straw was going to Hobart for some shopping and being told by a

306 The Devil in Tim

stranger that the back of her coat had a large jagged hole in it. Shortly afterwards in a supermarket the front of her dress disintegrated—Cliff had been pouring battery acid on her clothes. At which point she left him and Climar, which she loved dearly. A lot more than him.

These days she lives in Devonport alone, after two happy post-Cliff marriages—you'd think the only way was up, wouldn't you?—and has written a number of self published books on gardening, home hints, history and politics. Now in her late eighties, she still writes a handy hints column for the Burnie *Advocate* newspaper as she has done for that paper and others since the 1970s, her writing always larded with her favourite poems and literary quotations. Barry Humphries, who first contacted her in the 1960s when he was developing his Edna Everage persona, ordered several of her books. Later no less a person than Prime Minister Bob Hawke wrote an introduction to her book *Tasmania & Beyond*, published in 1988. Marjorie Bligh is undoubtedly one of Tasmania's living national treasures and I hoped there'd be time to call in and see her in Devonport before we left Tasmania on the *Spirit of Tasmania I*. We had corresponded in recent years and I had sent her a taped copy of an interview I had done with Barry Humphries (as Edna Everage) in London in 1961.

# nine

## Away from Paradise

**Travel Diary Wednesday 26 March**

It has come as a shock to realise that we only have five more days in Tasmania. Having stuck as close to the coast as we can in our six weeks on the island, we are heading up the Midlands Highway to return briefly to the north-west coast to remedy a significant omission—to visit the Cradle Mountain-Lake St Clair National Park at its northern end. When we headed up the north-west coast originally on our way to Stanley and the Royal Chartered property Woolnorth, we did not have time to detour to Cradle Mountain, which is definitely on the must see list for visitors to Tasmania. We have to be back in Devonport on the night of 30 March to embark on the *Spirit of Tasmania* ferry.

First we had an assignation with the Christmas Hills Raspberry Farm and café at Elizabeth Town, on the western side of Deloraine. I confessed to Ros I had been there once before without her, on a previous quick trip to northern Tasmania for a speaking engagement. Fresh raspberries are, to me, the ultimate fruit. They never taste the same when frozen, although I don't turn up my nose at raspberry jam. They are a seasonal delicacy.

Somehow the Christmas Hills farm manages to produce fresh berries for its customers for six months of each year— from December to May. This is exceedingly clever, because I remember fresh raspberries in Tasmania only occurring in a brief window of late summer and early autumn.

Their admirable café overlooks a lush dam where water-lilies grow and ducks amble about on its edges. We arrived at coffee time and could not resist a raspberry tart and King Island cream as well. Then we loaded up with generous punnets of mouth-wateringly fresh and plump raspberries.

We decided to approach Cradle Mountain through Mole Creek on the B12 road we had used earlier when we'd visited the Trowunna Wildlife Park and sampled exotic varieties of local honey at the Honey Farm at Chudleigh. Instead of heading north and climbing out of the Meander Valley, as we had done to return to Devonport, we would keep heading west, climbing into the high country again, but this time through Lorinna and across the Cethana Dam to join the highway from Sheffield—which is the generally used route from the north-east coast—for the final leg to Cradle Mountain.

All this made sense to us until I realised that I had neglected to refuel, something I fortunately twigged to just I was about to drive past the last petrol station at Chudleigh before heading into the wilderness. It was too soon after the raspberry tart to have a honey and ginger ice cream (fondly recalled from our last visit) but it was reassuring to have full tanks again.

We found that the route we had chosen was one of the most engaging drives of our Tasmanian wanderings.

Pausing on top of a mountain pass we wandered briefly into the bush, sniffing the aromatic perfume of sassafras and other unseen flowering trees. Later in the higher, plateau country we found sweet-smelling boronia.

On a whim, we chose a Hydro side road that took us down to a hairpin bend where we could see the Cethana Dam, and where there was just enough room to pull off the road and put up our picnic table for lunch with the added bonus of a fabulous view spiced with the slight frisson of illegality. But we weren't a hazard to passing traffic—and no vehicles came along anyway.

The final run into the Cradle Mountain National Park is along the high plateau, and we arrived at the camping area by 2.30 pm. Our booking was for the following day but they fitted us in with no trouble, in a little private bay with bush all around and a conveniently close toilet block. There was time to drive into the park proper and do some preliminary exploring by driving to Dove Lake, a crater lake which sits at the base of Cradle Mountain, its craggy escarpment rising up sheer from its shores. Under the right conditions, the mountain features in a mirror image reflected in the lake and adorns every tourist brochure that has ever been produced in this magic place.

Photographers, though, have to seize their moments when they can because Cradle Mountain is one of Tasmania's highest peaks, at 1545 metres, and attracts much wind and rain from the prevailing westerly winds. I have heard it said that the sun shines for only sixty days out of every 365 days of the year in these parts, but surely that can't be right? (The official rainfall figures may confirm this, at 2800 millimetres per year.) Tasmania's highest mountain, Mt Ossa (1617 metres), is not far away. I became fixated by the desire to get the classic shot of Cradle Mountain, in sunshine, reflected in Dove Lake, from the car park. The sun went behind a large bank of clouds as I leapt from Penelope, digital camera at the ready.

A few kilometres further back down the narrow access road is a side track to Gustav Weindorfer's original wooden chalet. There were road works in progress, so we parked Penelope and walked up the 500 metres to the chalet, which was terrific timing as we had the place to ourselves.

It often took an outsider's eye to see Tasmania's greatest natural features, and Austrian-born Gustav Weindorfer was spellbound by the beauty of Cradle Mountain when he first walked in to Dove Lake in 1909. Weindorfer, who first came to Australia in 1900, married a Tasmanian, Kate Cowle, in 1906. They met in Melbourne where both were members of the Field Naturalists Club of Victoria. They were both botanists, keen on the outdoors, and they settled on a farm at Mt Roland, about halfway between Cradle Mountain and the coast at Devonport. From Mt Roland they both walked into Cradle Mountain with a group of friends in 1910 and climbed it—Kate was the first woman to do so. According to Major Ronnie Smith, who was with the Weindorfers on that ascent, Gustav actually proclaimed from the summit, 'This must be a national park for the people for all time. It is magnificent, and people must know about it and enjoy it.'

The Weindorfers bought some land in Cradle Valley in the late summer of that year, and started building his shingle-roofed alpine chalet Waldheim (Forest Home) two years later. There was no road and all the material for Waldheim had to be carried in, including a cast-iron bath!

By 1913 hardy travellers (you had to be to get there) were enjoying the Weindorfers' basic hospitality of wombat stews, sing-songs around the fire and guided trips across the moorlands and lakes. The chalet was gradually extended to accommodate twenty-five guests.

Weindorfer saw his vision of a national park at Cradle Mountain established by the time he died in 1932 but, sadly, Kate Weindorfer did not. She died in 1916. In fact Gustav's life was marred by tragedy as his parents and Kate died in the same year.

I had dim memories of the original chalet, because I saw it as a ten year old in 1948 after my parents had rather gamely included me on a 'walking trip' (as such hikes were known then) through the Lake St Clair-Cradle Mountain Reserve, a 100 kilometre trek. Ros and I were looking at a replica, constructed in 1976 after the original collapsed in the 1960s. It is a convincing effort to recreate Waldheim with wooden shingles on the roof and split timber flooring. We enjoyed the well presented tableau of the Weindorfers, and an audio presentation dealing with their story and the history of the area.

As we left, other visitors started to arrive so we were fortunate to have enjoyed Waldheim's ambience without interruption. At the rear of the chalet was a sign pointing to a short forest walk. It is no exaggeration to say this is an enchanted forest, with moss-covered rain forest trees—big King Billy pines, celery-top pines and myrtles. It looked like something Tolkien might have dreamed up. Ros was in horticultural heaven.

As you leave Waldheim you can see down into the valley where the Overland Track begins, its board walk snaking along the floor of the marshy valley, typically covered with button grass. We walked down to it and up a hill on the other side to discover some photogenic little tarns, illuminated by shafts of late afternoon sunlight and ringed with small, gnarled, King Billy pines. The ground was covered with a carpet of alpine coral fern. These tarns are typical of the Cradle Mountain terrain and there are thousands of them, gouged out by glaciers which shaped this region only 20 000 years ago—but yesterday in geological time. We returned to camp glowing with the beauty of it all and planned a walk around the perimeter of Dove Lake the following day.

Ros created a new camping dish she christened a 'wokpot'—stir-fried chicken in a sauce with potatoes and vegetables added, a kind of hotpot but done in a wok. Well, as they say, all wok and no play makes a dull cook ... I hopped out of Ros's way as I delivered this little *bon mot*.

A mendicant wallaby also hopped into view as Ros was cutting up the vegetables. She could not resist its pleading brown eyes and against stated wild life guidelines handed over some pieces of carrot and broccoli. Surely such vegetable fodder could not be bad for it? Shortly after holding these offerings in its front paws and daintily eating them the wallaby vomited, then, dog-like and with some care, daintily ate it all again. We decided not to feed it any more.

### Travel Diary Friday 28 March

Awoke to a still but cloudy day, with a great deal of smoke hanging in the air. Forestry Tasmania has begun its autumn burning program and I cursed them because of my hope of getting a picture-postcard view of Cradle Mountain behind

Dove Lake, not through a smoky mist. We drove to the car park at Dove Lake by 9 am, well before the rush. Each day has its own particular beauty, of course, and although Cradle Mountain's dolerite ridge was hidden by cloud, there was not a breath of wind, and there were fabulous reflections in the lake of rocks and trees by the shore.

We settled on a clockwise circumnavigation of the lake which begins with a very well constructed board walk, so you don't have to watch where you are putting your feet all the time and can take in the sculptured elegance of the King Billy pines, their roots dipping into the freshwater lake. Because we were reasonably early in the day we saw no one else until about halfway around, when we met the anti-clockwise brigade. The going gets rougher halfway around, on the southern side of the lake, where the board walk ends and the stony track leaves the lake and winds up over some steep hills. Forestry Tasmania and low cloud continued to frustrate my photographic ambitions. I cursed myself for not taking more advantage of the sunshine of our first afternoon. But if we'd come to Dove Lake then, we'd have missed our forest experience at Waldheim seen in lovely low afternoon sunlight.

Not far from Dove Lake, near the recreated Waldheim Chalet, we could see lines of backpacking hikers making their way up the steep climb leading to an area called The Cirque, on top of the plateau, the gateway to the track south to Lake St Clair. While it was notionally possible to climb up and down to The Cirque (and take in Crater Lake) in one day, we wimped out in favour of some more gentle alternatives. In the afternoon we went on some short walks near the ranger station, including the Knyvet Falls and Pencil Pine Falls. These are actually just outside the national park proper—not that any sign lets you know. I photographed some brilliantly red fungus on the mossy trunk of a fallen log.

I reminded Ros that, after Cradle Mountain, we would not be camping again until we reached home on the mid north coast of New South Wales, because we would be using motels so as to maximise travel time. On a whim we booked ourselves into Dougherty's resort hotel that evening for a posh meal to celebrate the end of this phase of our Tasmanian odyssey.

It rained heavily in the night. The *Lonely Planet* Tasmanian guide says that Cradle Mountain only has one out of every ten days with clear skies and sunshine, and eight days out of ten have cloud or rain. Perhaps we were lucky to have experienced any sunshine at all!

I became pig-headed about getting my shot of Cradle Mountain and Dove Lake in sunshine. At least the rain had cleared Forestry Tasmania's smoke from the atmosphere. We alternated doing our final pack and driving to the car park at Dove Lake seeking my elusive photograph whenever the sun looked like breaking through. Every time the clouds departed at camp, they returned again by the time we got to the lake.

### Travel Diary Sunday 30 March

Clear skies and a sunny morning after more overnight rain. Although we are leaving for Devonport—and the ferry—this morning, I again insisted that we had one more crack at getting my sunny shot of Cradle Mountain. As usual, the cloud came in on cue as we reached the lake, but after about thirty minutes—bingo! The sun only shone for about five minutes, but that was enough. The weather is changing with strong, cold westerly winds and dark clouds looming. It is time to go.

We had two options for our drive to Sheffield and on to Devonport—via the Promised Land, or pass exceedingly close to Paradise. Both sounded good, but we chose the Promised Land. We drove down out of the mountains and over the Cethana Dam where we had lunched only a few days before. Somehow we missed the turning to the Promised Land, but did pass close by Mt Roland where the Weindorfers had their farm. (Apparently you can see Cradle Mountain from the summit of Mt Roland—that's what first excited Gustav Weindorfer's interest.)

Suddenly there it was—a big green sign with an arrow: 'PARADISE—JCN 400 M'. As we'd already passed through Paradise on the first day of our Tasmanian travels, we thought it might be overdoing it to double dip so we kept on towards Sheffield as the mountains and forests gave way to green pasture and farmland.

This used to be solid dairy country but as the industry was rationalised, Sheffield—like many rural hubs—started to slowly die. Sheffield is in the Kentish Town Shire and a group of townspeople started the Kentish Association for Tourism (KAT) to try to think up some bright ideas to save the town. One KAT member had heard of a Canadian town called Chermainus in a similar fix and which had slathered itself with large and bright murals, thus attracting tourists. Chermainus stopped dying and started prospering. Could Sheffield do a Chermainus? Well, yes. KAT funded an artist, John Lendis, to paint Sheffield's first mural in 1986, and a painting called 'Silence and Warmth' featuring Gustav Weindorfer was painted on the side of a building in the centre of town. More murals related to the history of the town and Sheffield is now a riot of public art. Like their Canadian model, the town's fortunes were revived and Sheffield is now firmly on the tourist map as Tasmania's 'outdoor gallery'. In fact murals are breaking out all over on buildings in nearby towns like Gowrie Park, Moina and Roland. (Some idea of how successful this strategy has been can be gauged by a newspaper article Ros saw a year after our visit, listing Sheffield in the top ten real estate 'hot spots' Australia wide!) I have to say I was underwhelmed by the garishness of it all but, fortunately for Sheffield, I am obviously not a typical tourist according to the reality of the mural-led economic revival.

Only thirty or so kilometres remained before Devonport, and our assignation with *Spirit of Tasmania I*. We had booked for a night sailing this time so we could spring off the blocks in Melbourne the following morning for the homeward run. But before then we would have time to take in a movie in the afternoon, although I had arranged to first have a cuppa with Marjorie Bligh in Madden Street, Devonport. From the street the house does not stand out like Climar did in Campbell Town, but then Marjorie did not design it. She has certainly put her stamp on it though.

She added an attic second storey in which she has her own museum absolutely crammed with examples of her handicraft, as well as extensive collections of vases, thimbles, spoons and bottles—a particular interest of her second husband Adrian Cooper. She also had every evening frock that she ever made and wore. I couldn't resist trying on one of her hats, crocheted from supermarket plastic bags. She has also recycled innumerable panty hose and woven them into mats.

'A woman in New South Wales sent me a whole parcel of bread bags. I crocheted them into hats, shopping bags, mats, coat hangers and dolls. You name it. I just can't bear to waste anything.

'My mother was like that. My eldest sister Doreen's frock was passed down to me, and then on to my youngest sister Beatrice. And when it was too small for Beatrice, Mum would cut it down the middle and add lace and panels to make it a bit longer.

'It was the same with the apples lying on the ground. She'd pick them up and cook them. You weren't allowed to throw them away. I'm the same with the produce in my garden. All three of us girls copied her pattern of life.'

Marjorie told me that she has willed her entire collection to the Queen Victoria Museum in Launceston, where the curator has agreed to take everything. It is a remarkable collection of social history made and amassed in one lifetime.

Her garden is a fecund clutter of vegetables, flowers and fruit trees. An unusual feature—not visible from the street—is a scale model of the Batman Bridge, big enough to walk over, constructed over her fish pond. (The original Batman Bridge spans the Tamar River in its lower reaches.) It was built by a suitor who appeared on the scene after the death of her second husband, Adrian Cooper, and before she met her third husband, Eric Bligh.

I was interested to find out from Marjorie about her connections with Barry Humphries, whom she has never met. They have spoken on the phone a few times, and should have met when he did a show in Launceston in the 1960s.

'He wanted to meet me, but it was the annual meeting of the Friendship Society, so I couldn't go to his show. I felt I couldn't let the society down, but I regret it now.

'When he was talking to me over the phone he asked me what flowers I liked, and I said gladioli. (I believe he's always going on about gladioli and chucking them to people in his audiences.) He said, "I'm going to use what you said in my show." I said, "Well don't mention my name please"—because people might think I'm doing a line with him or something!'

One of Marjorie's recent projects has been to write out the entire Bible—both the Old and New Testaments—in her own handwriting—simplifying it so her grandson, Damien Blackwell, could better understand it. Eat your heart out King James! It took her three years. Despite her prolific output of recipes, handy hints and other books, as well as her astonishing collection of handcrafts and memorabilia, Marjorie does not think of herself as out of the ordinary. 'Anybody can do what I do if they put their mind to it. It's just willpower really. The will to do.'

When I asked her what she'd like to be remembered for, she found it hard to say. 'The little things I did for people I suppose, that you never get praise for. I give heaps of things away, and very seldom get a letter saying thank you. That hurts. If anyone does a good turn for me, I thank them or write them a lovely little note. A lot of people just take me for granted you see.'

I came away with a complete set of Marjorie's books and some delicious tomatoes from her garden with instructions on how to capture the seeds and grow them in our vegetable garden after we'd eaten them. And yes, I did write and thank her, and enclosed some photographs taken in her museum and in the garden. We still correspond. She is uniquely Tasmanian and a great survivor.

# a postcript

The barrier of Bass Strait has had a significant influence on Tasmania's history, development and sense of identity. As the lights of Devonport receded and we headed for the dining room on *Spirit of Tasmania 1*, I found myself in the kind of reflective, philosophical mood rarely achieved in the cabin of a jetliner on a fifty minute flight. Flying has robbed us of a true sense of distance. We step out of air-conditioned metal tubes after twelve hours or so, into different countries, climates and civilisations. Even within Australia we can fly from Sydney to the other state capitals—including Hobart—with no real sense of geography. But sea travel, which is rare enough these days, restores that feeling of moving somewhere in real time.

I had looked forward to re-engaging with Tasmania and revisiting places and people not seen for some forty years. I had wondered how much the island of my boyhood and young adult life had really changed and I knew because of my rites of passage in Tasmania that this would be a different journey from any of our previous camping and driving expeditions. Ros, who although born in Ceylon (now Sri

Lanka) and who went to school in India before her tea-planter parents returned to Australia, also went to school in Hobart—which is how we first met. She thought that six weeks on such a small island might be too long. I was sure it would not be long enough and, over dinner, we both agreed that a few extra weeks would have been a bonus.

Our arrival had coincided by chance with the inauguration of the two Melbourne to Devonport vehicular and passenger ferries, *Spirit of Tasmania I* and *II*. It became evident, even in our short time on the island, that the ability of these ships to deliver so many travellers, cars, buses, campers, caravans and backpackers was about to have a significant effect on the culture of Tasmania by sheer numbers of the people involved.

Eighteen months later I know that this influx has been much more significant than I imagined. The 800 000 visitors streaming in to Tasmania every year arrive not only on the ferries, but also by air. Good news for the state's economy, of course, but a challenge to an island which had become used to a more sedate pace of life and where only a few years ago, a four-bedroom Georgian stone farmhouse on twenty acres could be snapped up for $350 000—if a buyer could be found.

The big ferry began to pitch slightly as it encountered the first low swells of the open strait, heading for the mainland now and leaving the island behind, and I said to Ros that it was hard to be objective about a place you felt you knew so well. In many ways—the easy friendliness of the people, and the stunning beauty of well-remembered places—it was astonishingly the same. Yet many things had changed out of recognition. It was difficult to get a decent meal outside a private home in the 1950s. Roast lamb, potatoes and two veg was the height of *haute cuisine*. Wine was regarded as plonk—something derelicts drank out of brown paper covered bottles. Now the settled Tasmanian countryside seems like one continuous vineyard, and clean green industries produce an astonishingly varied range of gourmet products. Aquaculture achieves not only sea-farmed salmon, but scallops, abalone and oysters. Tasmania produces commercially viable truffles. Other exotic crops include olives, saffron, mushrooms, wakame (derived from seaweed), Nashi pears, asparagus, wasabi, green tea, great Tasmanian cheeses—even emu steaks and other game from venison to farmed wallabies. And the list goes on.

That is the good news. There is, alas, a darker side that fills me with a deep unease. Often it has taken the eyes of imaginative outsiders to see Tasmania in ways that locals often fail to appreciate. The Austrian romantic Gustav Weindorfer's instant realisation that Cradle Mountain and its environs simply *must* be a national park, and the dedication of the rest of his life to achieving that, is one example. Another is the fierce excitement of a former member of the Lithuanian Resistance Movement, Olegas Truchanas, who arrived in Tasmania as a refugee in 1948 and realised that the island actually had unclimbed peaks and wild rivers still to be explored whereas in Europe no such primaeval wilderness areas remained.

In 1958 Olegas Truchanas was the first man to canoe the entire length of the Franklin River from Lake Pedder to Macquarie Harbour (unfortunately he did not live to celebrate its liberation) and he campaigned passionately to save Lake Pedder from being destroyed by one of Tasmania's many hydro-electric schemes. The lake was lost, but it can be argued that the environmental tragedy of this event fuelled conservationists' determination to save the state's last big, wild running river, the Franklin. That was a turning point. Today the once reviled Hydro Electric Commission (now Hydro Tasmania) is a world leader in generating power by wind turbines. Forestry Tasmania has taken over the Hydro's role as the architect—according to conservationists and even some timber industry professionals—of the destruction of Tasmania's irreplaceable old growth forests.

A speech Olegas Truchanas gave at the Hobart exhibition opening of watercolour paintings of the doomed Lake Pedder in November 1972 was extraordinarily prescient, considering the present imbroglio over the future of Tasmania's ancient forests:

> Tasmania is not the only place in the world where long-term, careful argument has been defeated by short-term economic advantage. When we look around, the time is rapidly approaching when natural environment, natural unspoiled vistas, are sadly beginning to look like left-overs from a vanishing world . . .
>
> We must try to retain as much as possible of what remains of the unique, rare and beautiful . . . Is there any reason why Tasmania should not be more beautiful on the day we leave it, than on the day we came? We don't know what the requirements of those who come after us will be . . .
>
> If we can revise our attitudes towards the land under our feet; if we can accept the view that man and nature are inseparable parts of the unified whole—then Tasmania can be a shining beacon in a dull, uniform and largely artificial world.[1]

---

1 Max Angus, 1975, *The World of Olegas Truchanas*, Olegas Truchanas Publication Committee, Hobart

Although I will always feel a native Tasmanian, I suppose I have lived away long enough to share the concerns of immigrants like Weindorfer and Truchanas that some of us who are fortunate to grow up and live in such a unique environment are at risk of taking its exquisite beauty for granted. Sometimes it's difficult to see the trees for the wood.